IMAGES
of America

ESSEX AND ESSEX JUNCTION

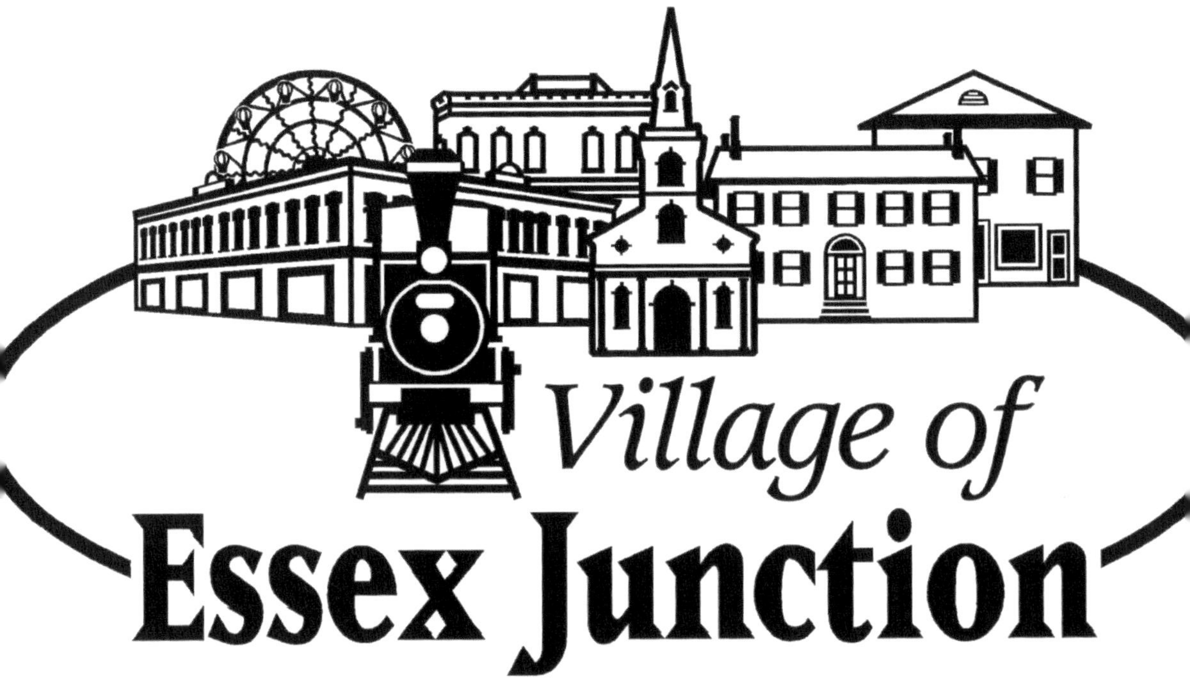

In January 2004, this logo for Essex Junction was chosen to represent the village from several entered in a contest. It is used on the municipal letterhead, vehicles, and welcome signs. Karen McCloud's design incorporates the fair, the railroad heritage, and, from left to right, the Brownell Block, the Essex Agency (at 2 Railroad Street), the First Congregational Church, Lincoln Hall, and the Reynolds Building (at 7–9 Main Street).

IMAGES
of America

ESSEX AND ESSEX JUNCTION

Richard and Lucille Allen

ARCADIA
PUBLISHING

ISBN 978-0-7385-3578-4

Published by Arcadia Publishing
Charleston, South Carolina

Printed in the United States of America

Library of Congress Catalog Card Number: 2004101202

For all general information, contact Arcadia Publishing:
Telephone 843-853-2070
Fax 843-853-0044
E-mail sales@arcadiapublishing.com
For customer service and orders:
Toll-free 1-888-313-2665

Visit us on the Internet at www.arcadiapublishing.com

On the cover: Richard Martin and his parents, Ina and Ernie Martin Sr., relax on the porch of their farmhouse, located across from the Lang Farm on Route 15, *c.* 1914.

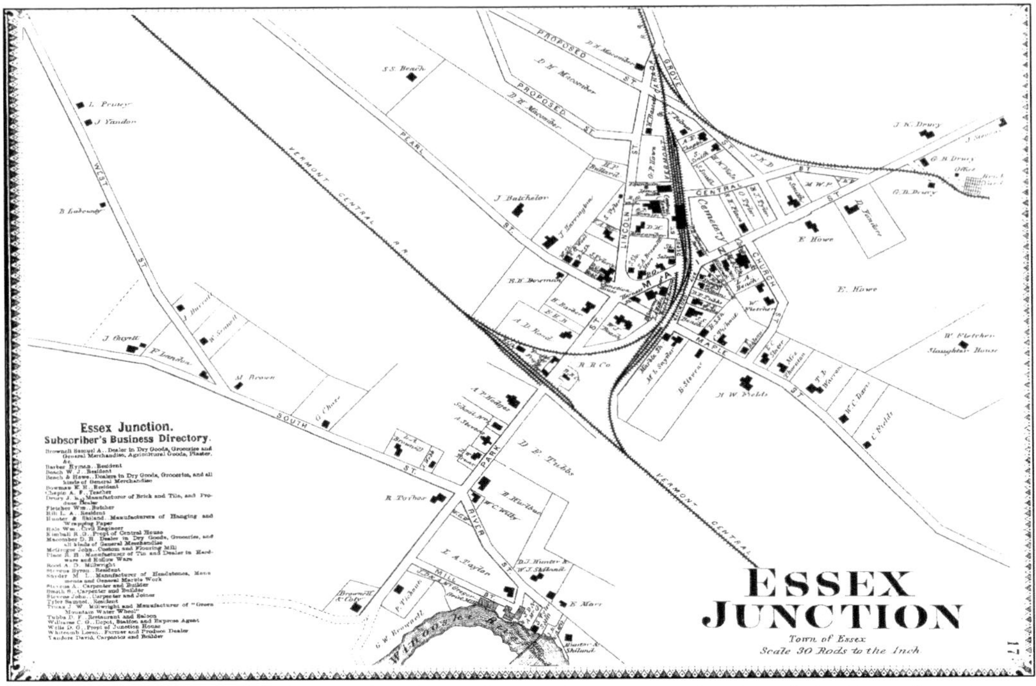

This 1869 map from the Beers atlas shows the predominance of railroads in Essex Junction at that time. The Drury Brickyard (upper right) had its own spur. The industry by the Winooski River at Hubbel's Falls included the Hunter & Shiland Mill, which made "hanging and wrapping paper," and the John McGregor Grist Mill.

Contents

Acknowledgments		6
Introduction		7
Selected Sources		8
1.	Around the Town and Village	9
2.	For the Public Good	25
3.	At Work	43
4.	People, Farms, and Families	73
5.	Schools and Churches	95
6.	Fun and Celebration	117

ACKNOWLEDGMENTS

The gathering of photographs and information for this book was an enjoyable experience, because it gave us a chance to meet and work with a large number of people.

We gratefully acknowledge the assistance of the following people and organizations: Kathleen and Ernest Martin Jr.; Philip Kolvoord, Esq.; Gerald Fox for help with the captions and research; Noah Thompson for his donation of material to the historical society; Mary O'Neil for her research on schools; Nancy Bartlett; Carlton Houghton; Jon's Darkroom for photographic services; and Suzanne Guiod of Arcadia Publishing for her excellent editorial assistance.

Special thanks go to the following: George Clapp, longtime president of the Essex Community Historical Society, for his foresight in collecting historic postcards of the area; Clinton Russell Jr., current president of the society, for his support of this project; the historical society board past and present, including Polly McEwing, Barbara Mudgett-Russell, Ann Gray, Eva Clough, Tobe Zalinger, Sherry Norton, Katherine Reynolds, William Parkinson, and David Clough; Penny Pillsbury, librarian at the Brownell Library, for access to material on the library dedication; Susan Overfield, librarian at the Essex Free Library; University of Vermont Special Collections and Annex librarian Sylvia Bugbee; Bill Gill from the Map Room at the University of Vermont; Paul Carnahan, librarian at the Vermont Historical Society; Ginger Isham of the Williston Historical Society; Jane Fitzgerald of the Milton Historical Society; and Thomas Way of IBM Burlington. The imagery on pages 52 (top and bottom) and 53 (top) is reproduced courtesy of International Business Machines Corporation. Unauthorized use is not permitted. Thanks also go to Photogarden; Jill Allen and B. Fuller Allen; Charles Safford, village manager; Patrick Scheidel, town manager; and the staff at the village and town offices.

Additional gratitude goes to the following: Phyllis Drury; Michael Stanton; Janet and Martin Powell Jr.; Fred and Nora Allen; John Schumacher-Hardy for information and photographs of the Wool family; Phyllis and William Fullerton for information and photographs of the Drury family on River Road; William Kalanges of the Essex Junction Historical Society; Sherry Mahady; Piper Smith; Lt. Robin Hollwedell; Greg Cluver; Dorothy Schnure of Green Mountain Power; George Rousseau from the Champlain Valley Exposition; Jacqueline Lowe of the Chittenden Trust; Lee Paul of Banknorth; James Fay and Paul Tice from the Champlain Water District; Matt Stevens; Jim Robinson; Matt Cohen; Mary Lou Marcussen; Jean Leonard; Robert C. Jones; Tom Simon; Allen Martin; Lincoln Brownell; Edward Baker Sr.; Warren Baker of the *Essex Reporter;* Proctor Page; Mary Cavanaugh; Joan Flynn; Dorothy and Nancy Hayes; Faye Soderberg; Barbara Chapin and the Chapin family; John and Bette Whitcomb; Harold Cross; Pearl Farley; Carol Ann Greig; Robert Wood; Robert Marcotte; Mary Parker; Mary Russell; George Tougas; Horace Jones; Lenore Whitten; Paul Abajian; Paul Sisson; Chuck Vile; Dr. Paul B. Frederic; Jenny Olgelby; Claire Brunnell; Judith Martin; Emily Stebbins; Father William Giroux; Rev. Brigid Farrell; Wayne Spear; Harold Bergeron; Ann Yandow; Julia Fifield; Martha Kourabanas; Ben Drury; Karen McCloud; and Martha Marvin Kelley.

We assume there are still many historic Essex photographs in private hands, and we hope that this book will inspire gifts to public archives and museum collections.

INTRODUCTION

So what ever happened to such Essex geographic features as Cranberry Swamp, Primrose Hill, and Indian River? Like many things over time, they were altered, forgotten, or renamed. Old maps of Essex are one key to learning about the changes this town has undergone in its 240-year history.

Essex Town is in the center of Chittenden County, Vermont's most populous area. The Winooski River forms the town's southern boundary with Williston. Essex is bordered by Jericho to the east, Westford to the north, and Colchester to the west. With a population today of 18,261 (2000 census), it is one of Vermont's largest towns and is advantageously close to the recreational opportunities in the Green Mountains to the east and Lake Champlain to the west. Transportation is enhanced by rail and interstate highway connections, as well as the proximity to the Burlington International Airport.

The town was chartered on June 7, 1763, by Gov. Benning Wentworth of New Hampshire. Sixty-four settlers received land grants to make Essex Town their home, but none of them ever did. Rather, beginning in 1783, farmers from Massachusetts made permanent settlements in the area. Huge pine and hemlock trees covered much of the land; clearing them to make space for crops and for the town common was a formidable task. In 1786, residents held the first town meeting, at which they chose town officers and raised money for road repairs. The 1791 census shows just 354 residents.

The water power of the Winooski River attracted early settlers who built dams and mills around Hubbel's Falls. Hubbel's Falls remained an industrial section of town well into the 1900s. Today, Green Mountain Power uses the falls to generate electricity.

It took a while before the center of town was established. Page's Corners had taverns and a post office and was the location of early town meetings. On a direct route to Canada, the Corners was also noted for its smuggling activity during the War of 1812. Butler's Corners, on the road to Cambridge, competed with Page's Corners to be the town center. A post office was established there in 1825. But the common was laid out in Essex Center. The center was also home to several churches and businesses, as well as the Essex Classical Institute, a school that drew students from surrounding towns.

When railroads came to the area in 1849, the settlement near the Winooski River was called Painesville after Charles Paine, president of the Central Vermont Railroad. Six rail lines approached the vicinity and made connections there. Because of the junction of the railroads at this spot, Painesville soon changed its name to Essex Junction. So Essex now had two areas of growth—Essex Junction and Essex Center. The Burlington & Lamoille Railroad was completed in 1877, providing passenger service as well as a way to export lumber and agricultural products. The route ran from Burlington to Essex Junction, through Essex Center, Jericho, Underhill, and up to Cambridge.

Essex Junction became an incorporated village on November 15, 1892. It was the home to businesses and industries that took advantage of the rail service, and served the farmers in Essex and surrounding towns. Over the years, the village had a corn-canning plant, a maple syrup co-op, several creameries, and a feed mill. The Drury Brick and Tile Company thrived as a result of the railroad and was a major employer in the village for more than 100 years.

Established on the western edge of town in 1893, Fort Ethan Allen increased prosperity in the area. Many local materials were used to construct its buildings. Some residents still recall troops and the cavalry marching through town on their way to the firing range in Underhill.

The Chittenden County Fair started in Essex Center in 1914. After several years, it reorganized as the Champlain Valley Fair and moved to Essex Junction. The fairgrounds are busy throughout the year with a variety of shows, meetings, and festivals.

When International Business Machines (IBM) moved into a manufacturing plant near the Winooski River in 1957, the town and village entered into a new era. The population of the town outside of the village increased 154 percent in the 1960s and 66 percent in the 1970s. Over the years, the company employed as many as 8,500 people. The work force was noted for its high level of education and above-average earnings. Traffic increased, houses were built, and school populations became an issue at numerous meetings. New pressure was put on farm and forest land in town. Housing developments and shopping areas kept the planning commissions busy. The town lost its agrarian base and gained a reputation as a suburb of Burlington, home to IBM, and a business and service center in its own right.

Recent growth outside the village, especially near Route 289, has highlighted the difficulty of maintaining a vibrant downtown in Essex Junction. New initiatives are under way to keep Essex Junction an attractive growth center.

In spite of the rapid growth since the late 1950s, Essex still has some natural areas where the public can "get away from it all." Indian Brook Park, owned by the town, provides a system of trails and a small lake for swimming and boating. Saxon Hill Forest has several miles of trails and dirt roads for walking, skiing, and biking. The northeast corner of the town remains fairly undeveloped.

The possibility of separation or consolidation of the town and village has been debated since at least 1958. Currently, the two share a high school and a police department. Residents of the village are also residents of the town. Proponents of consolidation argue that joining would help bring the community together, reduce duplicate services, and save on taxes. Opponents feel the merging of the town and village would deprive the village of its identity.

The town and village share an interesting past and a common future. We hope the images in this book make you more aware of some of the fascinating history of our community. As for Cranberry Swamp, a dam turned it into Indian Brook Reservoir. Primrose Hill still creates an elevation gain on Pinecrest Drive, and Indian River was renamed Indian Brook, a truer reflection of its size.

Selected Sources

Bent, Frank, ed. *The History of the Town of Essex*. Essex, Vermont: Essex Publishing, 1963.

Brownell, Lincoln C. *Notes on the Brownell Family in Vermont*. Privately printed, 1988.

Carlisle, Lilian Baker, ed. *Look Around Essex and Williston, Vermont*. Burlington, Vermont: George Little Press Inc., 1973.

Fox, Gerald. "Optimism Derailed: The Economic Impact of the Burlington & Lamoille Railroad." Master's thesis, University of Vermont, May 1993.

Gant, John. "Fort Ethan Allen from Military Parades to Rugby," Colchester *News Magazine*, 1997. *History of the Champlain Valley Exposition, 1922–1996*. Essex Junction, Vermont: Champlain Valley Exposition, 1996.

O'Neil, Mary. "Standing Still: Surviving 19th Century Schoolhouses in the Town of Essex." Research paper, University of Vermont, 2001.

Pillsbury, Penelope D. *Essex, Vermont: An Annotated Bibliography to Sources in the Brownell Library, Essex Free, and Essex Junction High School Libraries*. The Friends of the Brownell Library, 1992.

Powell, Harriet. *Yesterday in Essex*. Essex Junction, Vermont: Essex Publishing Company, 1977.

Putnam, William W., and Myron H. Jordan. *History of the Essex Junction Fire Department, 1893–1992*.

http://personalweb.smcvt.edu/thefort/Default.htm.

Thompson, Noah C. *A Pilot's Story, Flying in the 1940s*. Rutland, Vermont: Academy Books, 1995.

One

Around the Town and Village

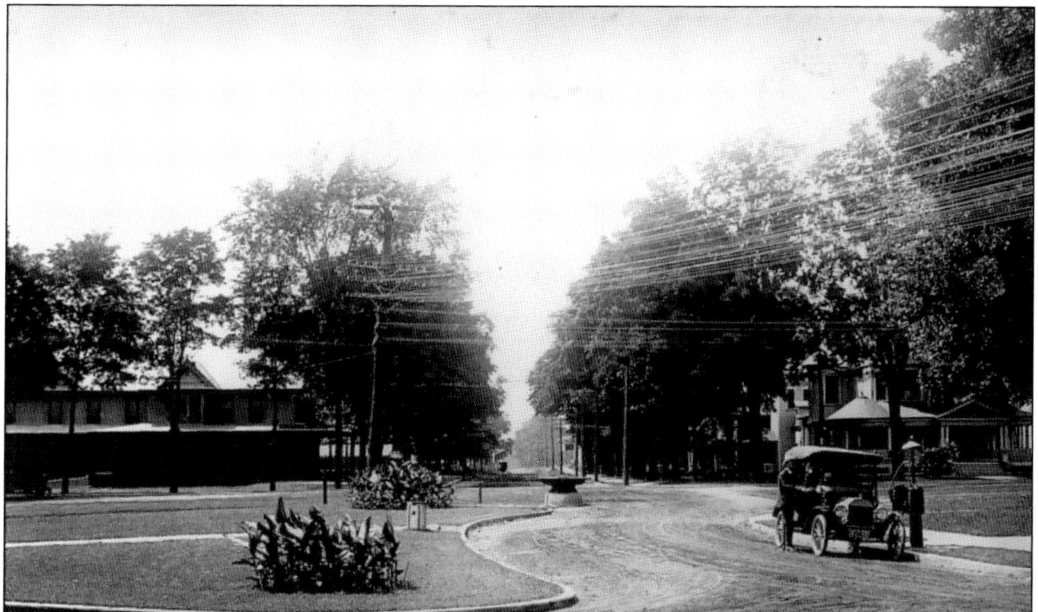

This *c.* 1915 view of the Five Corners shows the Lincoln Inn on the left, Park Street headed off to the south, and Lincoln Square in the foreground. The circular water trough in the center also had a smaller basin for dogs. The driver of the Model T on the right has pulled up to what is likely a hand-operated gasoline pump.

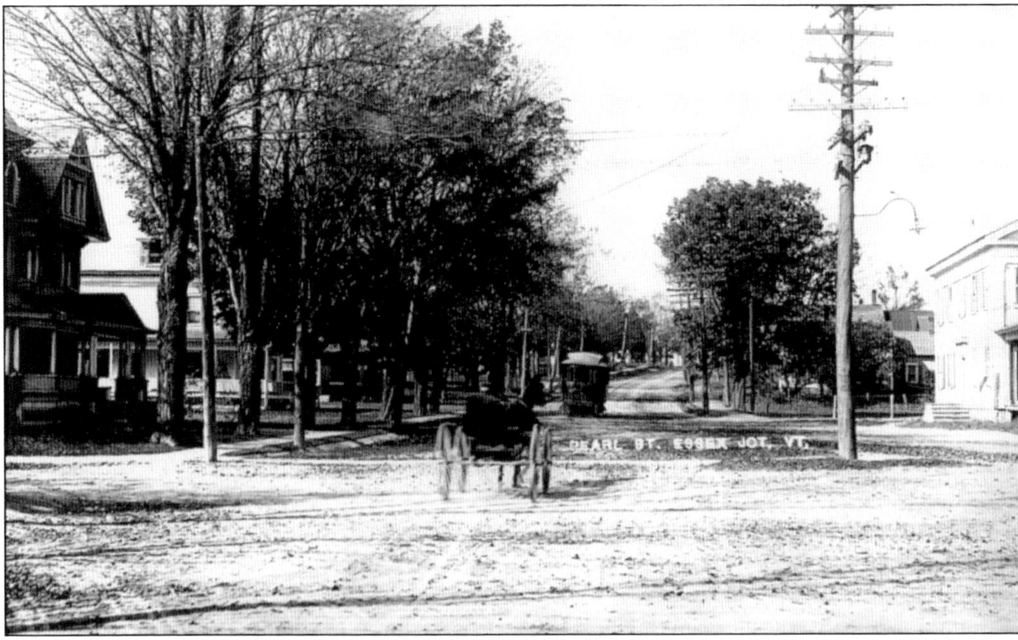

A trolley on unpaved Pearl Street is followed by a horse-drawn buggy. Lincoln Hall stands on the right. As a child, Julia Fifield grieved over the horses that fell down and the wagons that tipped over when they encountered the trolley tracks at the Five Corners. The trolley connected Essex Junction with Fort Ethan Allen, Winooski, and Burlington.

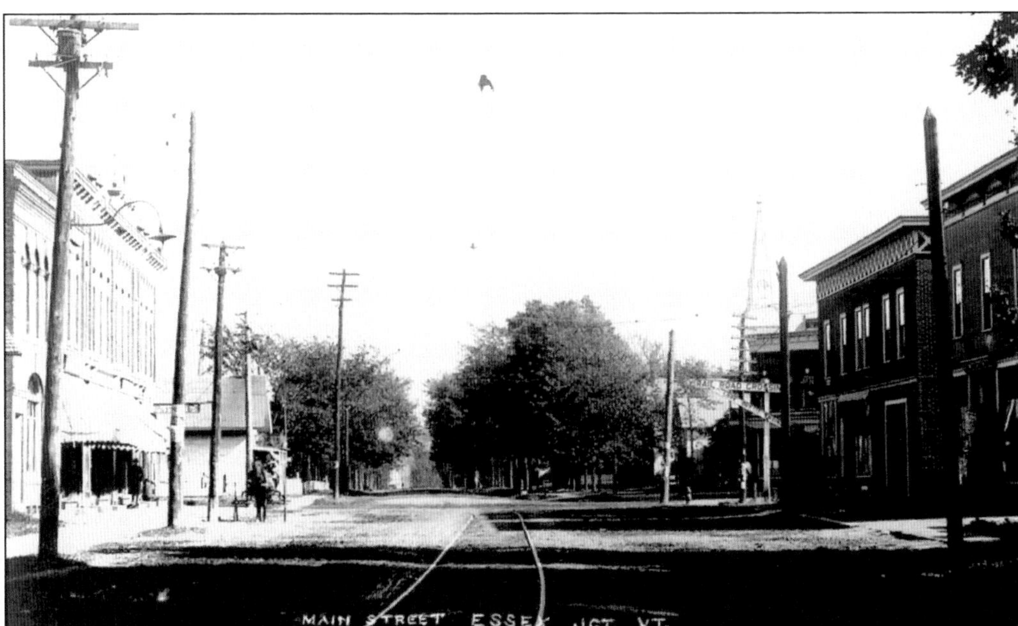

This view, looking toward the railroad crossing, reveals the trolley tracks and overhead wires on Main Street. The Brownell Block, with a large flagpole, is on the left. The Congregational church steeple appears on the right. The second building on the right housed the fire department prior to 1914.

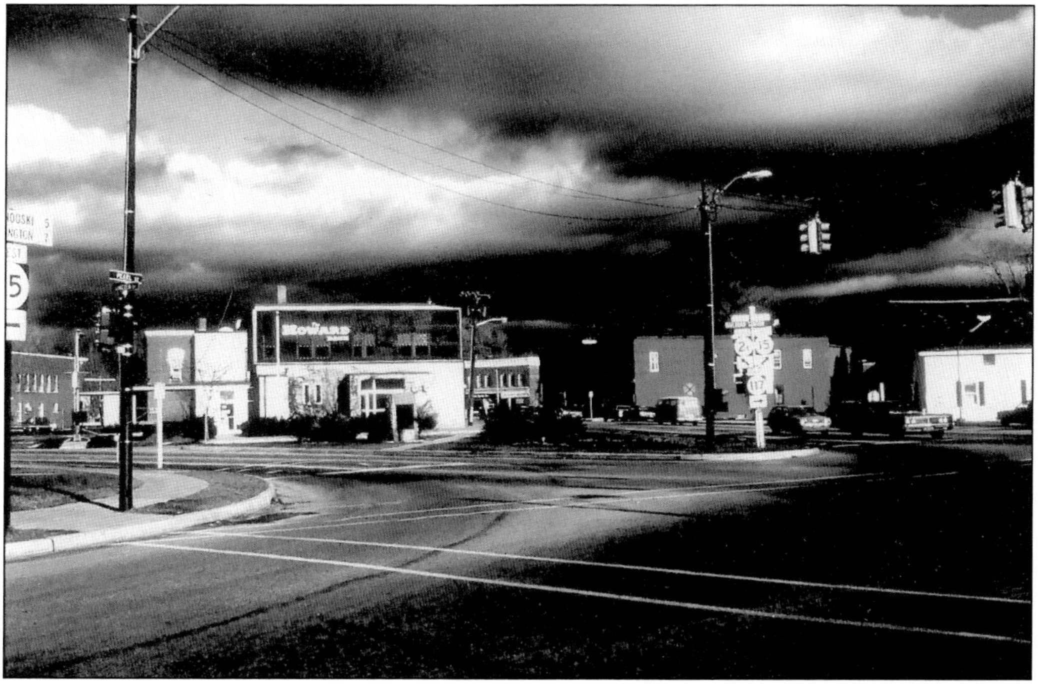

This photograph shows an unusually quiet moment at the Five Corners in the late 1970s. Ernie Martin Jr. remembers the "silent policeman" in the middle of the intersection, which created a rotary to control traffic. It stood about 6 feet tall with a battery-operated light on top. Ernie Martin Sr. had the responsibility, as superintendent of streets, of righting the device after it had been knocked over by some drunken driver. (Courtesy S. Henry Lampert, D.D.S.)

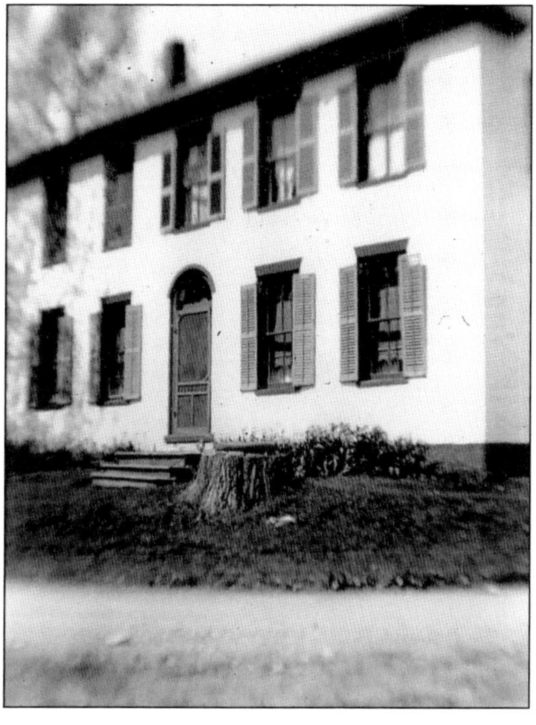

Page's Corners, at the intersection of Old Stage, Brigham Hill, and Colonel Page Roads, was once the center of town with a store, post office, and taverns. Early town meetings were held here. This home, seen here in 1936, was constructed in 1822 by Col. Samuel Page. It was also the medical office of Dr. Lucius C. Butler, Page's son-in-law, until 1888.

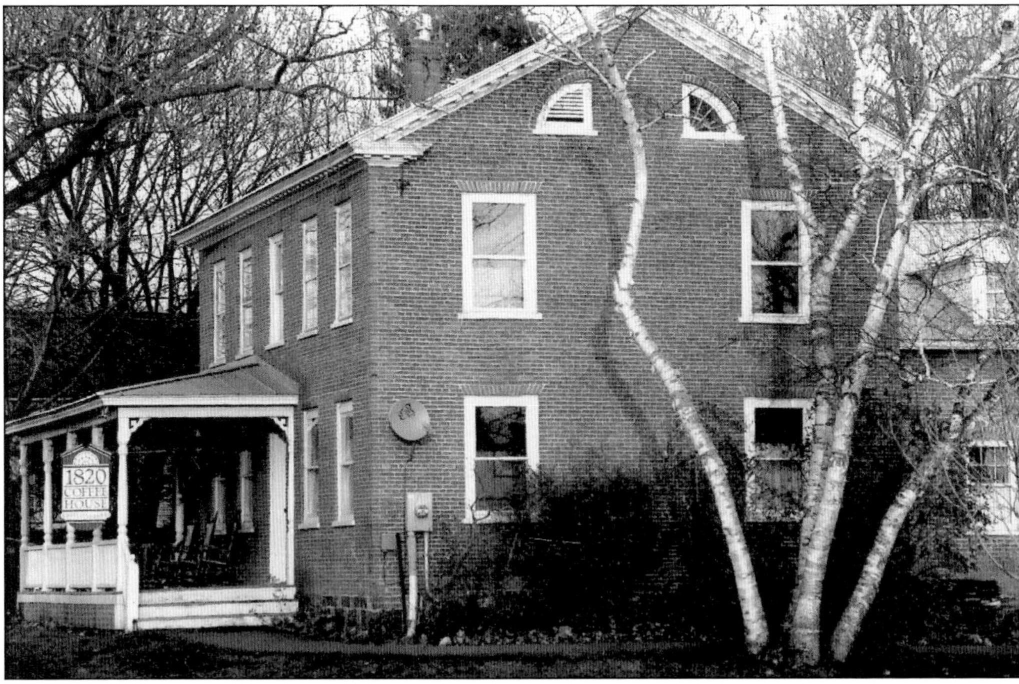

The Roswell Butler house, on Route 15, is a prime example of Federal-style architecture at what was an important center of town: Butler's Corners. Between 1822 and 1830, a store, tavern, and blacksmith shop operated here. The building is now the 1820 Coffee House and is on the National Register of Historic Places. As history repeats itself, the area has recently been developed as Essex Town Center with residences and businesses.

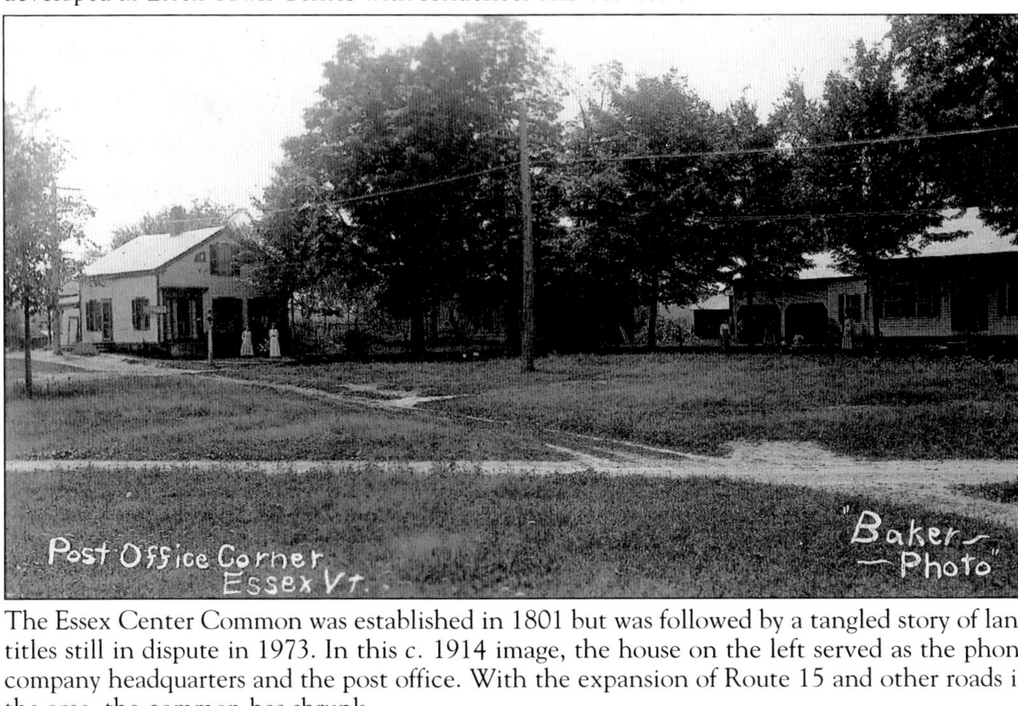

The Essex Center Common was established in 1801 but was followed by a tangled story of land titles still in dispute in 1973. In this c. 1914 image, the house on the left served as the phone company headquarters and the post office. With the expansion of Route 15 and other roads in the area, the common has shrunk.

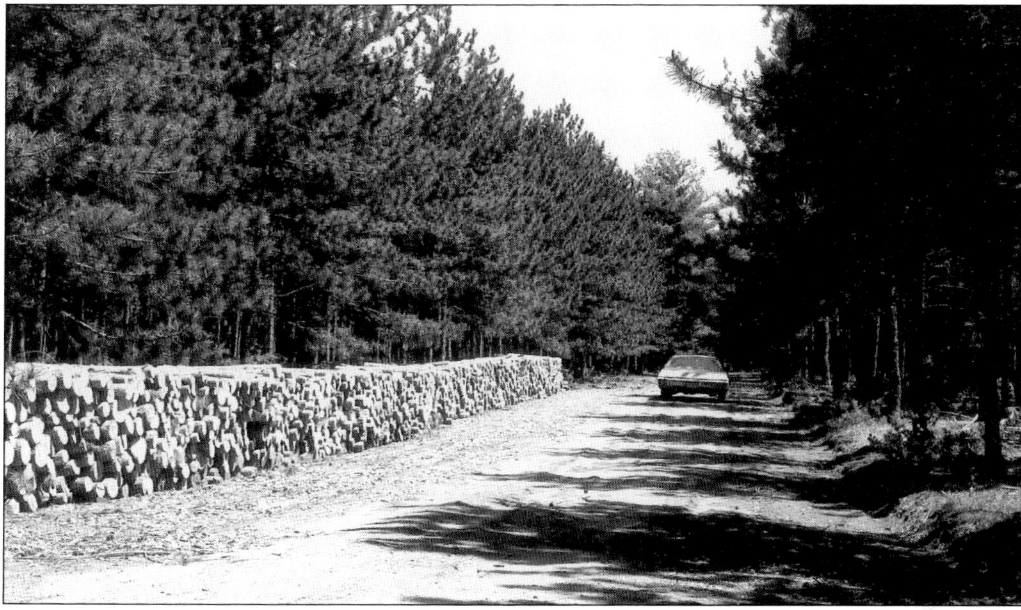

Allen Martin, as a member of the Essex Junction Water Board, pushed for the purchase of the Saxon Hill area and the development of a forestry plan for the property to ensure a steady supply of clean water for the village. Eventually, four reservoirs were established. Here we see some of the planted trees and cut pulp wood stacked along part of the now 12 miles of dirt road in the forest. (Courtesy William P. Hall.)

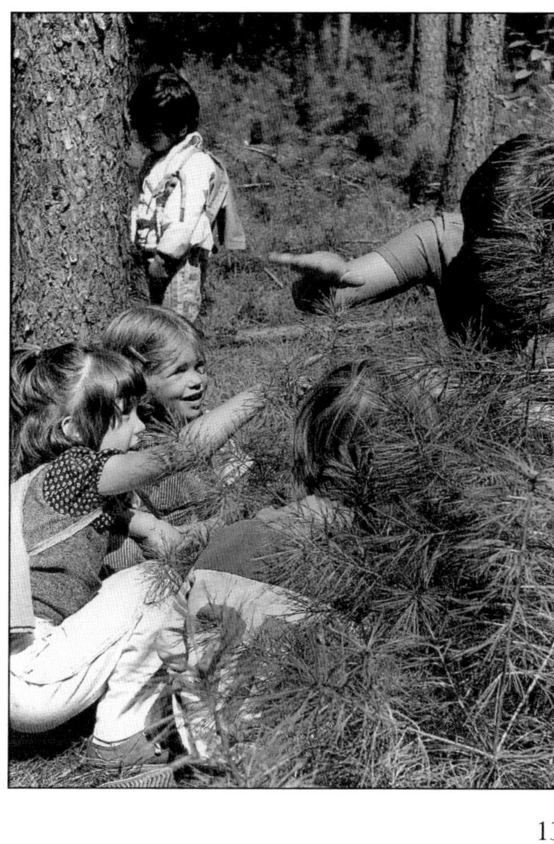

The initial purchase in 1900 of 10 acres of Saxon Hill land around the springs cost $600. Major tree plantings occurred from 1924 to 1927. Serious problems in the 1920s included silt in the reservoirs, leaky dams, blocked pipes, and a fire in the pump house. In this c. 1974 photograph, local youngsters learn about trees during one of the many forest tours organized by county forester William P. Hall. (Courtesy William P. Hall.)

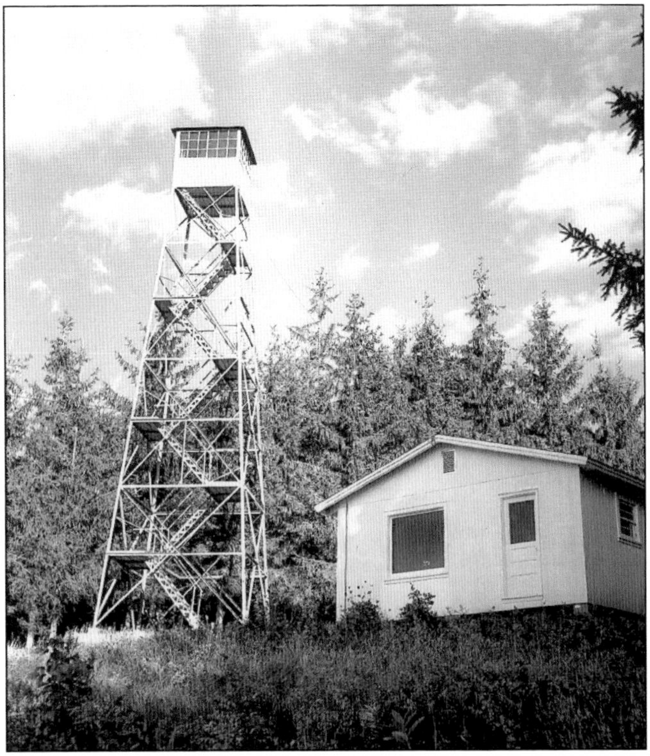

In October 1948, the Chittenden County Forest Festival Field Day was held in Saxon Hill Forest with speeches, demonstrations, and a tree-chopping contest for the youth. Jeeps took visitors to the new fire tower on Saxon Hill, which replaced one that had been constructed in 1926. Although there has been some development in the forest, much of the land is still open to the public for recreation. (Courtesy William P. Hall.)

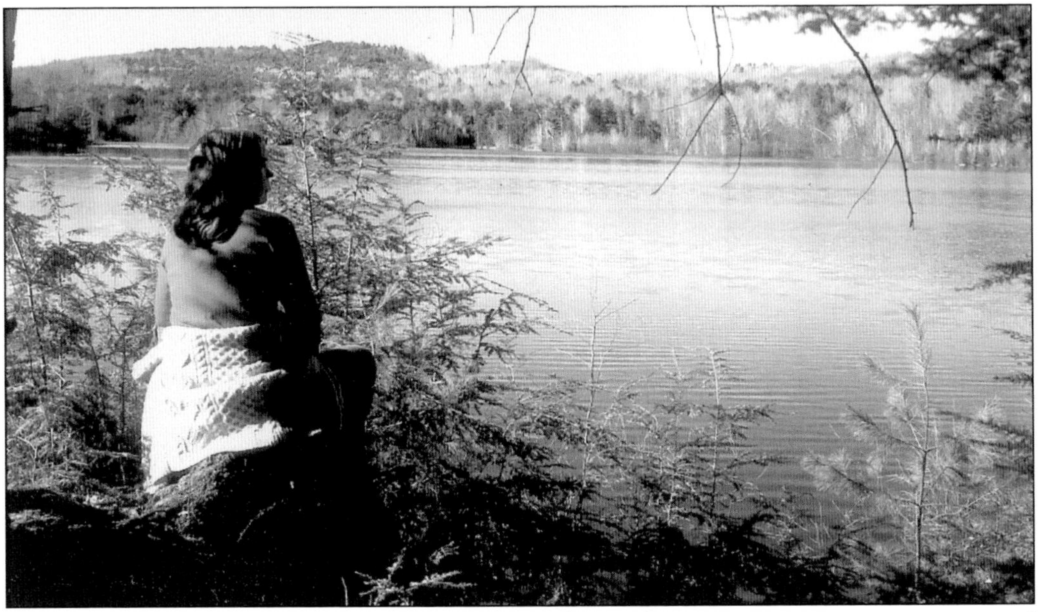

After World War II, the village experienced rapid growth, so water consumption increased significantly. In 1954, an engineering firm recommended the Indian Brook area as a second water source. The dam was constructed from 1955 to 1956, and a 50-acre reservoir was created within a 450-acre forest. Like the Saxon Hill area, Indian Brook Reservoir was not needed after the village went online with the Champlain Water District in 1973. Here, Louellen Hall overlooks the reservoir. (Courtesy William P. Hall.)

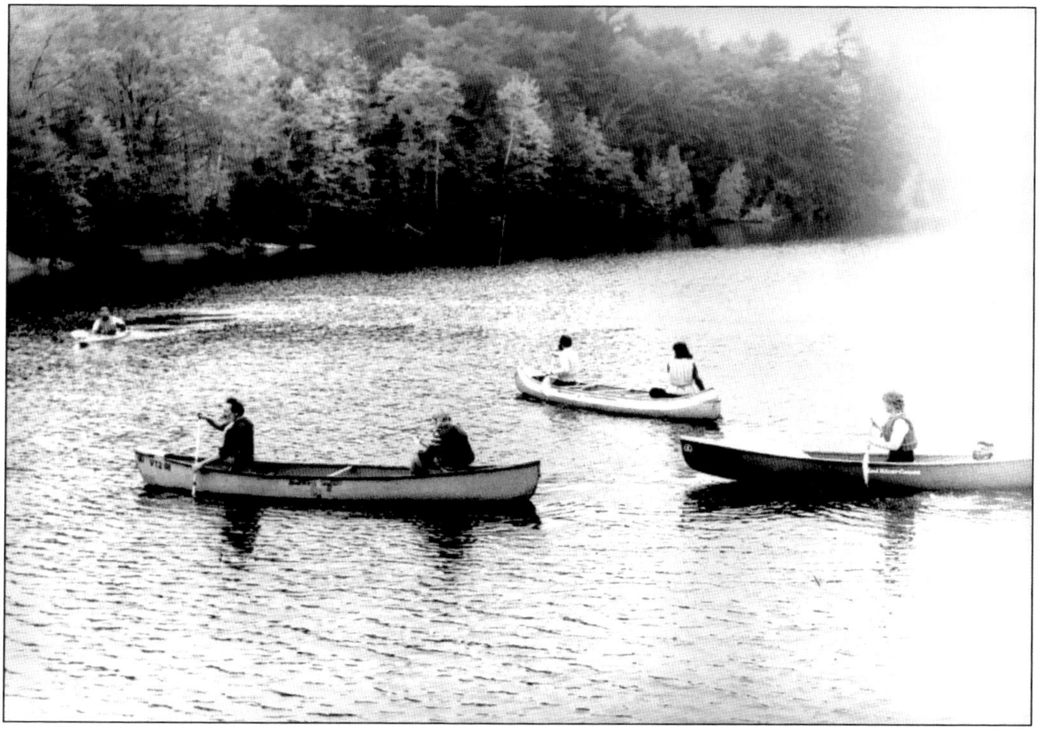

The public toured Indian Brook Reservoir by canoe during a Friends of Indian Brook open house on October 19, 1985. On November 4, 1986, voters approved money for the purchase of the property from developers, the repairing of the dam, and preliminary site work. Today, Indian Brook Park is owned by the town of Essex and is used for year-round recreation, such as hiking, fishing, swimming, and skiing.

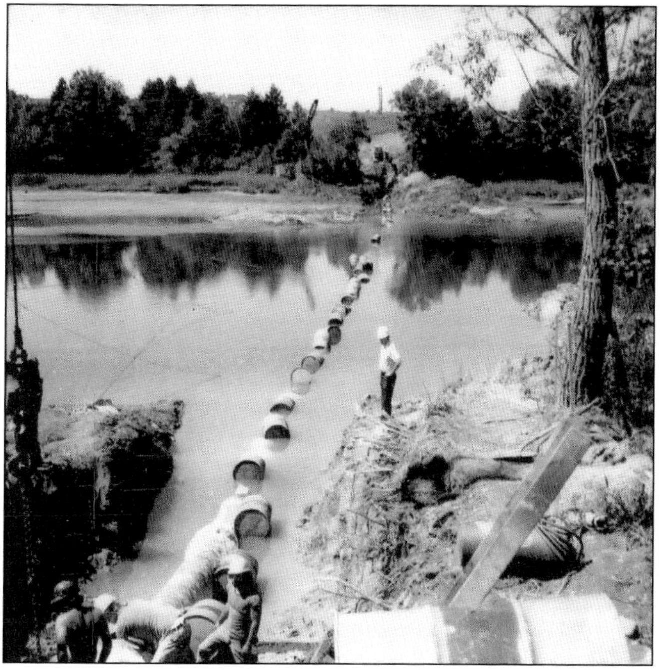

In 1973, the Champlain Water District, a regional water supply municipal corporation, started serving Essex Town and Essex Junction. The service to the town and village was upgraded in 1981 by R. B. Goodrich Contractors. This photograph, taken in 1981, shows the river crossing, via pipe, as it neared completion. The IBM building is visible in the far distance.

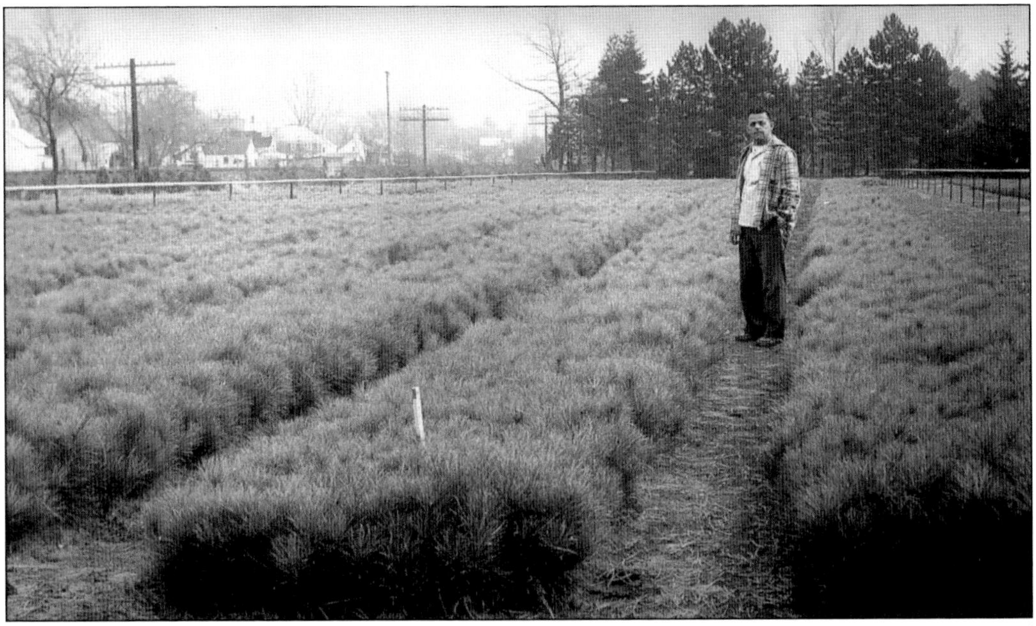

In the spring of 1922, the state tree nursery was transferred from Burlington to 20 acres off Pearl Street because of the workable soil, availability of water, abundant labor, and constant supply of horse manure from the stables at Fort Ethan Allen. Today, it is the regional office of the Agency of Natural Resources. Kenneth L. Hovey, superintendent of the nursery, appears among some red pine seedlings *c.* 1957. (Courtesy William P. Hall.)

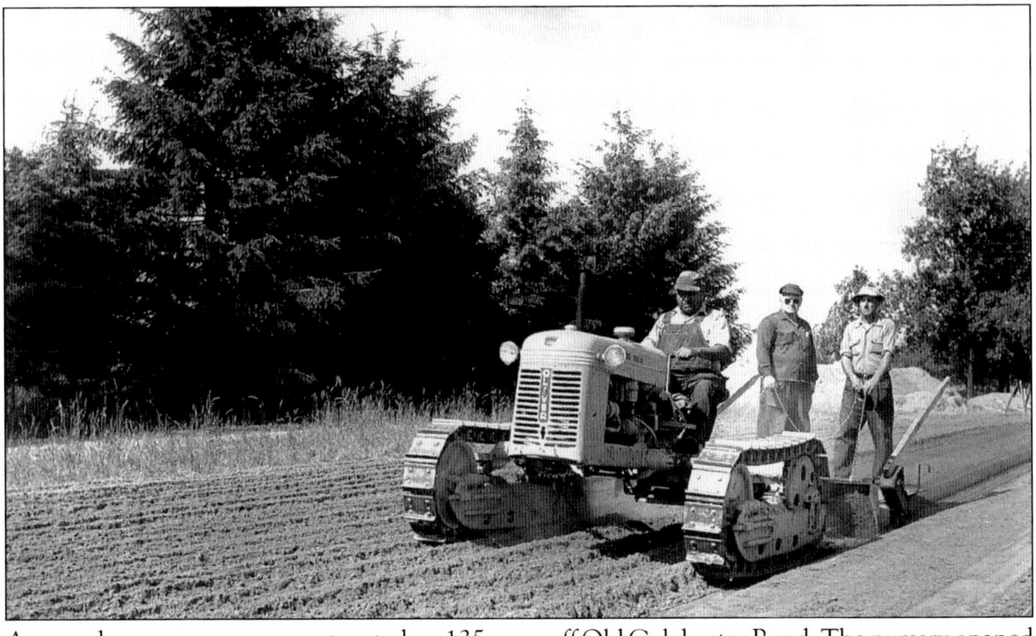

A second tree nursery was constructed on 135 acres off Old Colchester Road. The nursery opened in 1957 and operated as one unit along with the Pearl Street nursery. It closed in 1995, and the state land is now leased to the town and village for recreational, educational, or horticultural purposes. Howard Hurson (on the tractor), Rod Quesnel (left), and Harry Sanderson form four-foot-wide beds for seedlings *c.* 1959. (Courtesy William P. Hall.)

The large oxbow in the Winooski River, labeled Loomis Bow on an 1807 map, was distinctive enough to warrant its own postcard. The 1967 Comprehensive Plan for the town and village proposed that the river be "discontinued" (rerouted) and the cut-off land be used for recreation. This 1999 aerial photograph shows Route 15, with Fort Ethan Allen on the left and the Champlain Valley Exposition on the right. (Courtesy Vermont Department of Taxes Mapping Program.)

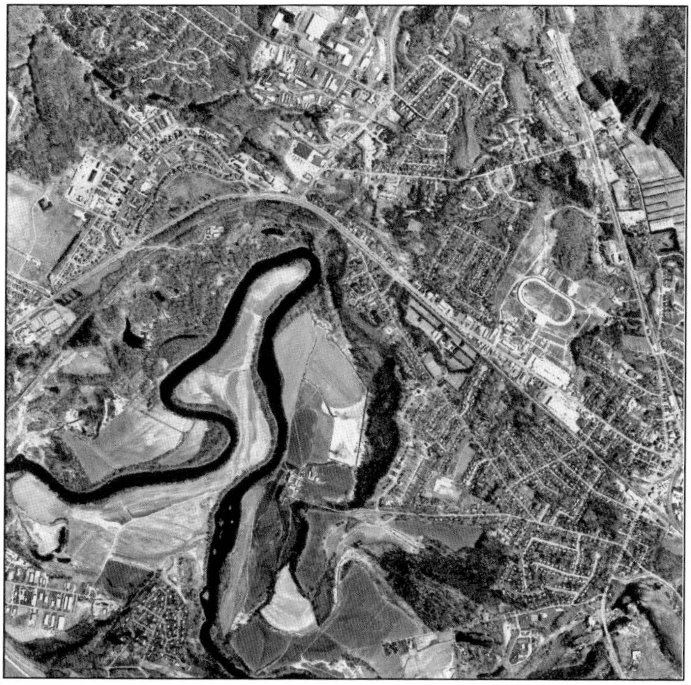

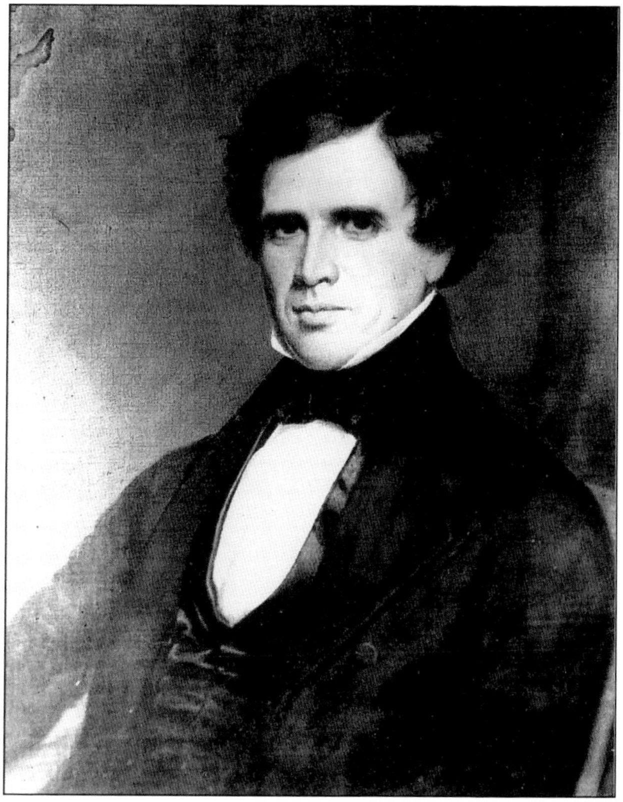

Charles Paine, born in Williamstown, used his father's wealth to enter business in Northfield and politics statewide. In 1842, he was elected governor by one vote in the legislature. The community around the junction of the railroads in Essex was known as Painesville because Paine was president of the Vermont Central Railroad. It was changed to Essex Junction in 1865. (Courtesy Vermont Historical Society.)

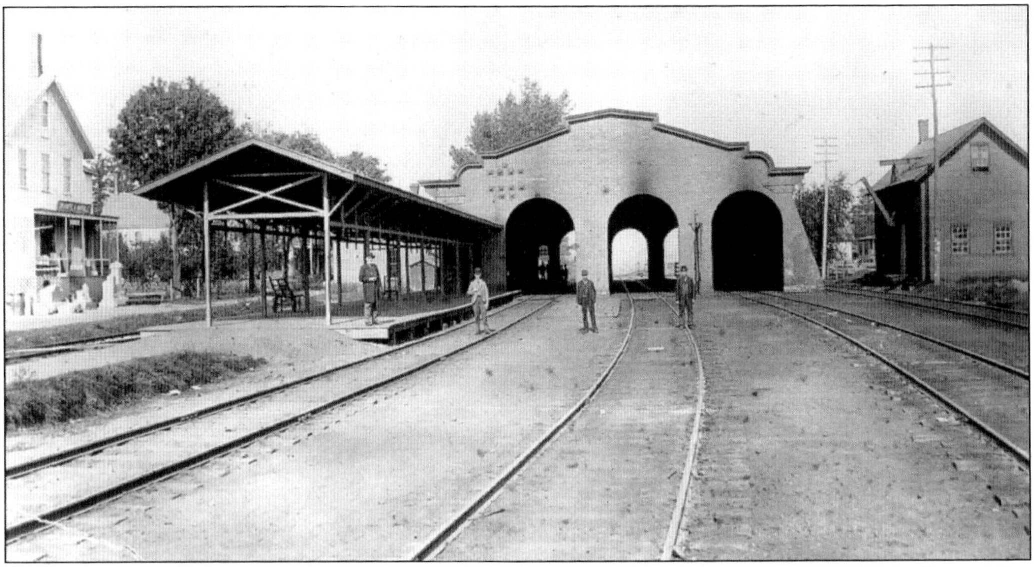

The railroad came to Essex in 1849 and produced significant prosperity in the village. The second station, seen here *c.* 1881, was built in 1862. The arches originally had iron doors so the interior could be sealed off from the weather. They were eventually removed. The business on the far left sold monuments, and the building on the far right was the water tank. (Courtesy Canadian National Railways.)

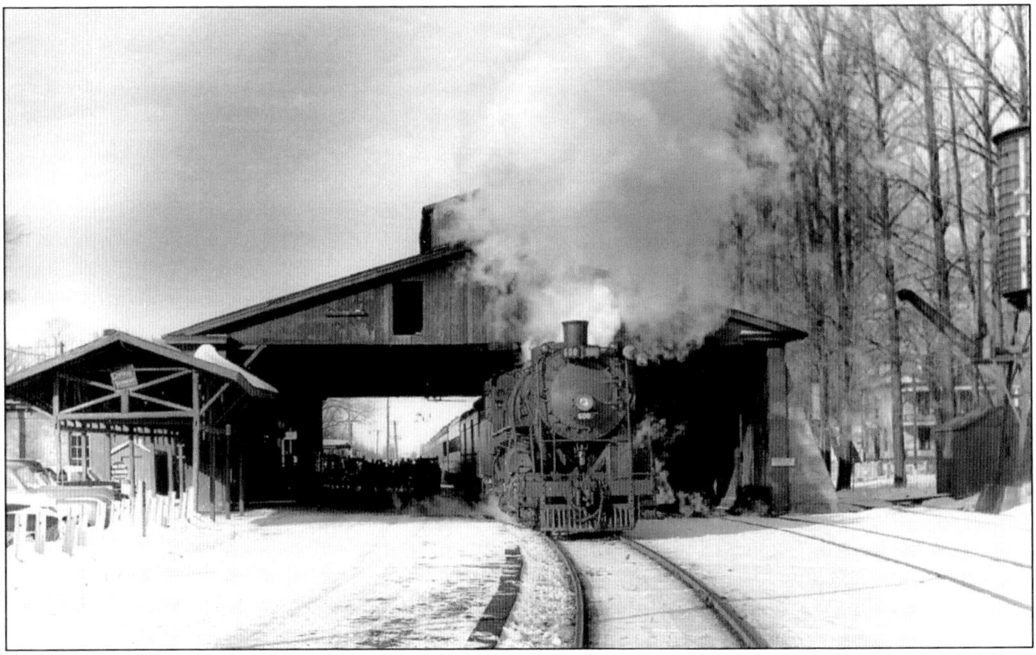

The arches on the Essex Junction station were removed in the early 1890s. Here, the steam-powered locomotive No. 600 of the Central Vermont Railroad pulls the *Ambassador* southbound into the station. This Jim Shaughnessy photograph was taken on December 26, 1954, while he was on Christmas break from college. The days of the steam locomotive in Vermont were numbered; the Central Vermont's switch to diesel power occurred in 1957. (Courtesy Jim Shaughnessy.)

As the *Ambassador* heads south and crosses Main Street, a white building appears on the right. At one time it held Sylvester's Public Market, and later Henry's. The Ethan Allen Creamery was in the back. In 1955, the creamery moved to Park Street to what is now the Five Corners Discount building. In 1965, Allen Alfred sold the business to the St. Albans Creamery. It was shut down in 1973. (Courtesy Jim Shaughnessy.)

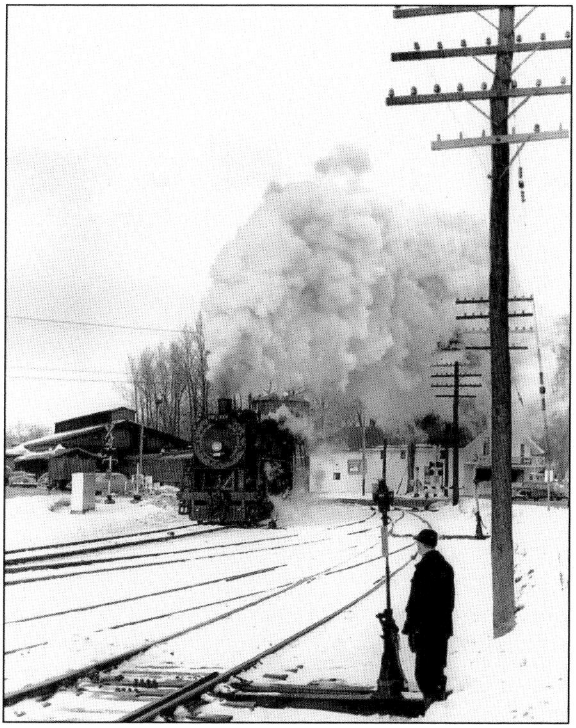

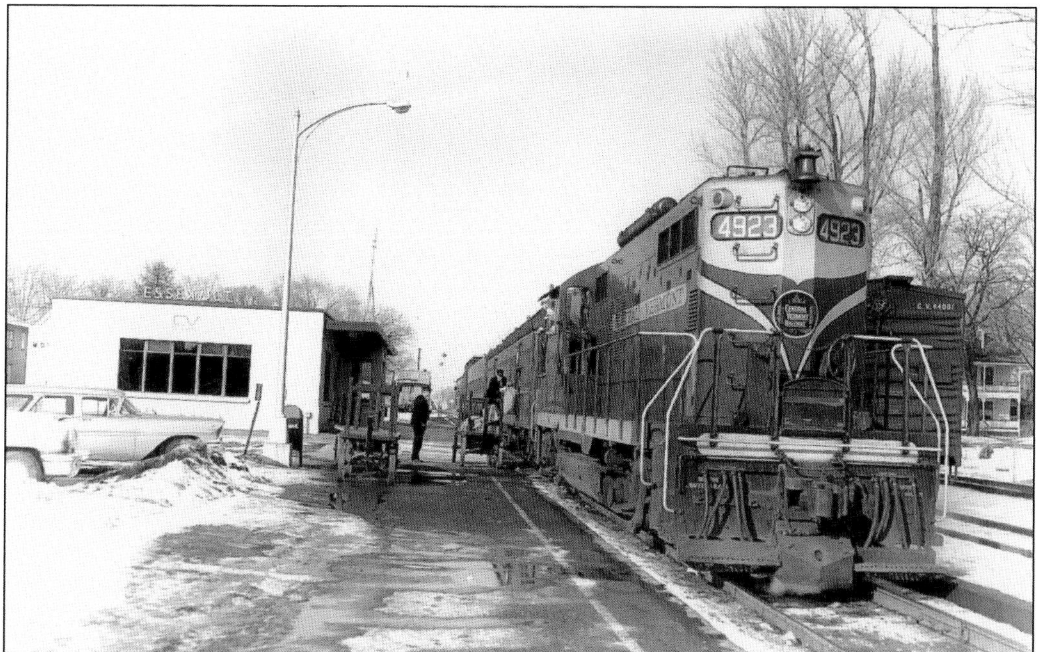

The old station was torn down in 1958, and this concrete block building was put up. In 1962, it served as a major hub for Girls Scouts headed to the National Jamboree at Button Bay State Park. Several thousand scouts arrived and departed from here. Today, passenger service continues from Essex Junction with one Amtrak train a day in each direction. (Courtesy Jim Shaughnessy.)

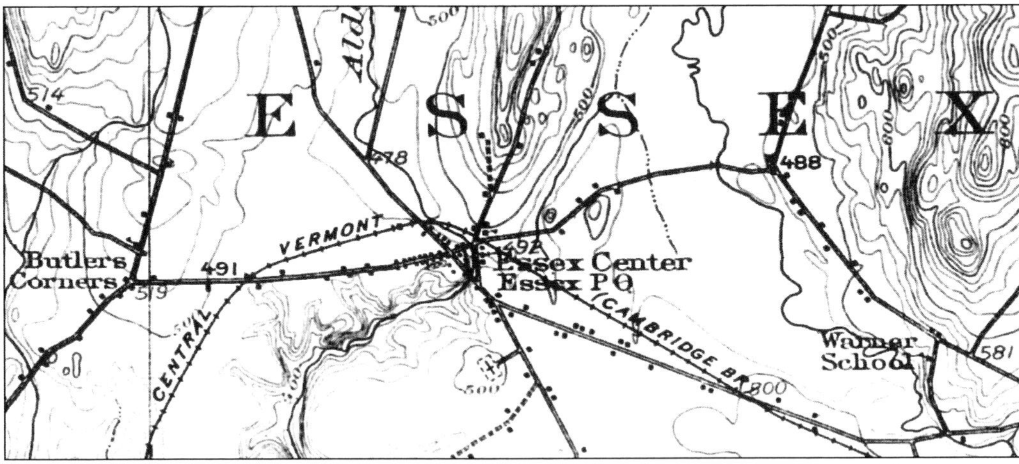

The Burlington & Lamoille Railroad was completed in 1877. The line ran 35 miles from Burlington through South Burlington, Essex, Jericho, Underhill, and on to Cambridge. This portion of a 1915 map shows the route through Essex Center. The abandoned railroad bed today serves as the basis for much of the bike path that runs from Essex Junction across Route 289, behind the Essex Post Office, to Route 15.

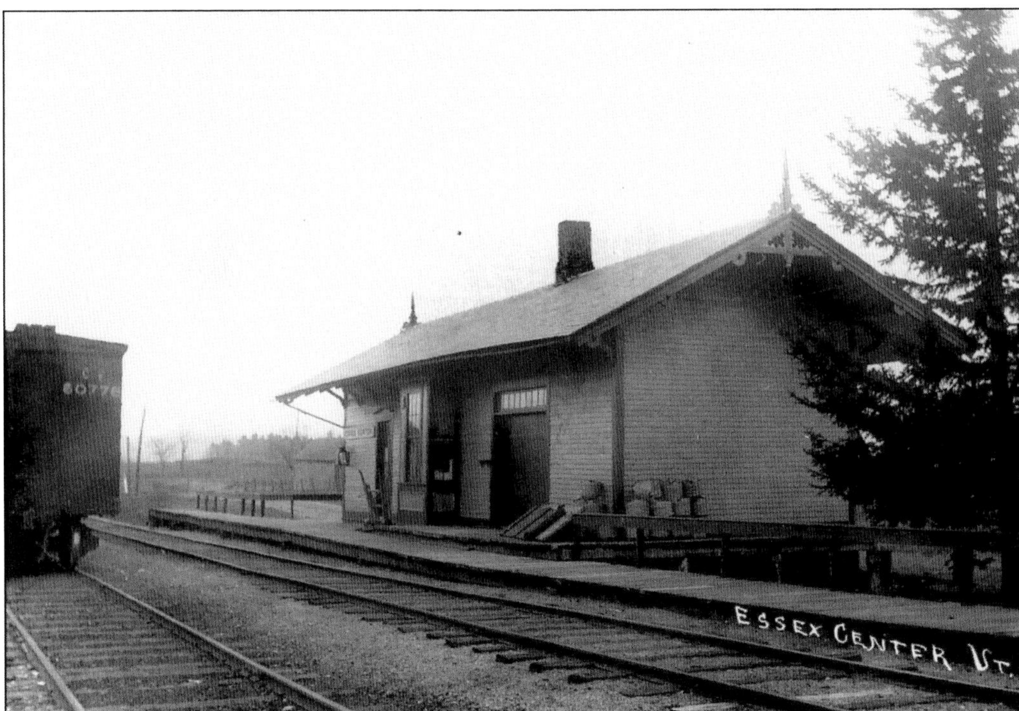

At one time, the Burlington & Lamoille ran three passenger trains a day in each direction. It took two hours with stops to travel from Burlington to Cambridge. Freight included lumber and dairy products, coal, firewood, granite, grain, potatoes, eggs, oysters, ice, and livestock. The Essex Center station was photographed before the line was torn up in 1938. The station has since been renovated as a residence.

On July 7, 1984, the 13-car Amtrak *Montrealer*, carrying more than 200 passengers, derailed just across the Winooski River in Williston when heavy rains washed out several beaver dams and overwhelmed a culvert. Five lives were lost. Rescue workers from a wide area, including the village and town fire departments and emergency personnel, put their training to work and were on the scene for many hours rescuing people from the wreckage.

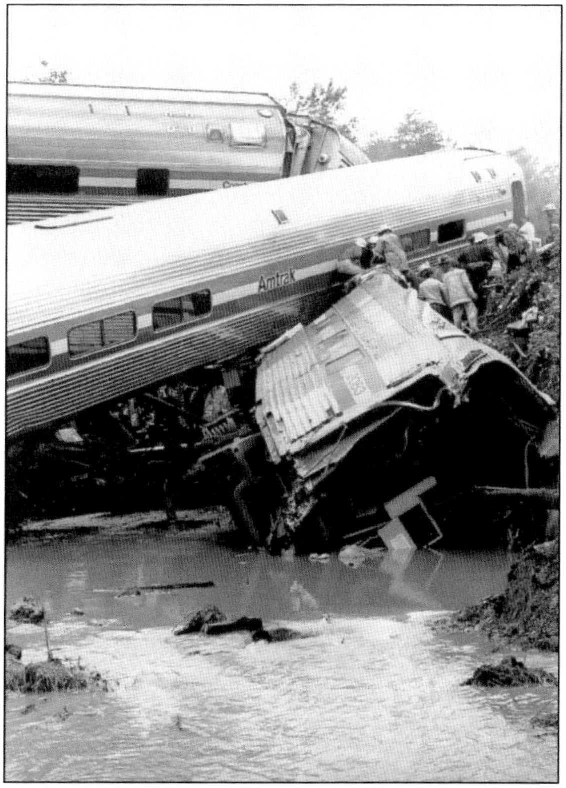

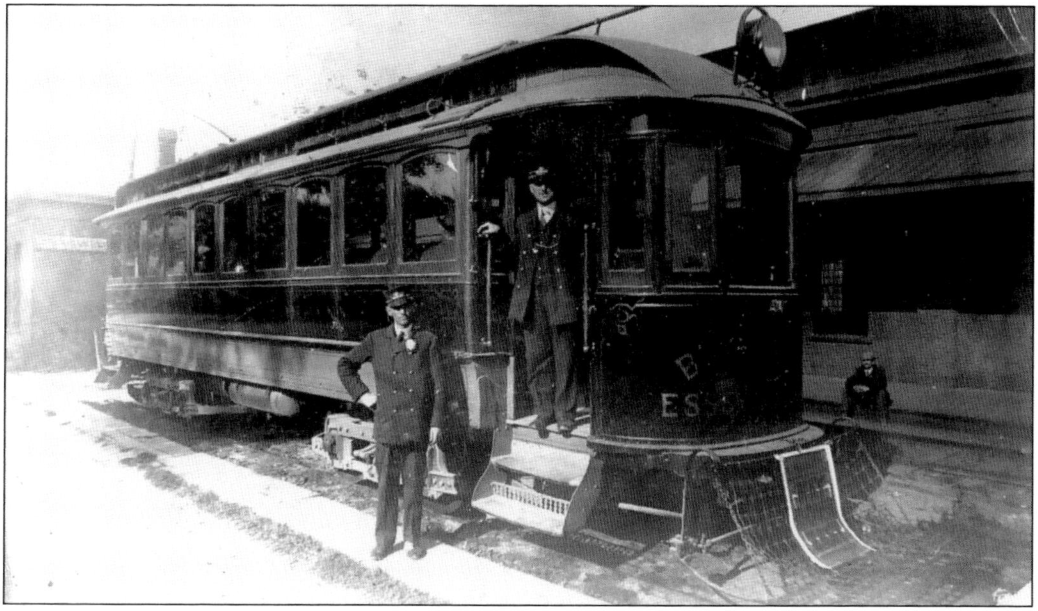

The Military Post Street Railway began in 1895 as a horse-drawn trolley between Winooski, past Fort Ethan Allen, to the train depot in Essex Junction, where this crew poses with its electrified car. The playbill on the front of the car advertised the 1920 D. W. Griffith movie *Way Down East*, starring Lillian Gish. Competition from cars and buses led to the end of trolley service in 1929.

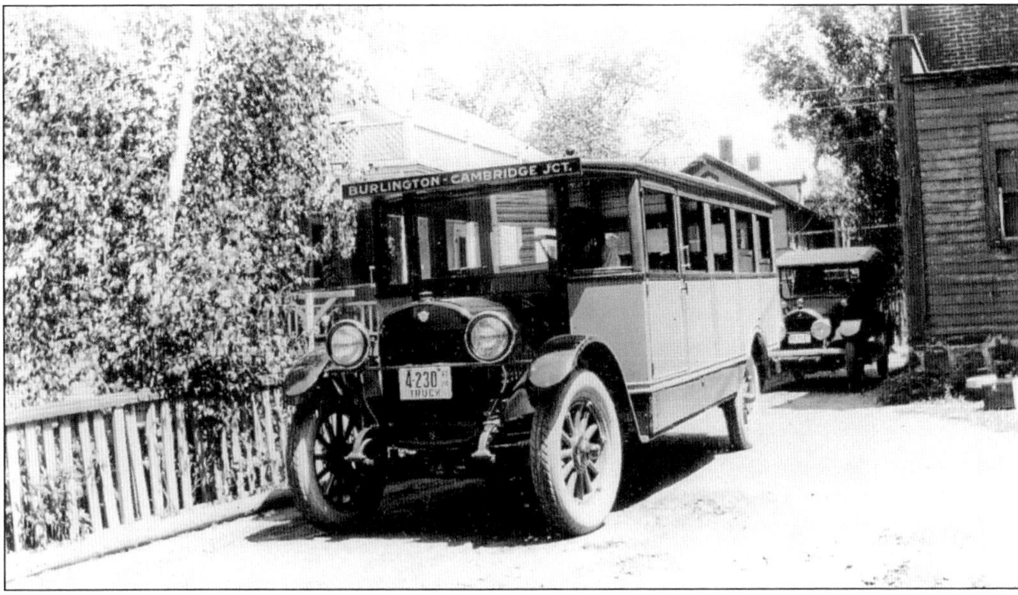

A bus route between Burlington, Essex, and Cambridge Junction was established in late 1923. In April 1925, Essex native Ray E. Nichols purchased the rights to the route, extending it to Johnson and Newport. He continued this service until being bought out by Vermont Transit in December 1938.

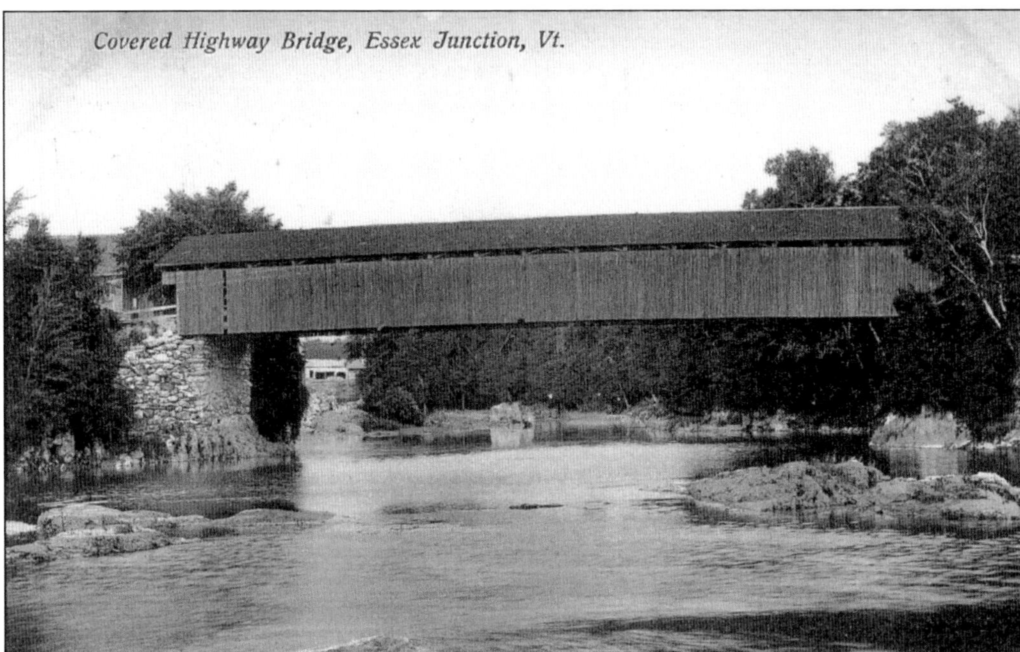

This covered bridge, spanning the Winooski River at Hubbel's Falls, replaced a floating bridge that was washed out during the freshet of 1830. It has been estimated that the freshet was equal in size to 80 percent of the 1927 flood. The 1922 town report notes that E. A. Martin was paid for "snowing bridge at dam 2 yrs." Did he remove the snow or bring some in to ease the passage of sleighs?

This photograph shows the iron bridge across the Winooski River *c.* 1980. The bridge was erected in the spring of 1927, withstood the flood the next November, and served until 1986. This area made the Paul Harvey national radio news on November 30, 1962, when a tank trailer with 3,000 gallons of vinyl acetate wrecked and burned on the hill near the powerhouse. (Courtesy S. Henry Lampert, D.D.S.)

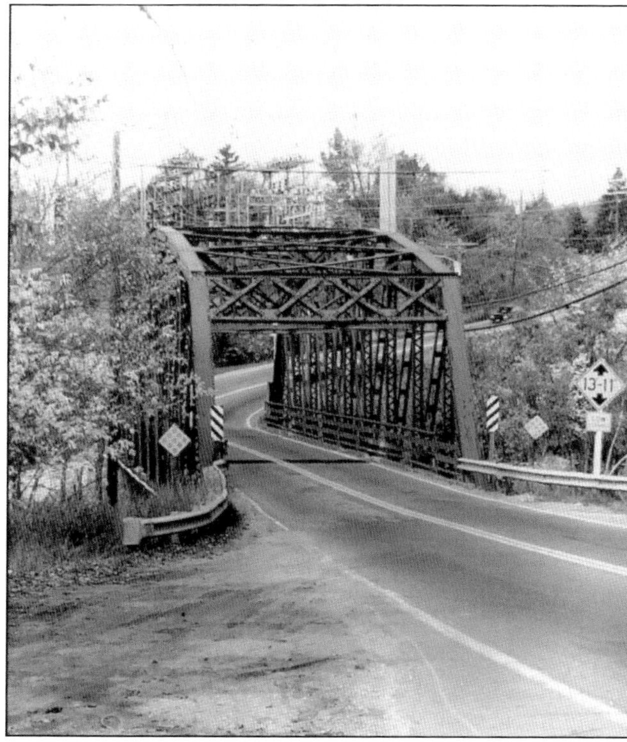

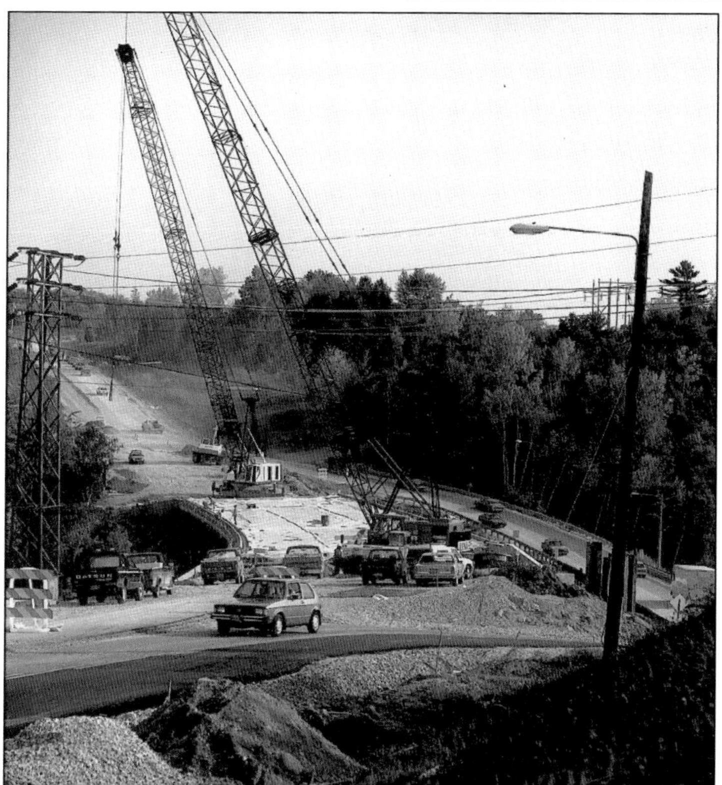

What locals often referred to as "the Power House Bridge" on Route 2A was taken down in 1986, and a temporary bridge (far right) was put in place. This photograph, taken in September 1987, shows the present span under construction. By November, it was open to traffic. (Courtesy Betsy [Thrasher] Melvin.)

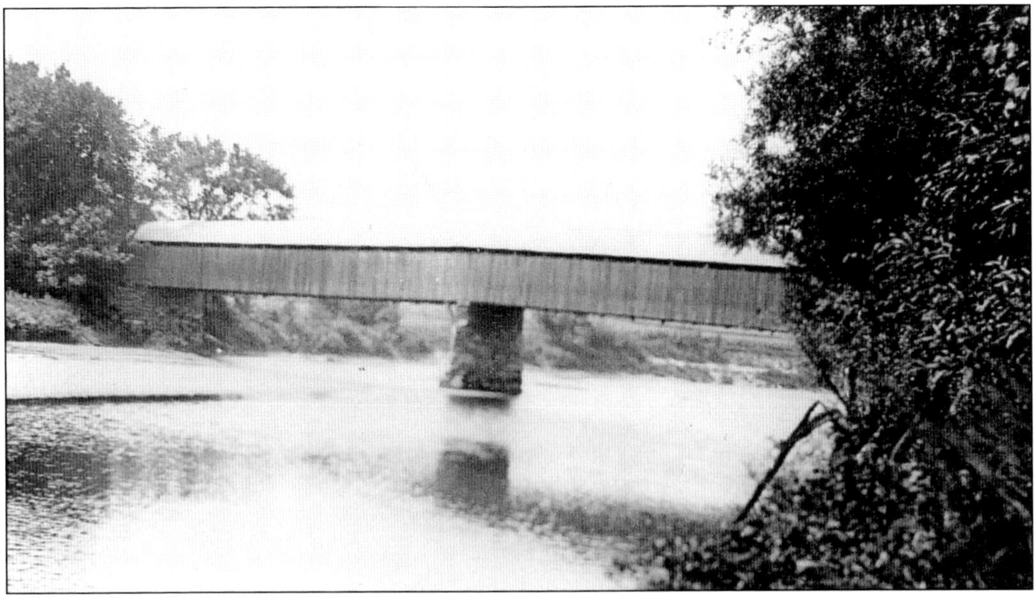

This double-lane covered bridge, on North Williston Road, was built in 1860. Julia Fifield, who lived in North Williston in the 1920s, recalls how she spent time each Saturday removing advertisements from the inside of the bridge. When the wind rustled the papers, her horse would spook, making it difficult for her to continue the ride to school in Essex Junction.

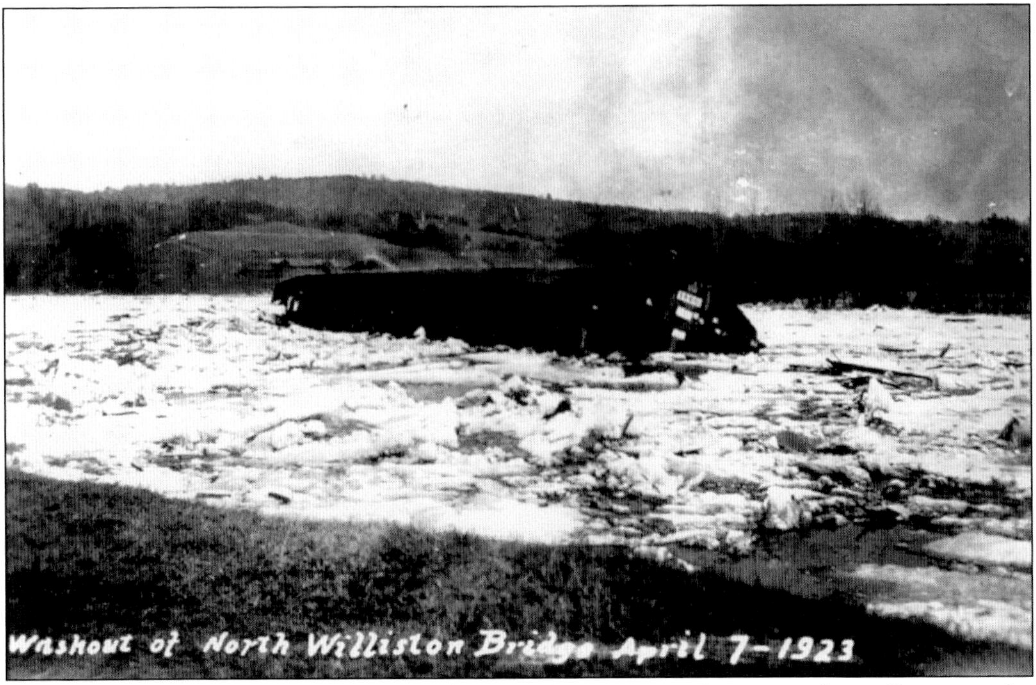

Henry Tarrier remembers that on April 7, 1923, ice jammed against the willows on the riverbank, and a large elm tree with its roots skyward stopped against the North Williston bridge, lifting it up and onto the ice. Rob Redmond let the bridge sit on his land for 30 days and then claimed it as his. The Williston selectmen sued to regain ownership but lost, and the timbers were turned into a barn.

Two

FOR THE PUBLIC GOOD

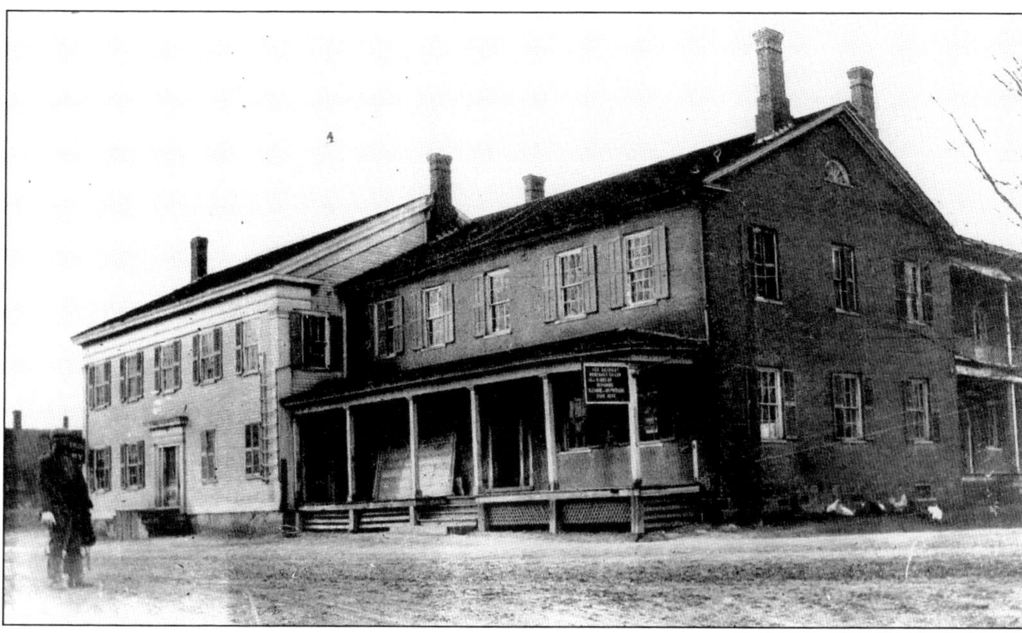

Lincoln Hall, now the home of the village offices, has had several uses since it was built by Abram Stevens in 1819–1820. Abram Stevens operated it as a tavern under the name of the Stevens House before the Stauntons ran it as the Staunton House. In 1858, the building was sold to David and Samuel Tyler, who also owned taverns at Butler's Corners and in Essex Center.

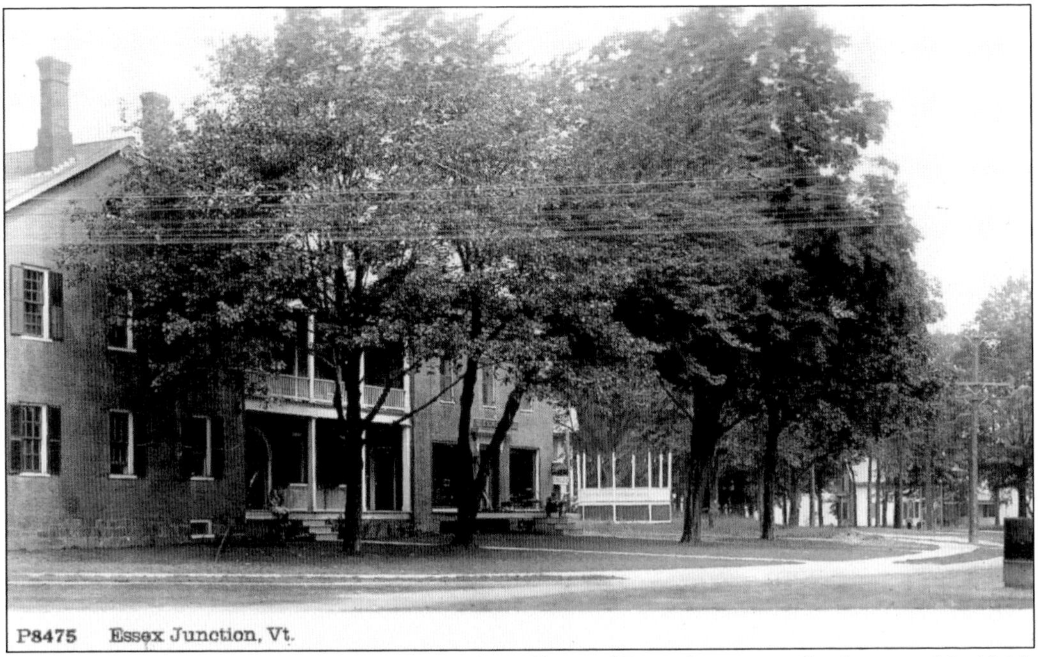

In 1911, Henry Root sold the property to the village of Essex Junction. On January 21, 1914, the trustees voted to name the land and buildings Lincoln Hall Square. During World War II, Lincoln Hall served as a first aid center. Following the war, Teachout Brothers Hardware was located in the building, as were living quarters for the police chief, the police headquarters, and the fire department. Note the bandstand on the right.

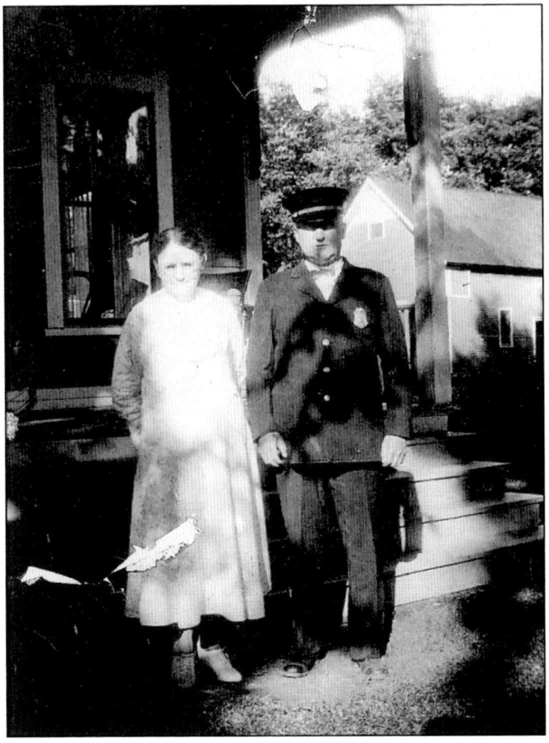

Shown here are James Flynn and his wife, Cecelia (McCoy), in 1931. Flynn was hired in 1926 as a police officer for Essex Junction. The 1936 village report lists him as the chief of police. That year, there were 23 arrests, including intoxication, larceny, vagrancy, and breach of peace. In the 1930s, most of the police force was part-time, and the officers used their own cars.

Police chief James F. Mulcahy poses in May 1953. Under Mulcahy's tenure, cars were purchased, an office was set up, the first radar unit was started, and a curfew of 9:00 p.m. was instituted for juveniles. He was chief of police for the village from *c*. 1952 through 1957. He is also listed as the chief in the 1969 village report.

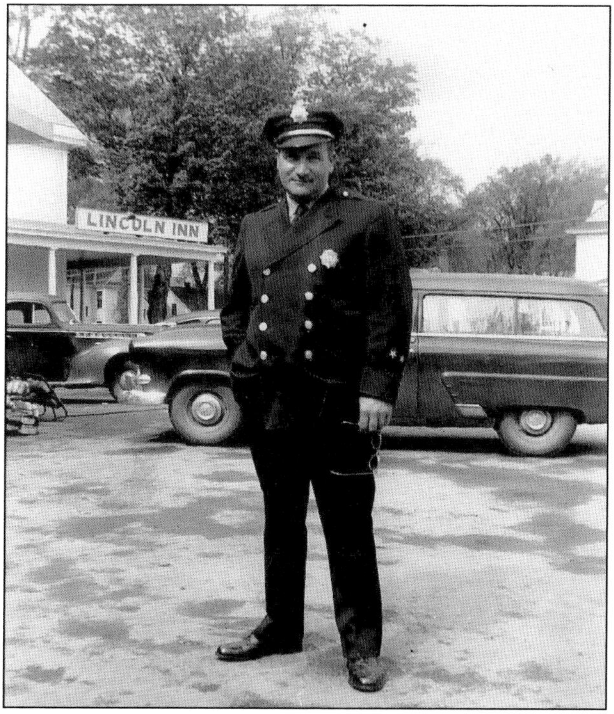

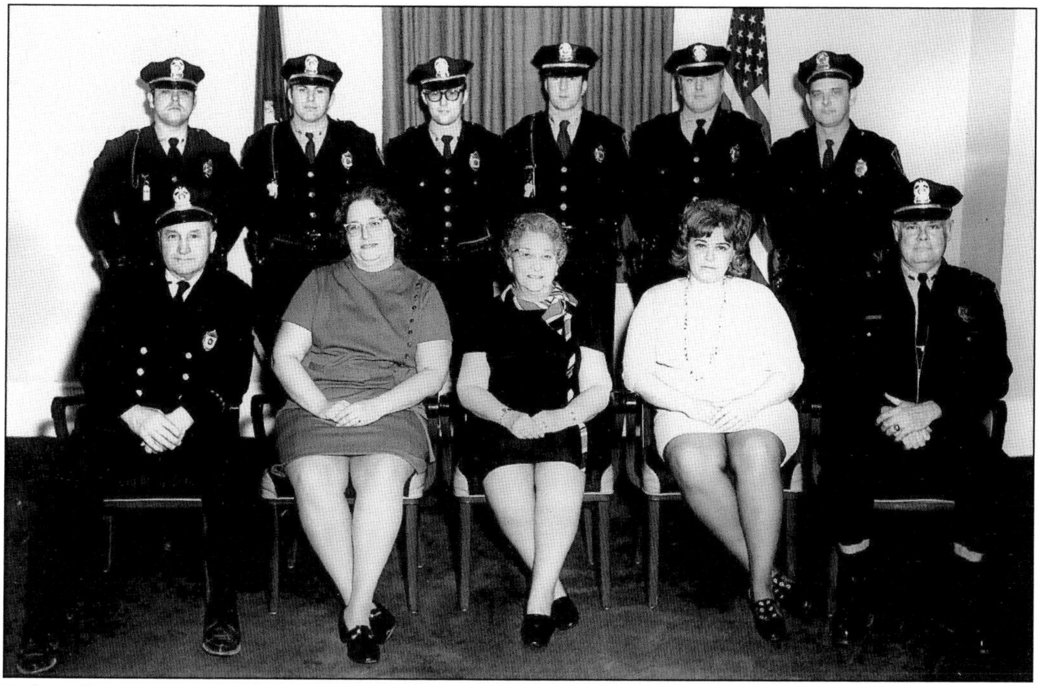

Police department employees *c*. 1970 are, from left to right, as follows: (first row) James Mulcahy, Joy Meyers, Marie Bailey, Marlene Colman, and Mac Kingsland; (second row) Roger Barber, Wayne Bither, John Terry, Leo Nadeau, Ron Audette, and Harold Barrett. John Terry, police chief from 1976 to 1999, helped with the expansion of the village force to include the town in 1980.

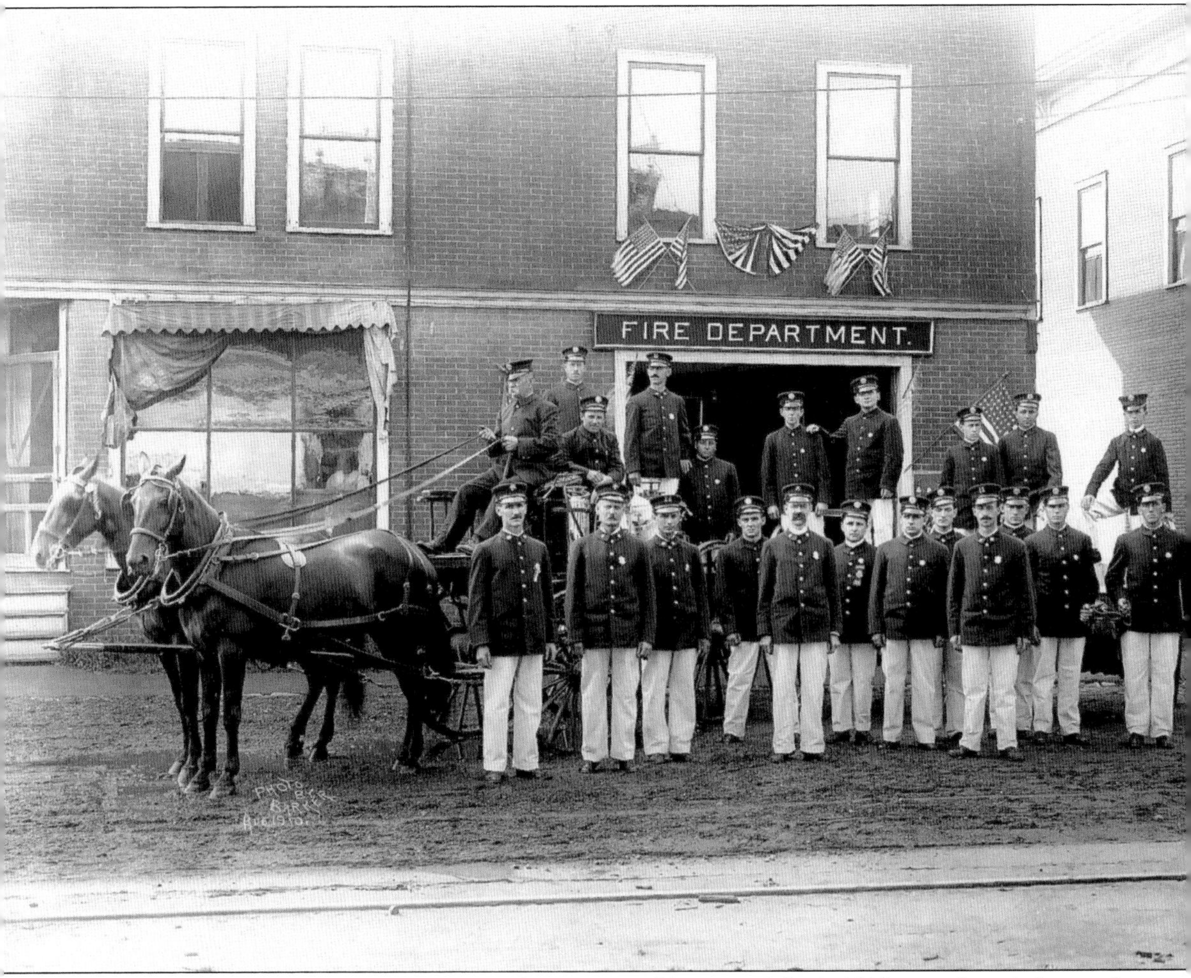

Essex Junction Fire Department members pictured here on July 4, 1910, are, from left to right, as follows: (first row) Guy Peck, George Woodard, Floyd Barnes, Dean Viele, Frank Woods, Ed Cronin, Arthur Lavigne, Fred Demag, Wilbur Greene, Chester Barnes, Ira Charbonneau, and Clark Remington; (second row) horses Jack and Jimmy, driver George "Gramp" Willey, Chancey Burns, Ralph Stevens, Joe Seymour, Arthur Thompson, George Teachout, George Sheldon, Bert Prescott, Guy Nichols, and Jay Saffard. In the 1908 village report, the board of trustees approved the organization of a volunteer fire department. Guy Peck, listed as the chief, was instructed to buy a set of harnesses and badges. Early alarms were sounded by ringing the bell of the Congregational church, or by a Central Vermont locomotive blowing its whistle. In 1916, a fire alarm system was approved at the annual meeting.

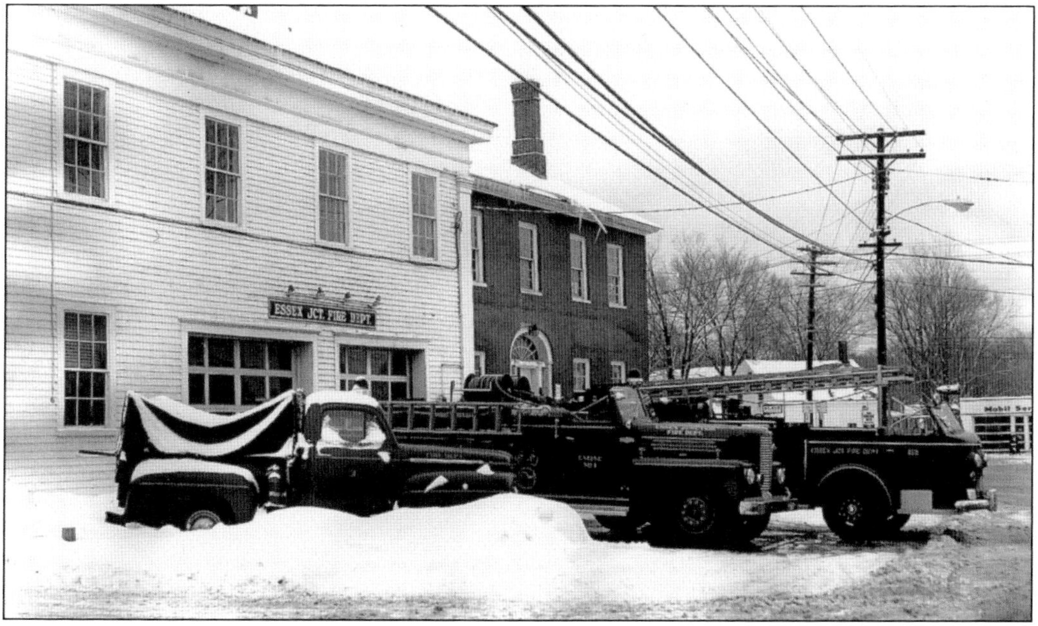

The early fire station was located at 13 Main Street. If there was a fire, horses stabled nearby were pressed into use. In 1914, the station moved to Lincoln Hall on the Pearl Street side. Several trucks wait outside Lincoln Hall in the 1950s. The fire department moved to its current location west of Lincoln Hall in 1965.

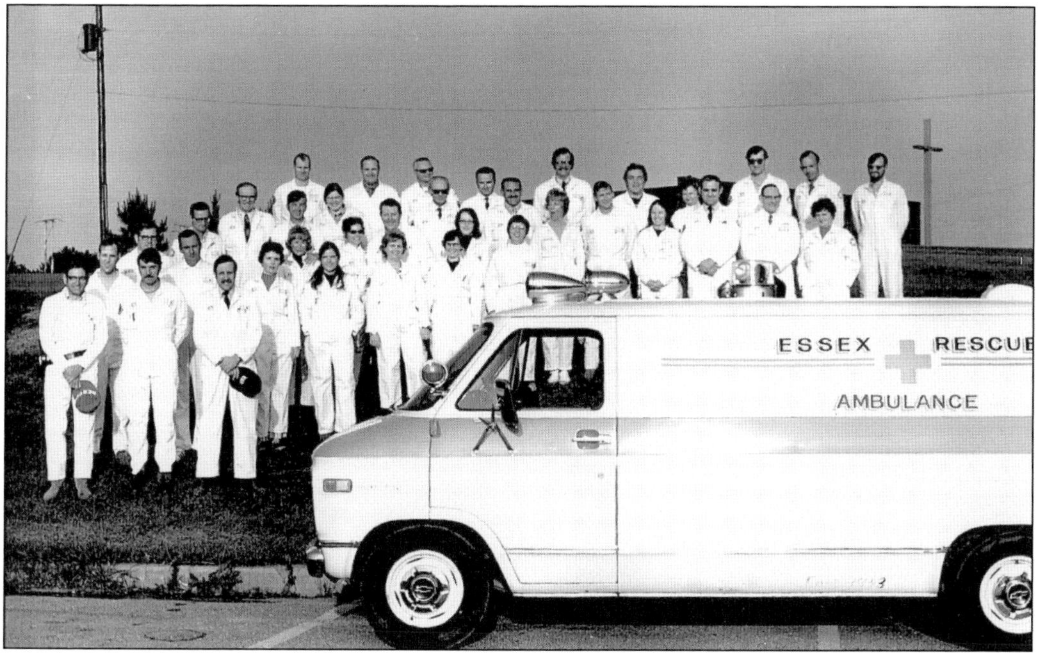

In the late 1960s, several community volunteers saw the need for a rescue service in town. Essex Rescue started on October 1, 1971. The present facility was built on Educational Drive with help from vocational students from the high school. Today, Essex Rescue, with more than 40 volunteers, answers about 1,400 calls a year in Essex, Westford, Jericho, and Underhill. Members appear in this 1973 photograph.

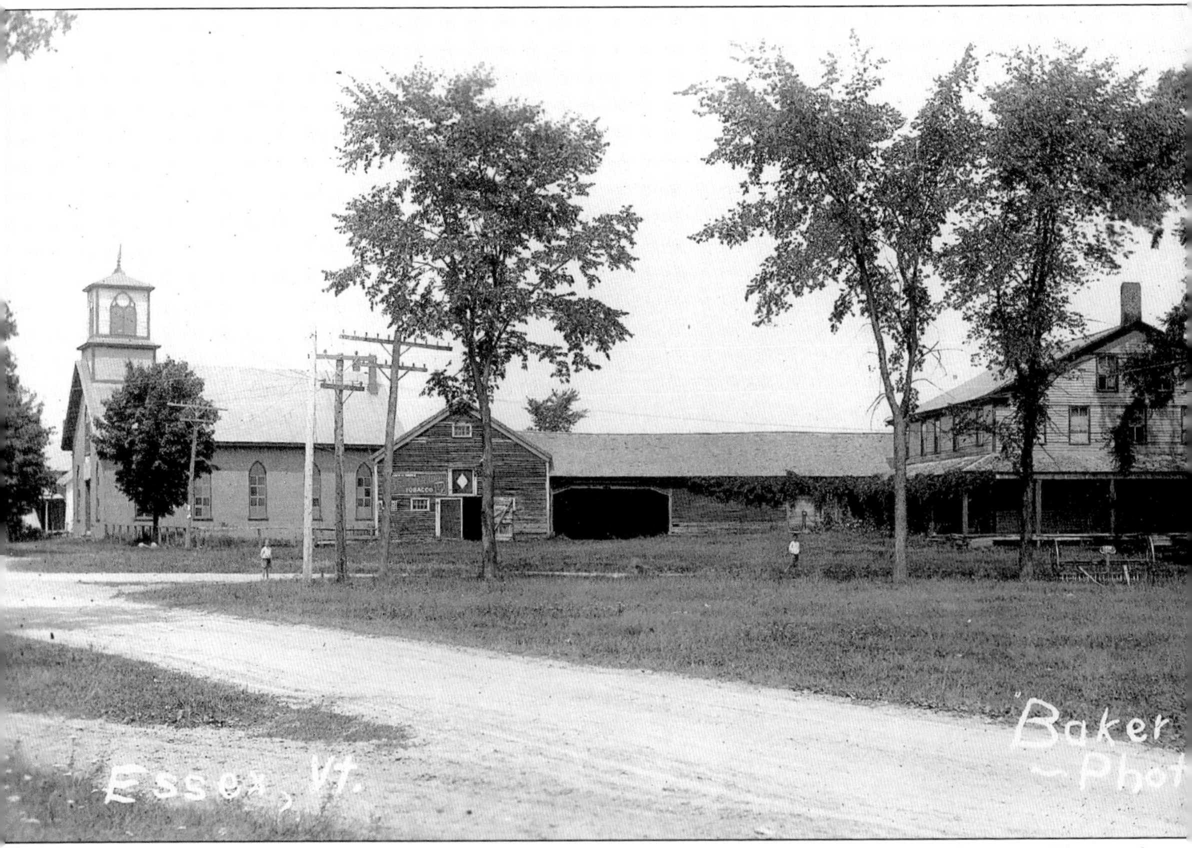

Memorial Hall (left) was built in 1871 "in grateful remembrance of the brave soldiers of Essex who lost their lives in service of their country during the war for the preservation of the Union, 1861–1865." A marble plaque above the front door lists the names of 33 of the 36 soldiers from Essex who died in the war. The building has hosted town meetings, socials, basketball games, a pistol-shooting range, and boxing matches. It has also served as the library for the Essex Classical Institute. Today, Memorial Hall, mainly used by the Essex Community Players, has been renovated with a performance area and seating for 130. The building on the right was a tavern and hotel owned and operated by Stephen Butler, followed by his son Billie Bishop Butler. It eventually became part of Merle Wood's Country Store and was an apartment building when it burned down on December 23, 1968.

The Memorial Hall tower was dismantled in October 1959. The slow disappearance of steeples in town—the Congregational church and the Grange also lost theirs in the 1950s—was lamented with the comment, "They're all getting to look like barns!" (Courtesy Betsy [Thrasher] Melvin.)

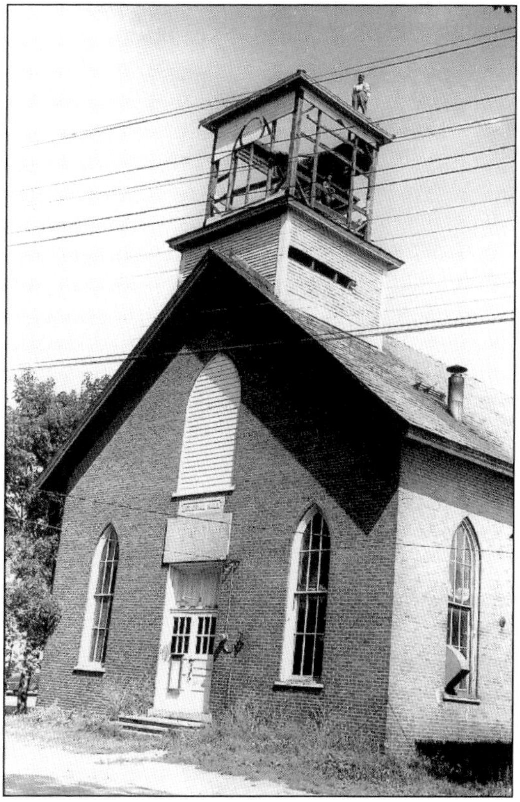

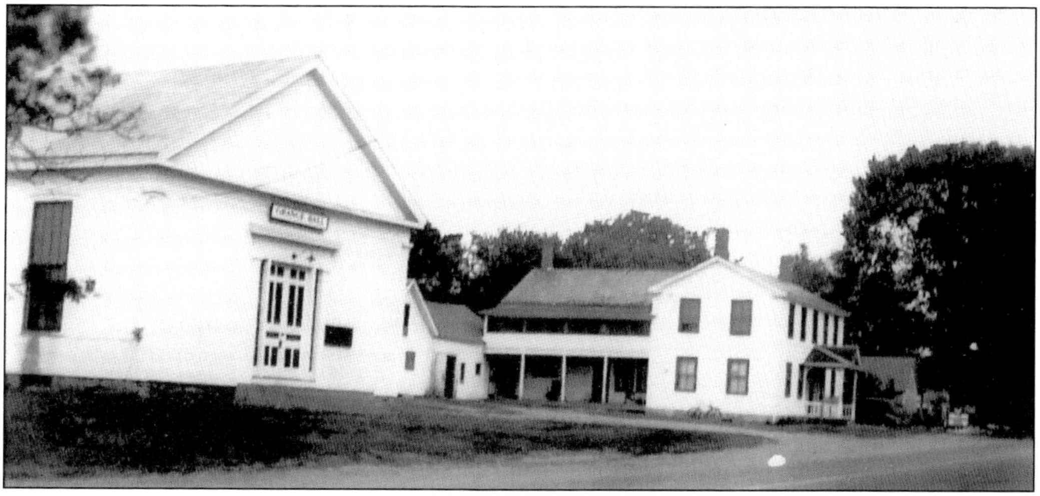

The building to the right of the Grange in this photograph served as a preventorium from 1918 to 1922. Children with tuberculosis, or those in danger of contracting the disease, were able to live in a healthy environment. They slept on screened porches year-round, protected in the winter "by heavy ducking." The children ate hearty meals, and hopefully each child was "thoroughly converted to the hygienic manner of living" before returning home. (Photograph by Evans Knapp.)

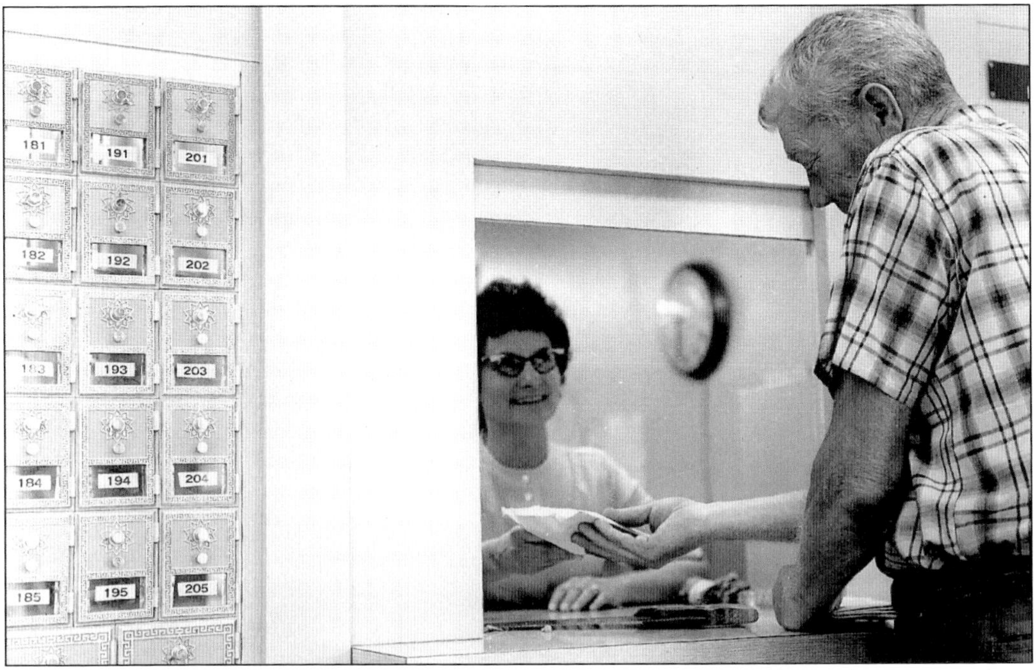

The Essex Center Post Office underwent some renovations in 1966. Additional service windows were added, and 59 new mailboxes were installed. The entrance to the post office was moved from the north side of the building to the east side, and more apartments were added. Here, acting postmaster Elizabeth Gunn waits on Bill Cunningham. (Courtesy Betsy [Thrasher] Melvin.)

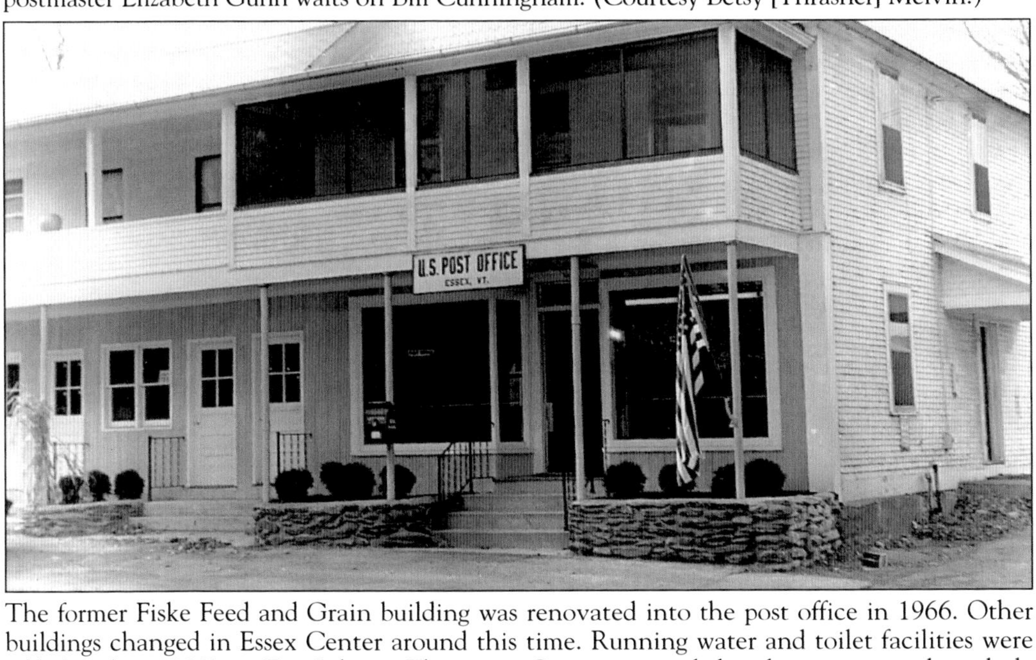

The former Fiske Feed and Grain building was renovated into the post office in 1966. Other buildings changed in Essex Center around this time. Running water and toilet facilities were added to the 1933 Essex Free Library. The empty Congregational church was now used regularly by the Calvary Baptist Church. Memorial Hall became the home of the Essex Community Players. Betsy (Thrasher) Melvin reported this news for the *Burlington Free Press*. (Courtesy Betsy [Thrasher] Melvin.)

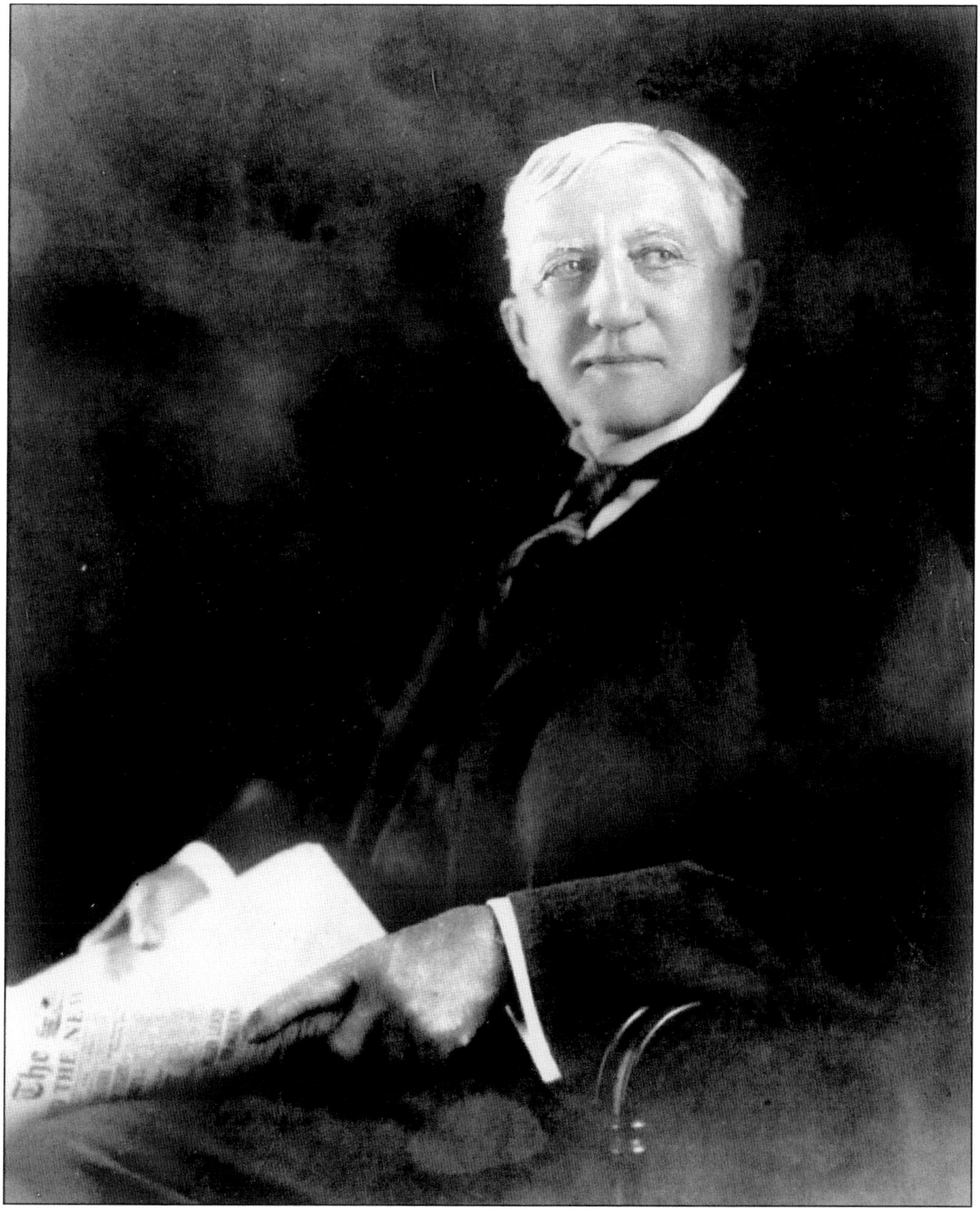

Samuel Aaron Brownell II was born on May 29, 1842, in Williston, the son of Chauncey Wells Brownell and Laura Chapin Higbee. He attended J. S. Cilley's School in Williston and Eastman's Business College in Poughkeepsie, New York. After a short adventure in the oil fields of Titusville, Pennsylvania, he bought his father's store at the Five Corners. With his brother Chauncey Wells II, he established a power plant on the site of his father's property along the Winooski River and was soon generating electricity. Samuel Brownell represented the town in the legislature for several years. He built the Brownell Block in 1894 and helped organize the Essex Trust Company (later the Howard Trust), which opened in 1913. He died on August 18, 1927.

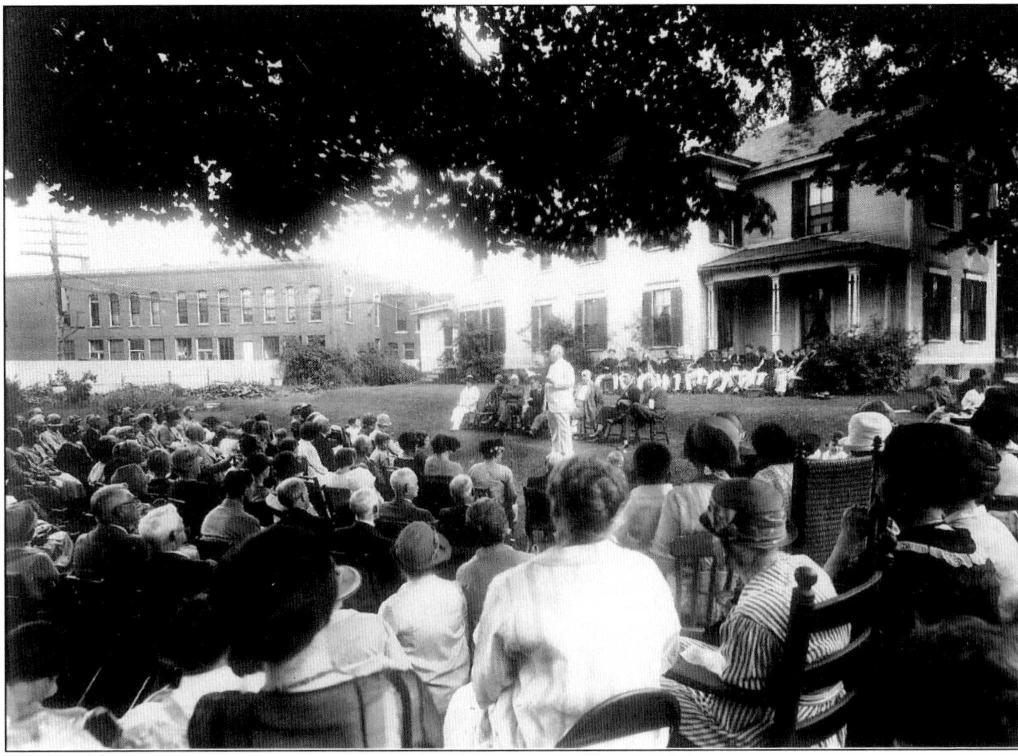

The dedication ceremonies of the Brownell Library took place on Samuel Brownell's lawn, across the street from the library, on July 20, 1926. Here, the president of the University of Vermont, Guy Bailey, delivers the main address. Brownell was not well, so he listened to the proceedings from his bedroom window. His speech was read by his son Cleon H. Brownell. The Essex Junction Boys' Band, seated near the porch, played a selection.

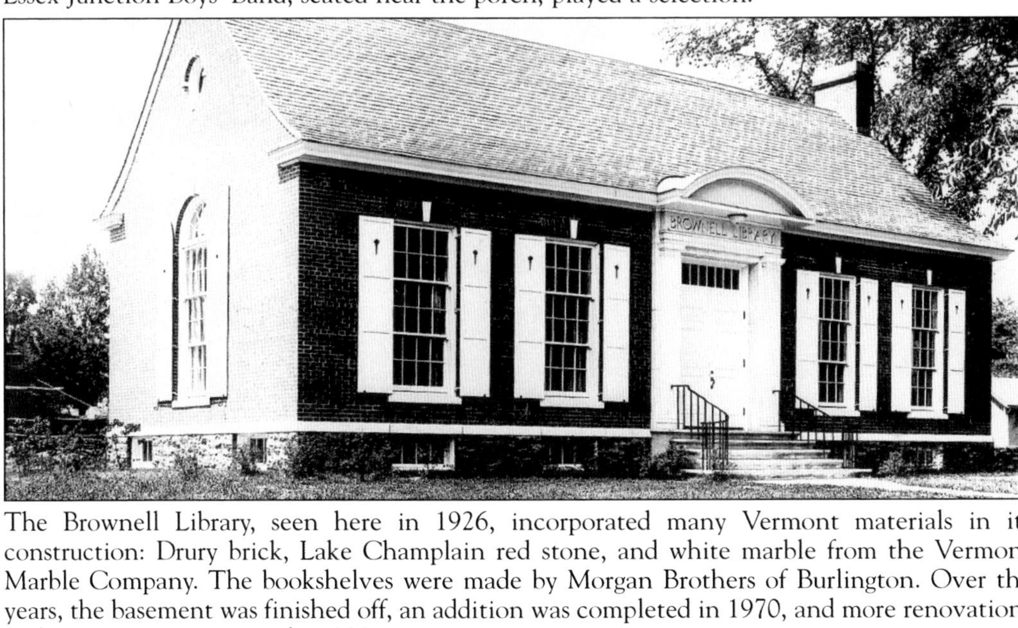

The Brownell Library, seen here in 1926, incorporated many Vermont materials in its construction: Drury brick, Lake Champlain red stone, and white marble from the Vermont Marble Company. The bookshelves were made by Morgan Brothers of Burlington. Over the years, the basement was finished off, an addition was completed in 1970, and more renovations and an expansion occurred in 2001.

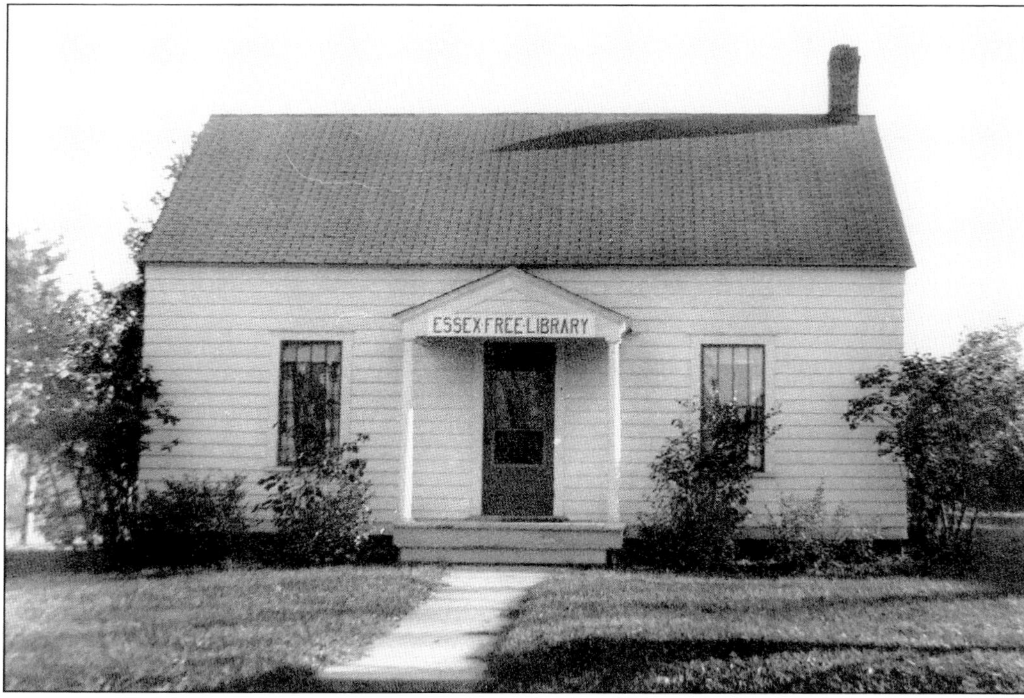

Prior to 1933, when the Essex Free Library opened its doors, the town library was in the side room of Memorial Hall. Fund-raising, aided with the sale of a Packard automobile won in a newspaper subscription contest, led to the construction of this building by O. S. Nichols. It was built and outfitted for $1,400 and housed the library until 1989. It is now the home of the Essex Public Works Department. (Photograph by Evans Knapp.)

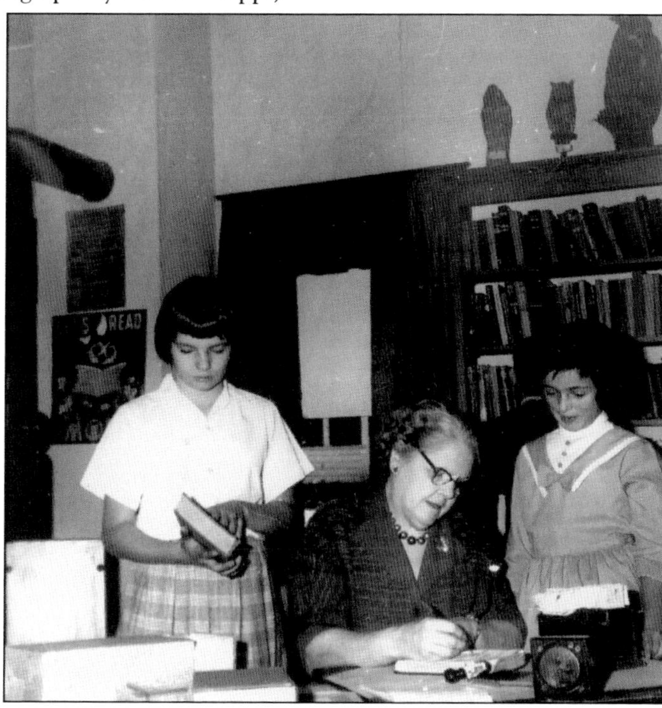

Bernice Bixby was the librarian at the Essex Free Library from 1956 to 1975. Behind her, on top of the shelf, are several of the 100 stuffed birds given to the library by Charles Weed. The collection was later given to the Audubon Center in Huntington. (Courtesy Betsy [Thrasher] Melvin.)

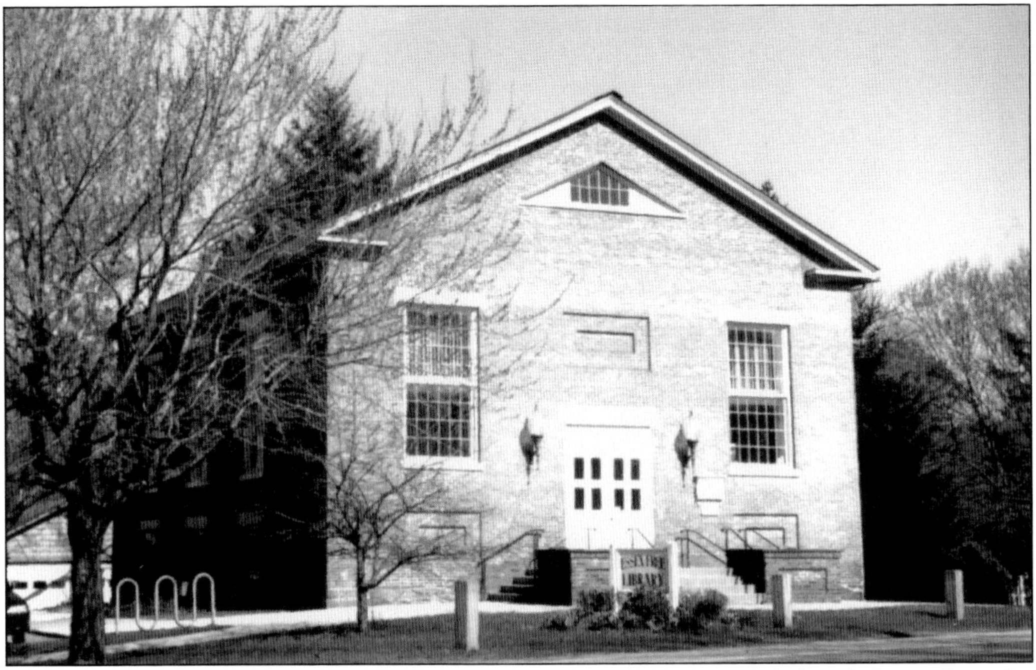

In 1987, voters approved a bond to restore the former Congregational church located on the common as the new home for the Essex Free Library. The building was completely renovated and updated, and an elevator was added. Using the building's three levels greatly increased shelf space. Head librarian Susan Overfield now oversees a staff of six and a collection of about 25,000 titles. (Courtesy Betsy [Thrasher] Melvin.)

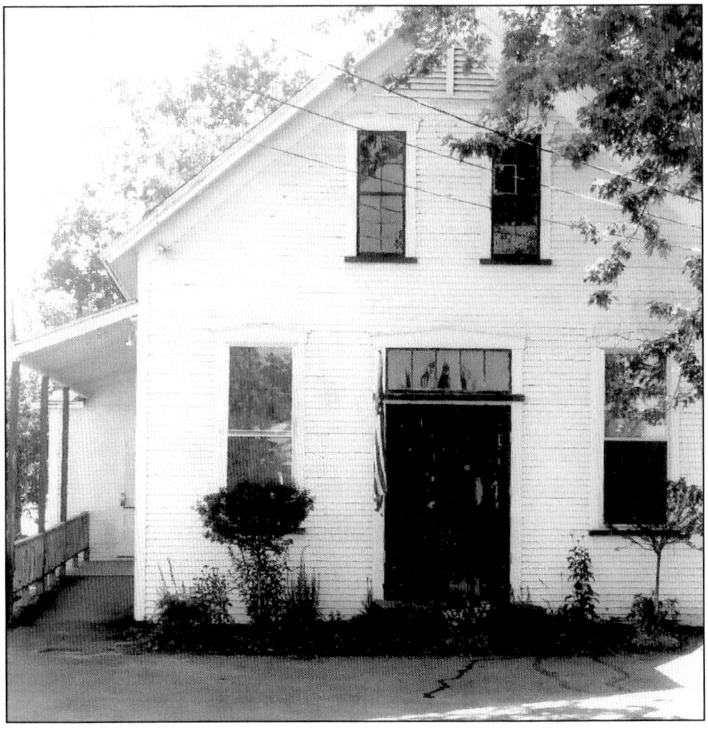

The White School dates from c. 1879 and stands on the former site of the Stone School in Essex Center. The building was expanded c. 1899 and was used as a school as late as 1984. For several years thereafter, it housed the Essex Town school superintendent's office.

Harriet Farnsworth Powell, a teacher for many years, researched and recorded Essex history and was instrumental in the founding of the historical society. The Essex Community Historical Society was established in 1991, and the White School was renovated to house the museum and many artifacts from Powell's estate. Her sons Rollie Jr. (left) and Holly attended the dedication of the museum on June 13, 1992.

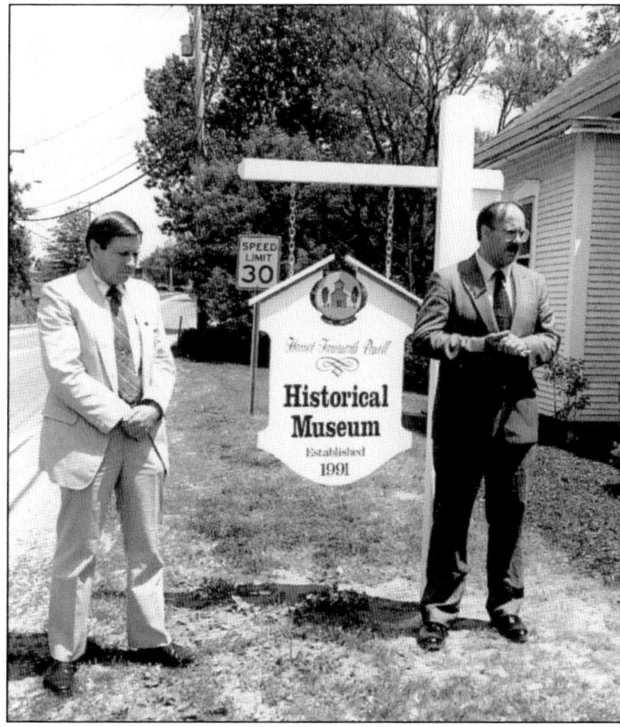

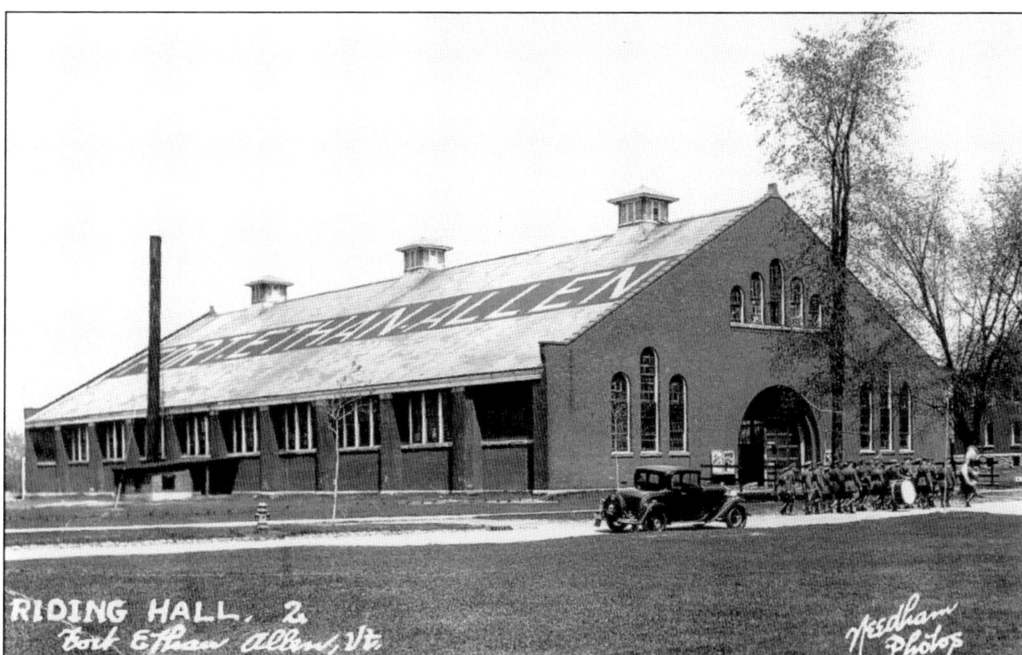

Fort Ethan Allen was established by federal legislation passed in 1892. Dr. Seward Webb of Shelburne Farms, the Central Vermont Railroad, and pledges from local citizens minimized the cost for the government and helped ensure the building of the fort in Chittenden County. The Riding Hall, built in 1895, is now the Elley-Long Music Center, home of the Vermont Youth Orchestra.

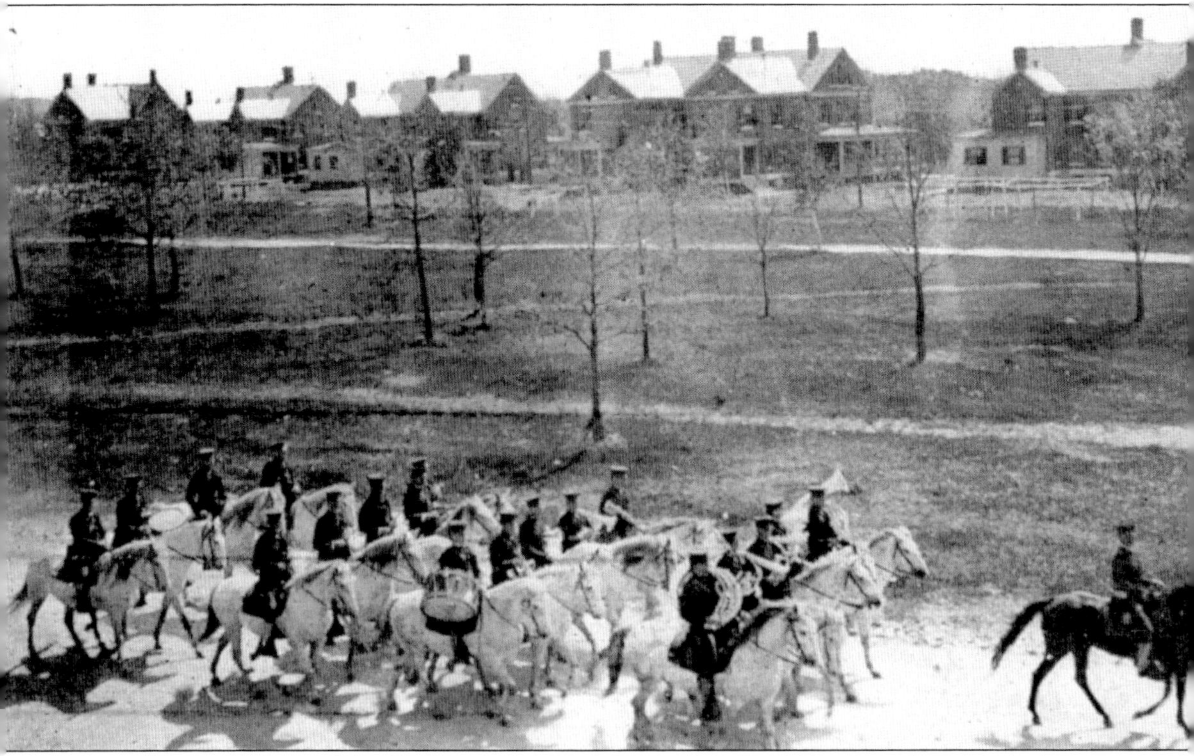

Try to imagine a band on horseback! This postcard is dated October 9, 1908, prior to the arrival of one of the most famous units stationed at the fort: the 10th Cavalry Regiment of African American soldiers, or "the Buffalo Soldiers." They earned their superb reputation during the military action against Native Americans from 1867 to 1889. During their stay here from 1909 to 1913, this northern post gave the soldiers some comfort, with an indoor riding hall during cold-weather training. Their stay was highlighted with an elaborate Wild West show by the soldiers in 1911. In 1913, a 700-mile march to Virginia provided the unit a chance to show off in front of Pres. Woodrow Wilson. The horse era at the fort ended in 1934, when the remaining draft horses were sold and the stables were taken over by automobiles.

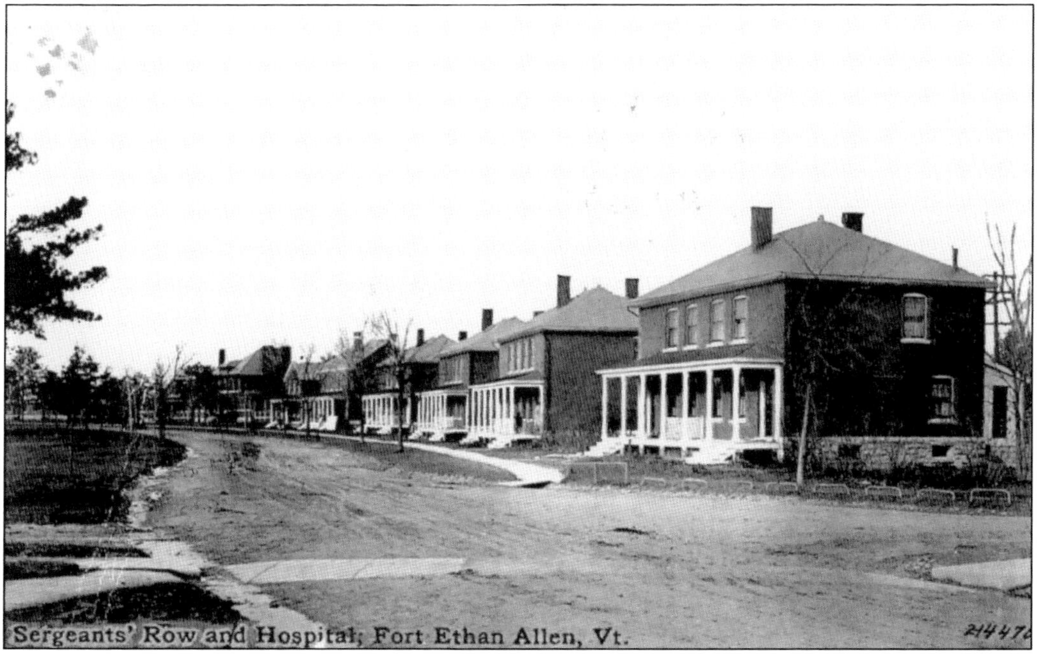

Construction of Fort Ethan Allen was a boon to the local economy, with many Vermont materials used, such as limestone, granite, and Drury brick from Essex Junction. The layout of the fort was dictated by standard plans issued by the quartermaster general. Officer quarters were placed front and center along a curved drive edging the parade ground. Sergeant's Row was behind the larger and more ornate homes of the officers.

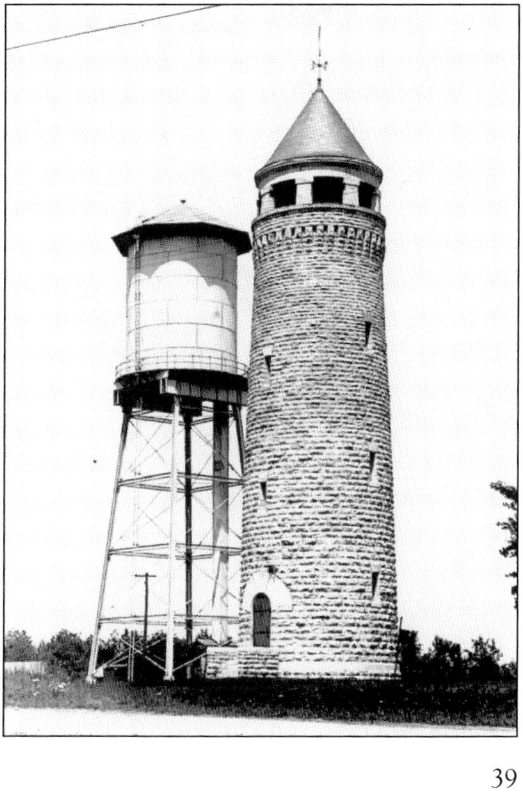

In 1893, the first structure completed was the 80-foot-high, stone-faced water tower that tapped nearby wells. The "look-out holes" allowed soldiers to estimate distances on the rifle range. The metal tank to the left, now gone, provided extra water. Today, the tower is owned by the town and is leased by the Champlain Water District. It is occasionally opened to visitors by the Essex Community Historical Society.

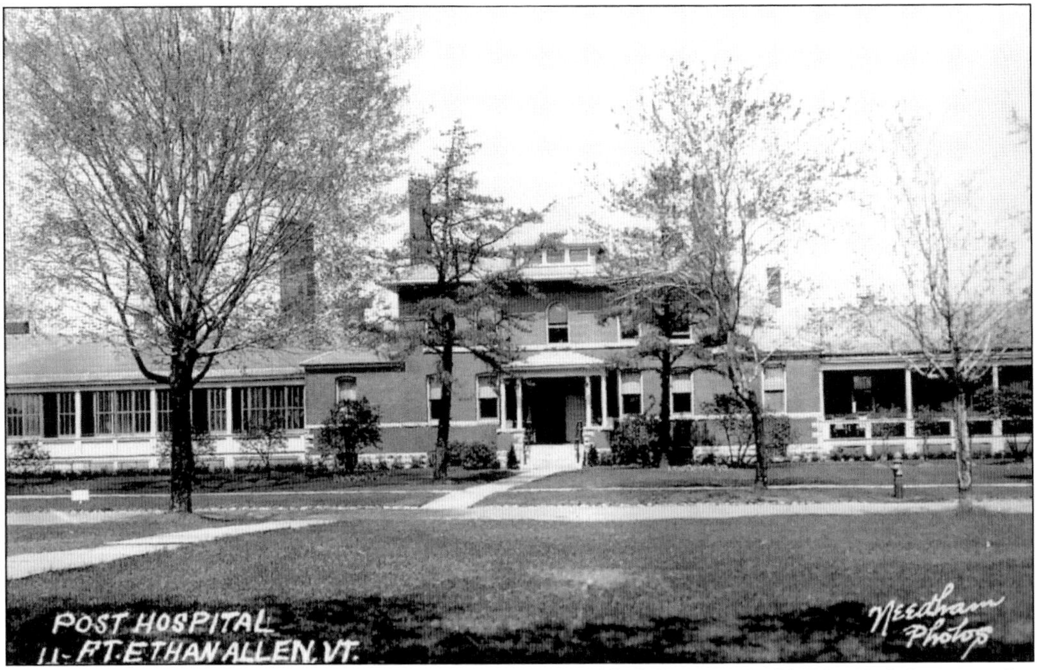

The hospital was completed in 1894, with two wings added during World War II. It became the Green Mountain Nursing Home when the fort ceased its military function in 1960. Now many of the buildings at the fort are used by businesses, as private homes, and for college housing.

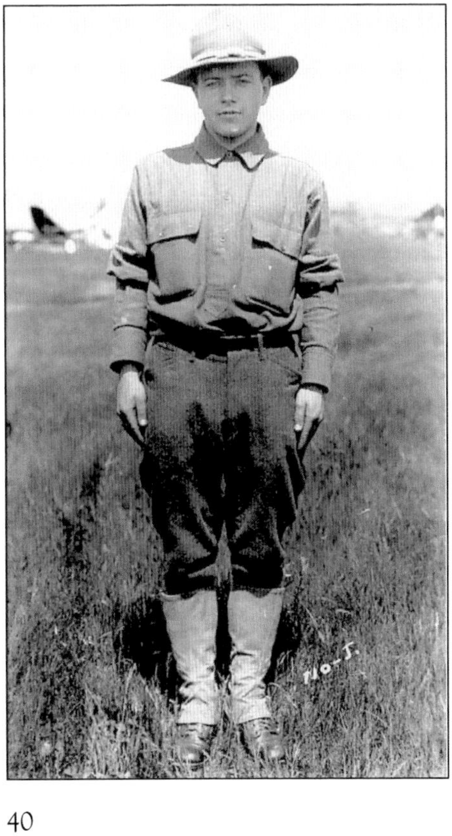

During World War I, 8,000 troops trained at the fort, including the Vermont National Guard. The message on this postcard reads, "Martin in his working togs at Fort Ethan Allen, July 1, 1917." If Martin was in the Vermont National Guard, he would have received training in marching, mock combat, weaponry, and physical conditioning.

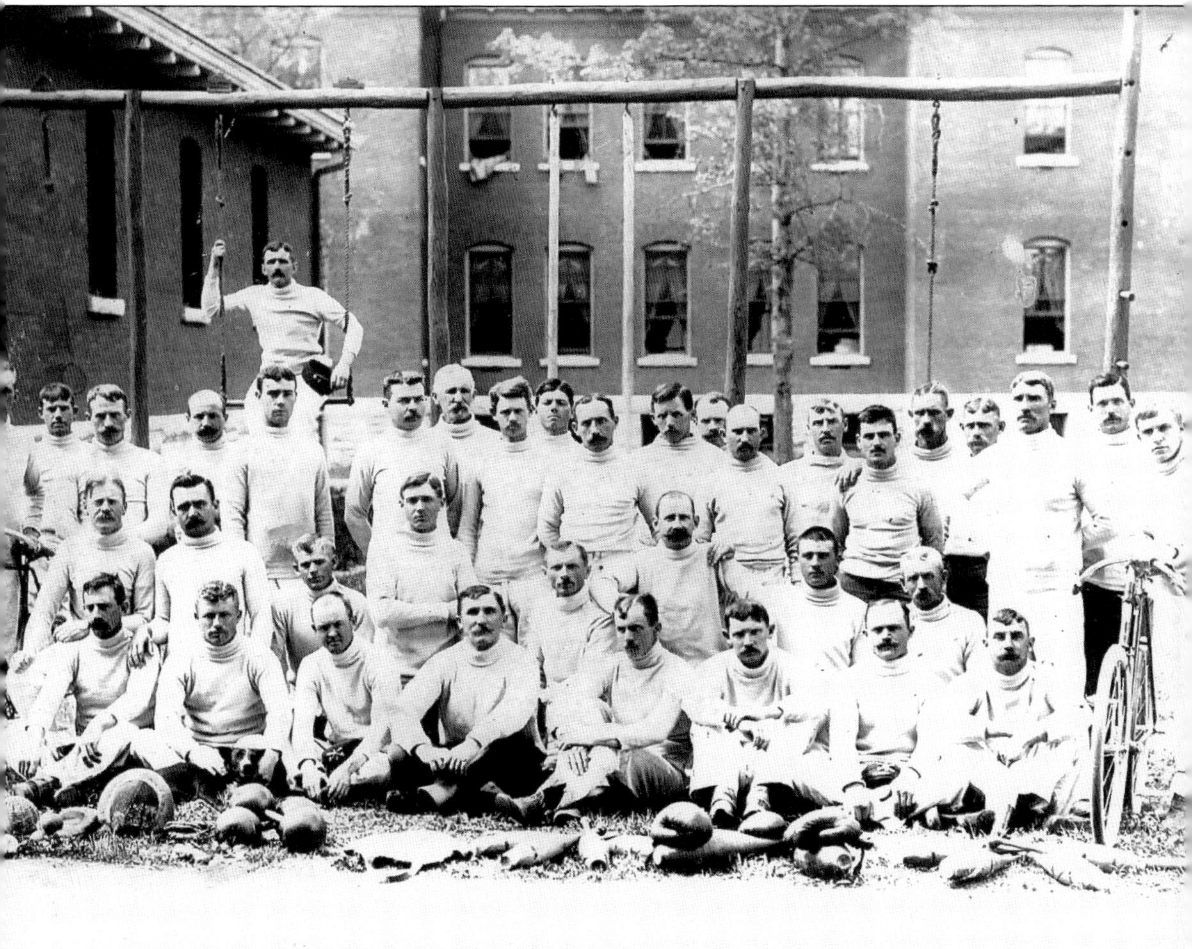

In this 1896 photograph of the Hardie Athletic Club, Troop G, 3rd U.S. Cavalry, note the equipment on the grass. A large variety of off-duty activities kept the troops entertained: movies, theatrical productions, boxing, riding, bowling, football, baseball, and shooting competitions. Sunday afternoon band concerts and parades delighted soldiers and locals alike. Starting in 1895, a horse-drawn railway connected the fort with Essex Junction to the east and Winooski and Burlington to the west. In 1927, soldiers could catch a trolley to Burlington as often as every 20 minutes. Saturday night forays into Essex Junction, Winooski, and Burlington by the soldiers often created problems for the local constabulary. Arrests for intoxication increased dramatically as the fort became operational. Local women were invited to dances held at the fort. Florence Remington's scrapbook contains a 25¢ ticket to the camp's annual ball on April 23, 1926. The ticket "also entitles the holder to share in the Free Distribution of a $10 gold piece, 1 barrel of flour and 100 lbs. of sugar."

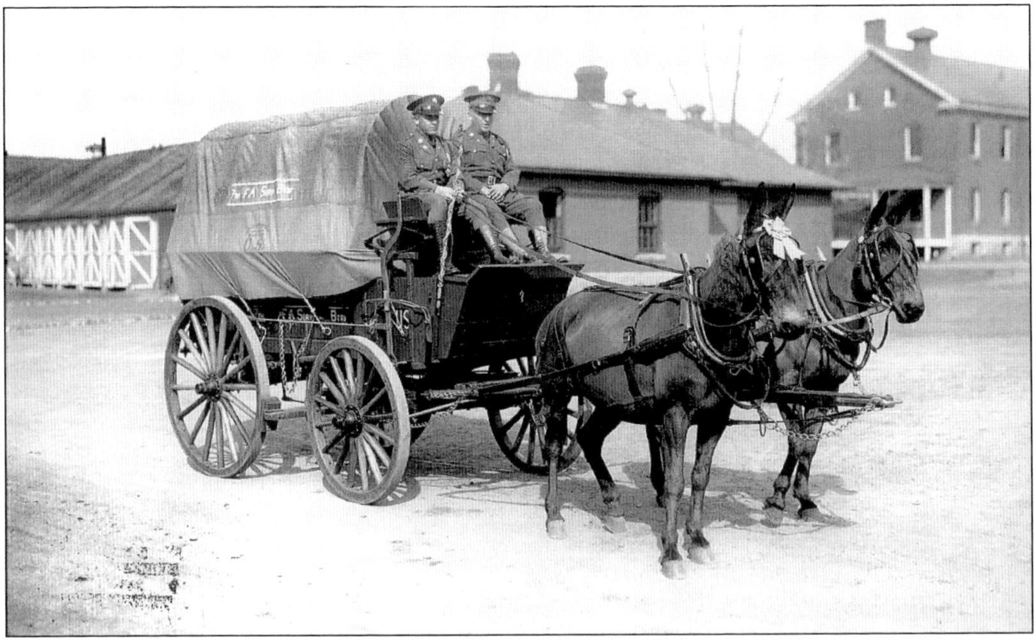

From the beginning, the fort was horse and mule powered. Here, a supply wagon crew displays a ribbon won in a competition. A program for an indoor horse show in 1921 boasted music selections by the "educational and recreational band," a competition for polo ponies, ladies' saddle horses, officers' chargers, and other classes for enlisted men and officers. Essex Junction businesses Hilliker's Garage and R. O. Mudgett and Company had advertisements in the program.

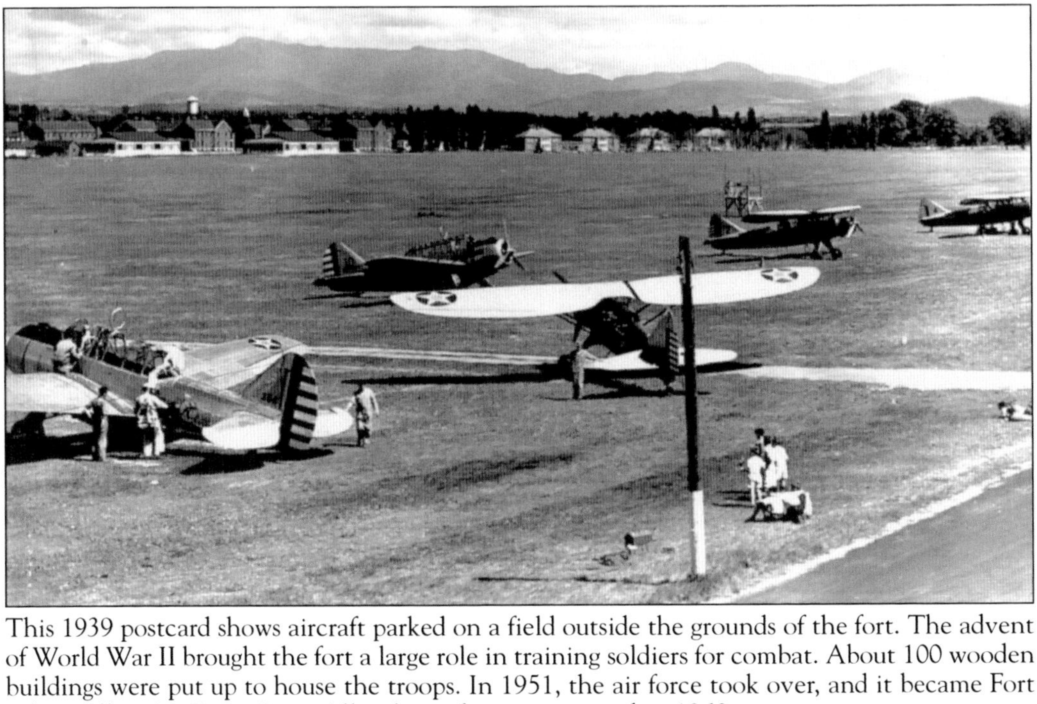

This 1939 postcard shows aircraft parked on a field outside the grounds of the fort. The advent of World War II brought the fort a large role in training soldiers for combat. About 100 wooden buildings were put up to house the troops. In 1951, the air force took over, and it became Fort Ethan Allen Air Force Base. All military functions ceased in 1960.

Three

AT WORK

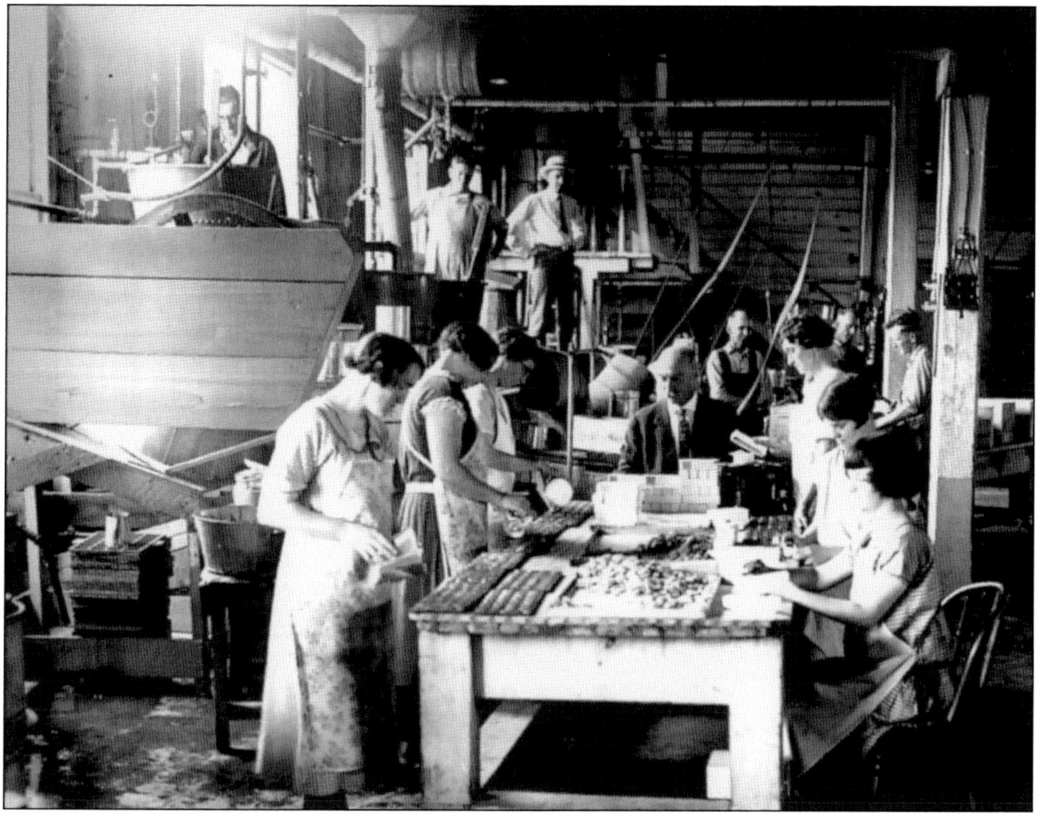

Workers at the Vermont Maple Products Co-operative Exchange, located at Elm and Jackson Streets, are pictured *c.* 1927. Those standing are, from left to right, Anna Houghton, Mae Wheeler, one unidentified person, and Lock Wheeler (at the end of table). In the upper left, the man next to the person wearing a hat is Nelson Valyou. Up until 1982, various maple-related businesses were located in this building.

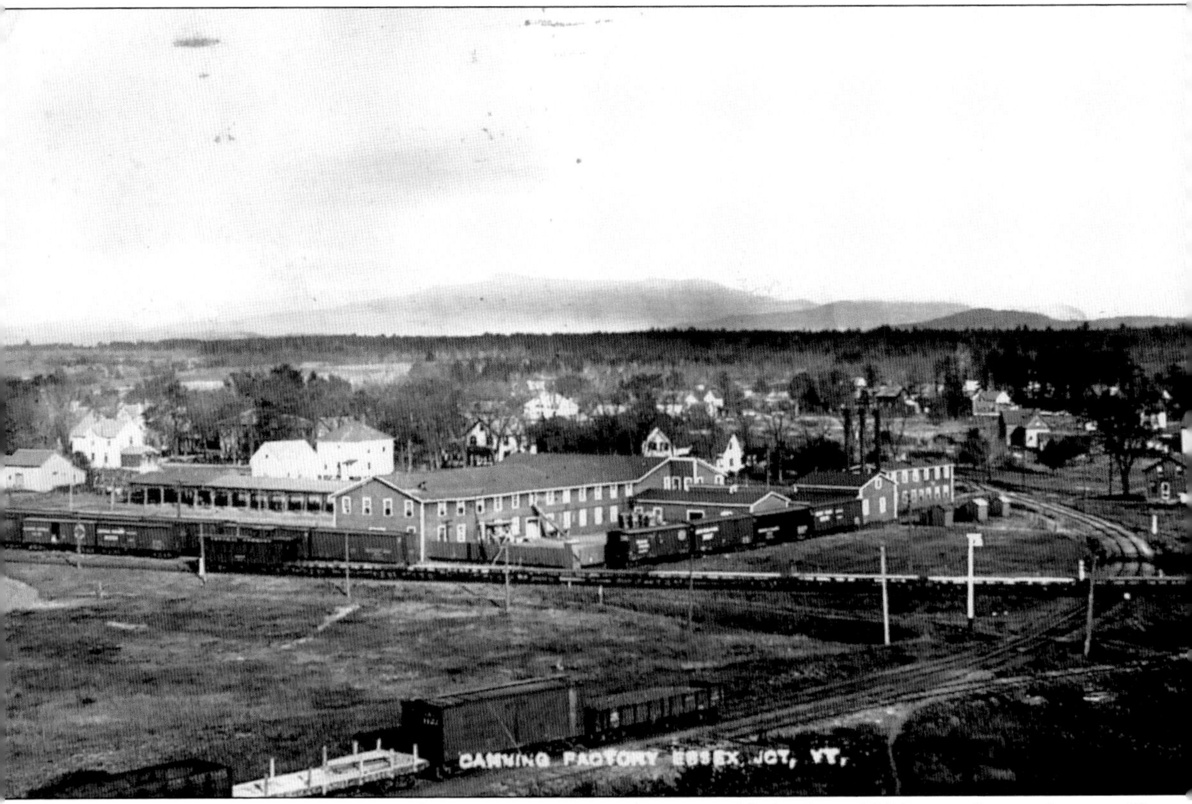

The H. C. Baxter and Brother corn-canning plant, established in 1901, was located just off Maple Street and packed corn under several labels, including Snowflake. In 1953, 35 members of the Green Mountain Corn Growers Association planted 385 acres for the cannery. The seed was provided by the Baxters, and the farmers were held to a strict schedule for planting and harvesting. As many as 100 workers were hired for the three- to four-week canning season starting in late August. George Tougas remembers, "During the canning time, the whole town could smell the aroma of fresh corn. It made you hungry." Hartley Baxter and his brother Rupert owned the firm, headquartered in Brunswick, Maine. In 1922, with 11 canneries, it was reputedly the world's largest corn packer. Hartley's stepbrother Percival later became governor of Maine and used family canning wealth to purchase the land that became Baxter State Park. The plant closed in 1960.

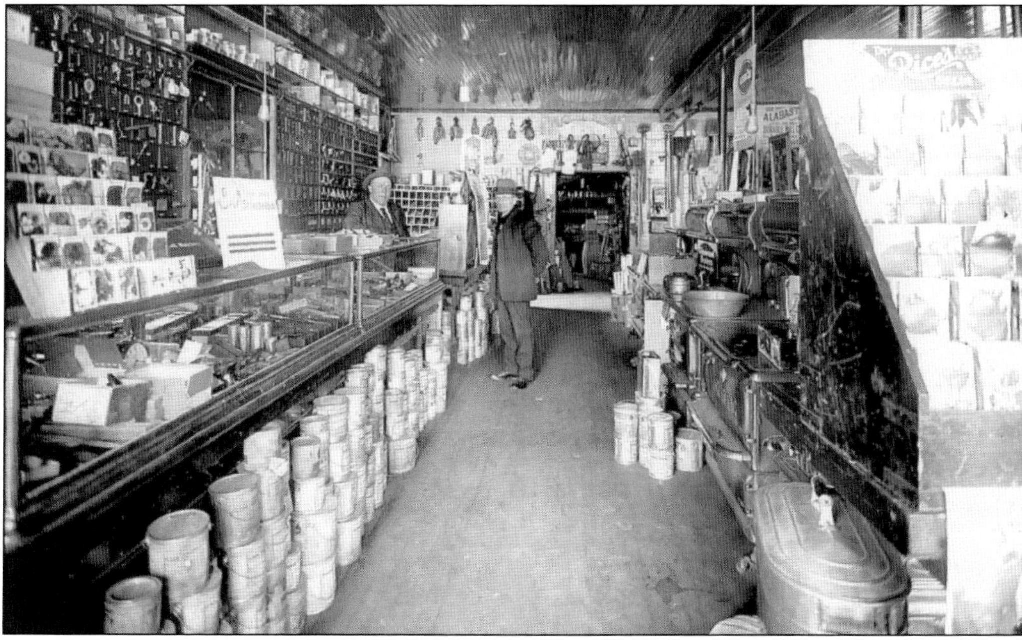

Ralph Mudgett (behind counter) and James Spaulding appear in R. O. Mudgett and Company, a hardware store located at 7–9 Main Street, in the early 1900s. Mudgett and his growing family came to Essex Junction in 1902 and lived above the store. The store sold, among other things, Glenwood ranges, which Mudgett also serviced. Both he and his wife assisted Samuel Brownell in establishing the Brownell Library.

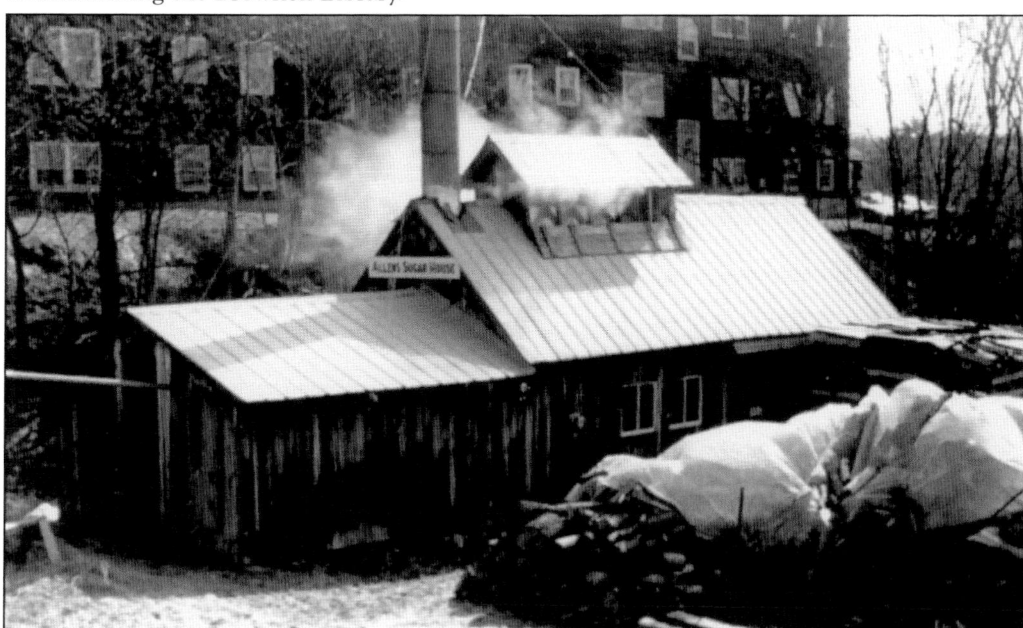

Fred Allen built his sugarhouse on Main Street in 1960 on land leased from the Drurys for $3 per month. Sap was collected along Route 15, Old Stage Road, and on the John Heins farm in Williston. The Allens always tapped on Washington's Birthday so as to not miss the first run of sap.

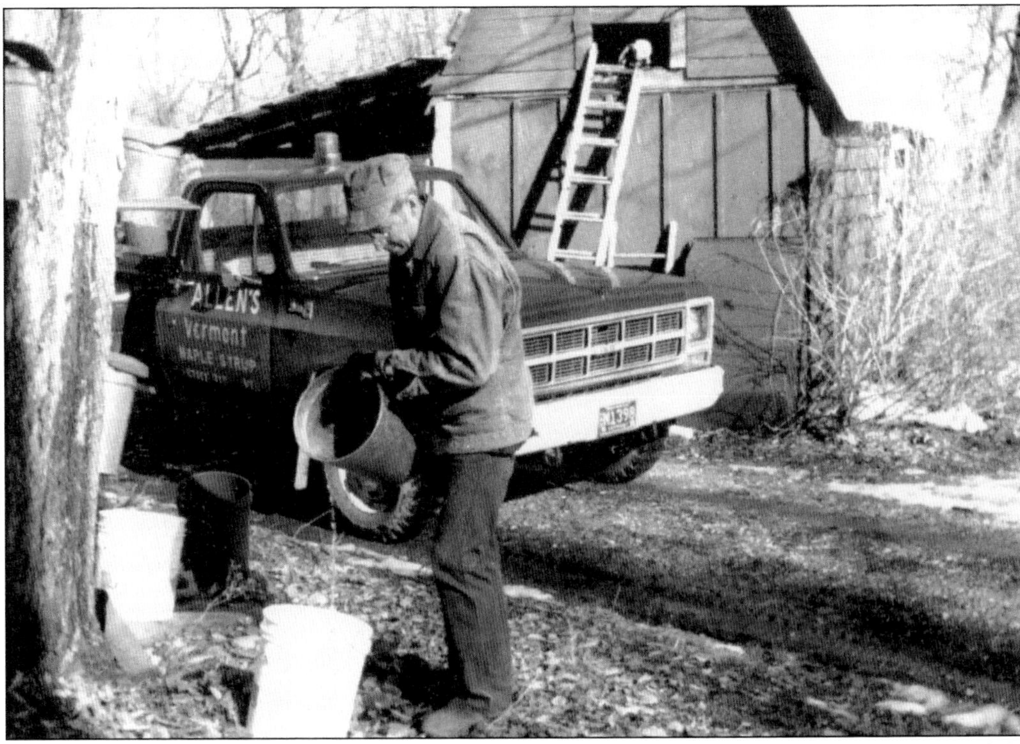

Fred Allen collects sap from one of his 1,600 buckets. His wife, Nora, was in charge of the boiling and did the canning in her kitchen at 1 Crestview Drive, across the street from the sugarhouse. Some years, they produced up to 600 gallons of maple syrup. The sugarhouse, a popular stop for tourists and schoolchildren, closed in 1990.

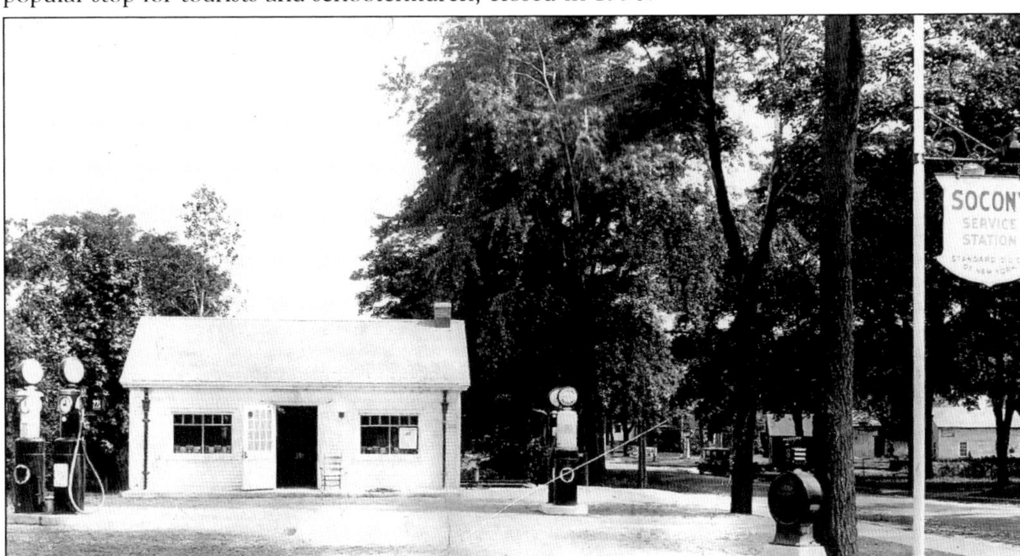

Anthony "Steve" Stevens arrived in Essex Junction in the 1930s and started the Socony service station located at the corner of Maple and Main Streets. In 1947, propane was added to the company's services, sold through Steve's Home Supply, located just up Main Street from the gas station. Appliances were sold here as well.

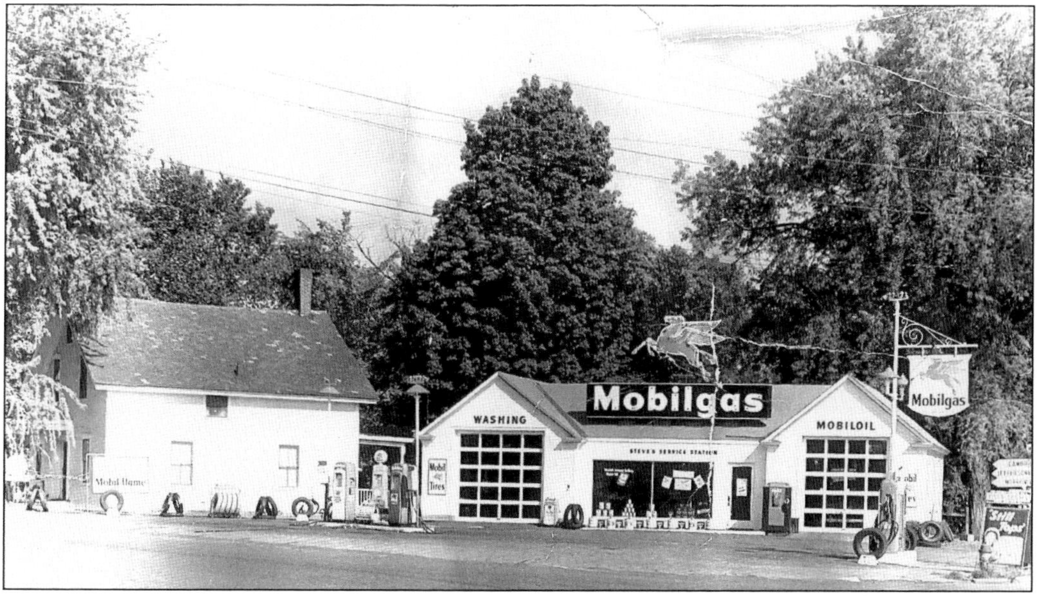

Stevens's station is pictured here in the 1950s as Mobilgas. Stevens left the service station business in the mid-1960s but continued propane sales into the mid-1970s. Currently, his son Matt runs his own propane business as Stevens Gas Service, on Route 2A north of the village.

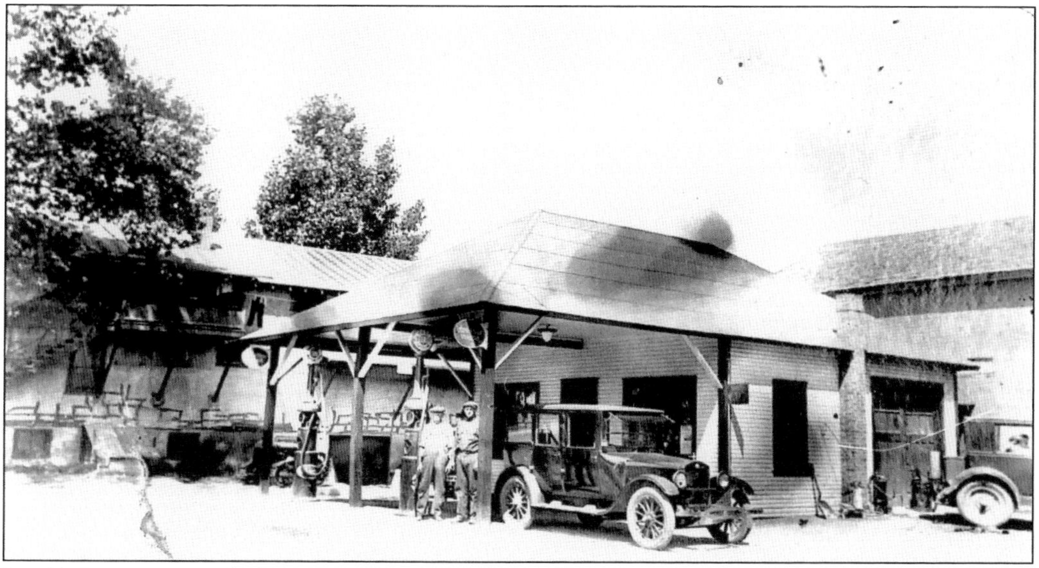

Les Robinson started this service station on Pearl Street, where the fire department is now, c. 1920. In a letter dated April 29, 1926, Robinson received acknowledgment of his enrollment in a pneumatic tire training class offered by Firestone in Cleveland. It stated, "We hope you will take advantage of their teachings and will soon return as a full fledged repairman, able to put out high grade work which produces the profits."

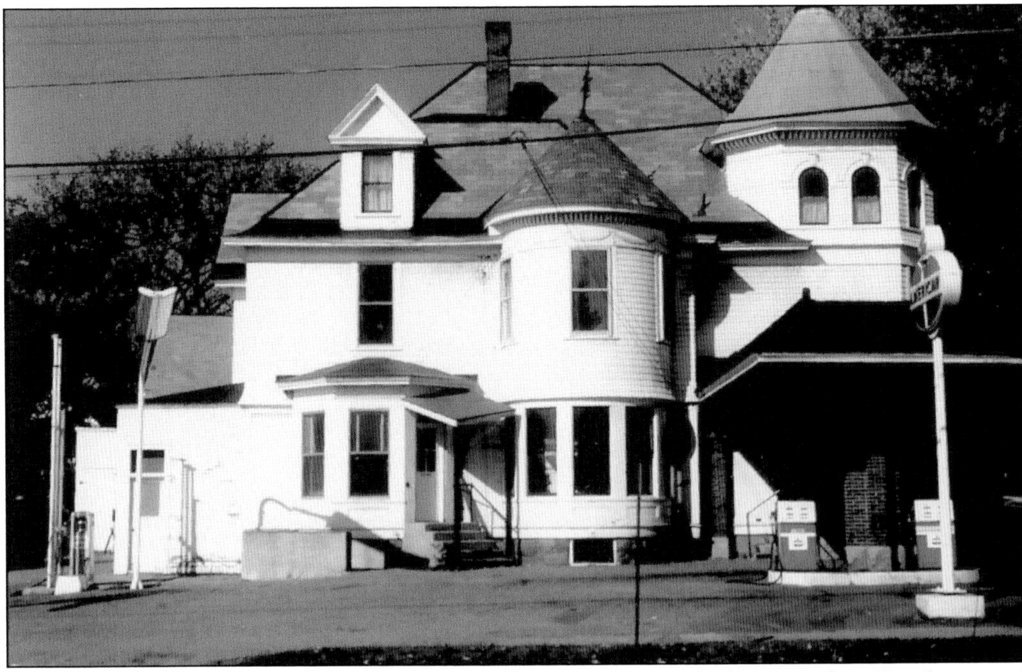

Les Robinson expanded his business to include delivering fuel in trucks. His first truck was purchased on June 1, 1928, for $1,233.55 from the Burlington Cadillac Company. Les Robinson moved his business and family to the Johnson house, shown here *c.* 1969, on the corner of Pearl and Park Streets *c.* 1930. Over the years, the franchise changed from Gulf to Atlantic to Amoco.

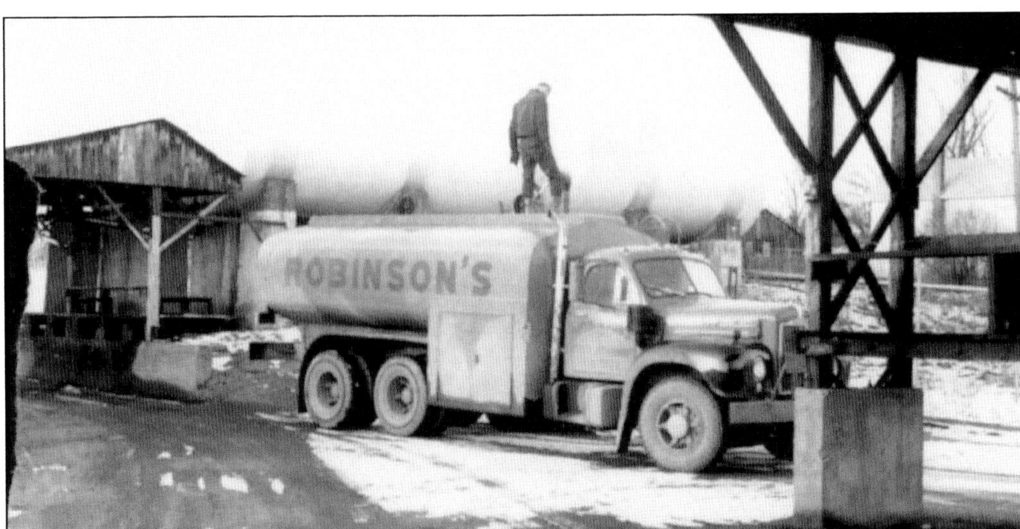

In 1968, Robinson's moved to the corner of Maple and Railroad Streets, setting up a service station and offices. In 1987, the company office moved to its current location on Park Street, keeping just the fuel-delivery business. The business continues today under the ownership of Les's grandson Jim. This photograph, taken in the early 1960s, shows Jake Tomlinson with his truck at the kerosene loading rack.

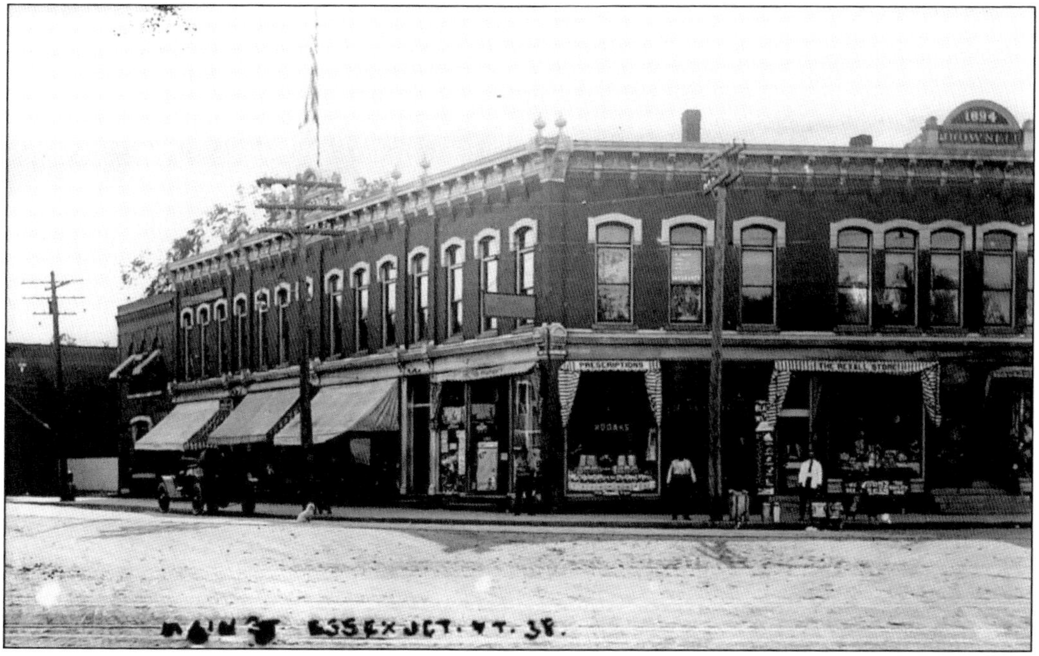

The Brownell Block on Main Street, built by Samuel Brownell in 1894, remains an imposing structure. With characteristic hometown pride, architect G. H. Guernsey was commended in the *Essex Eagle* for designing a building "to ensure strength and durability, security against destruction by fire and abundance of light; few public buildings outside the larger cities surpass it in these respects."

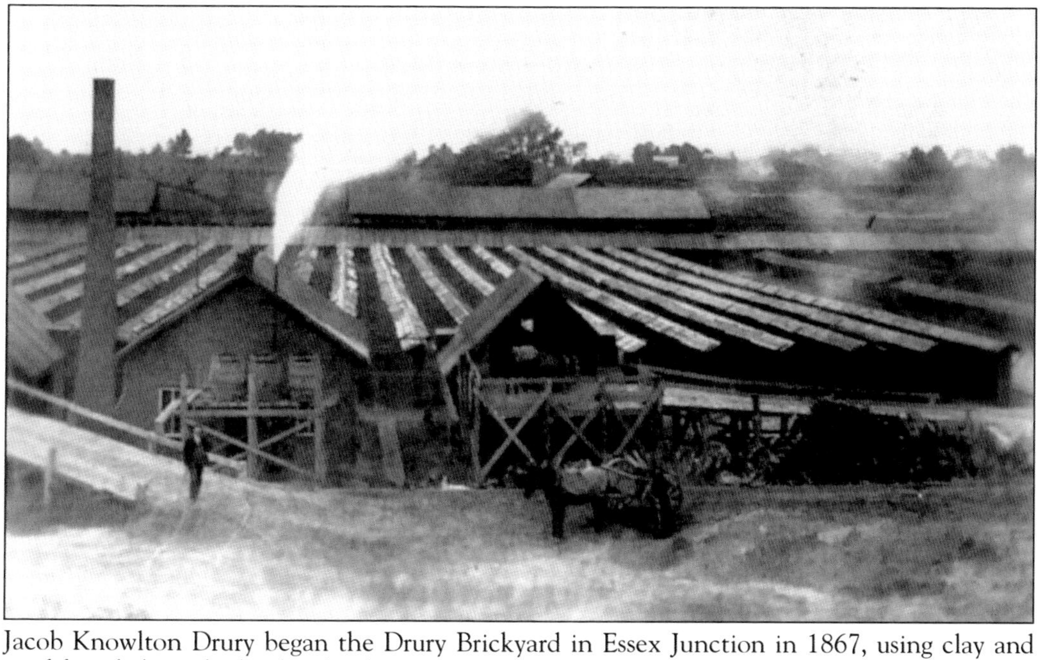
Jacob Knowlton Drury began the Drury Brickyard in Essex Junction in 1867, using clay and sand found along the banks of Indian Brook. Jacob was soon joined by his son George. In 1889, Homer, the youngest of the family, was on board. These sheds were used for air-drying the bricks before they were taken to the kiln for a final baking.

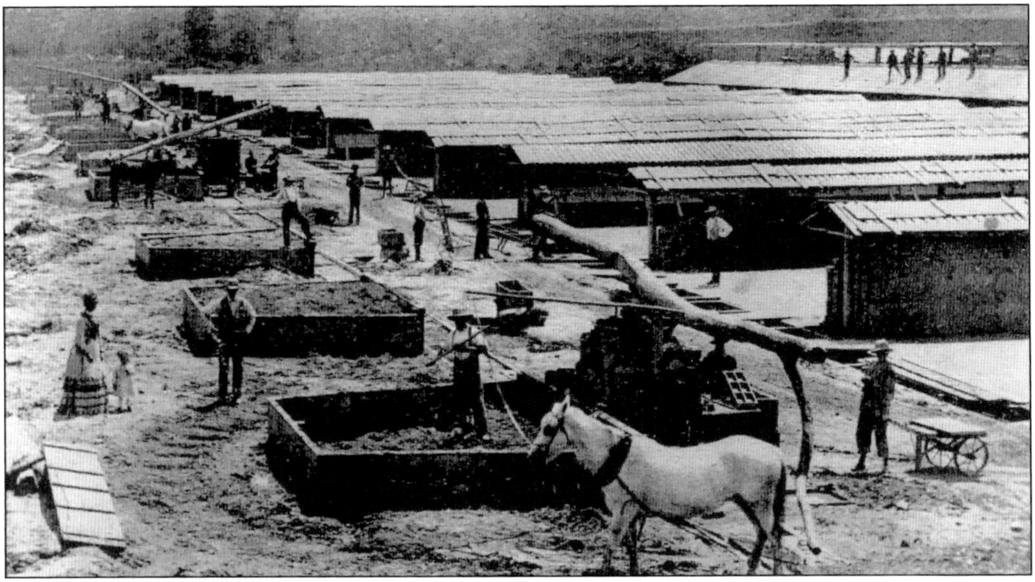

Horses were used to mix the ingredients in a pug mill. Under the leadership of Harris and Max Drury, grandsons of Jacob, the rose-red bricks were stamped with the family name. Drury bricks were used in the building of many schools and public buildings in Vermont, including several on the University of Vermont campus. Although a seasonal operation, the brickyard was a mainstay of the local economy for more than a century.

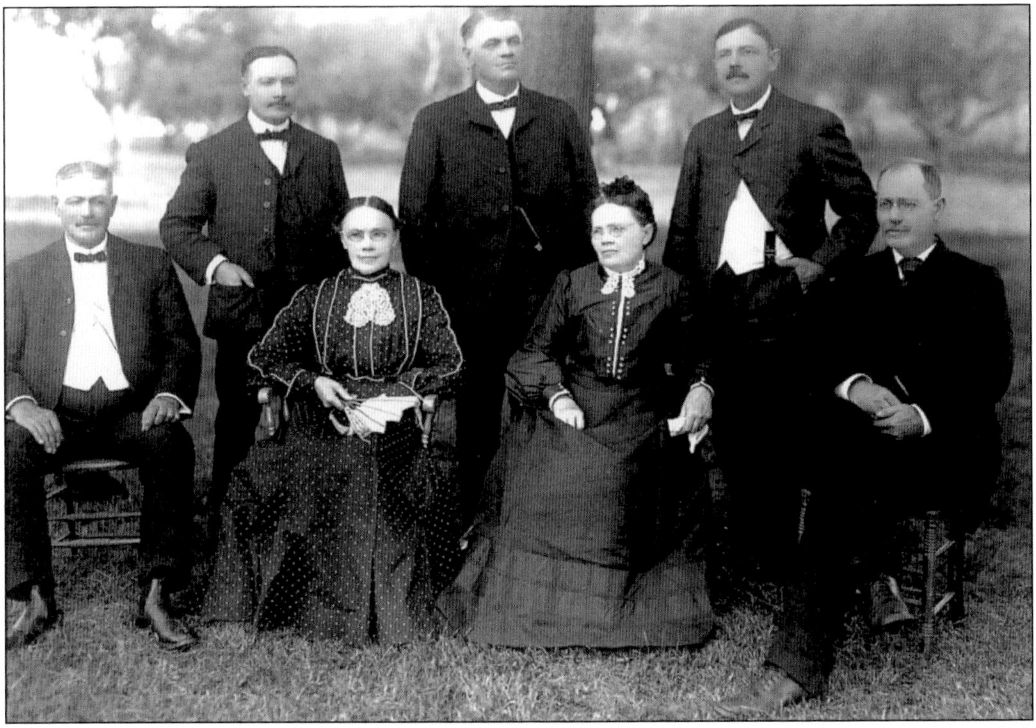

The grown children of Jacob K. Drury and Caroline (Bascom) Drury pose *c.* 1903. From left to right are the following: (first row) George, Hannah, Annette, and Charles; (second row) Homer, Edwin, and Harley.

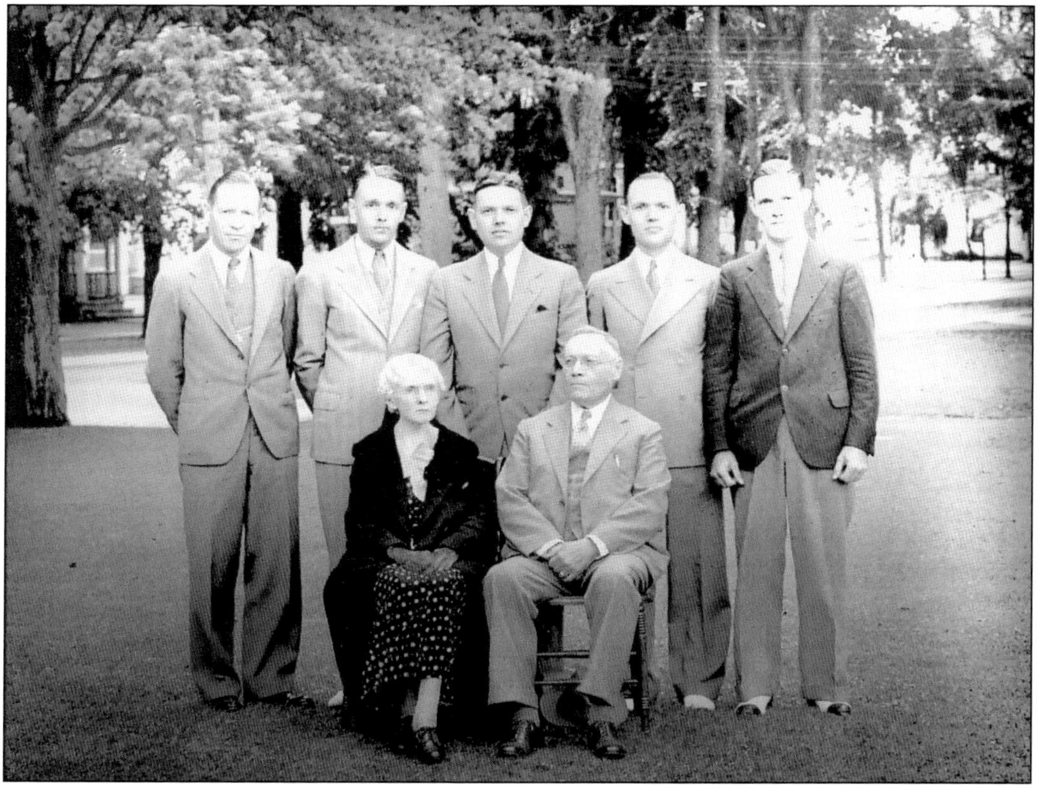

Clara and Homer Drury are seen with their five sons—from left to right, Harris Sr., Max, Alan, Harley F., and Edwin—in the 1920s. Harris Sr. and Max operated the business for many years. It was then sold to the Densmore brick concern in 1962. In 1971, the business fired its kiln for the last time and shut down. The only visible remains are the machine room, now the office of the Snyder Company, and a 1901 chimney.

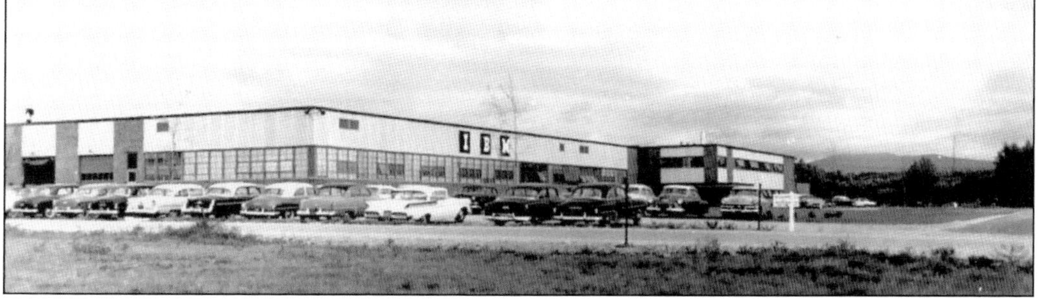

In 1954, the Winooski woolen mills closed, and the local economy suffered a serious blow, with 1,900 laborers put out of work. The Greater Burlington Industrial Corporation attracted IBM to Essex Junction with "a skilled workforce, access to educational resources, transportation links, and a good quality of life."

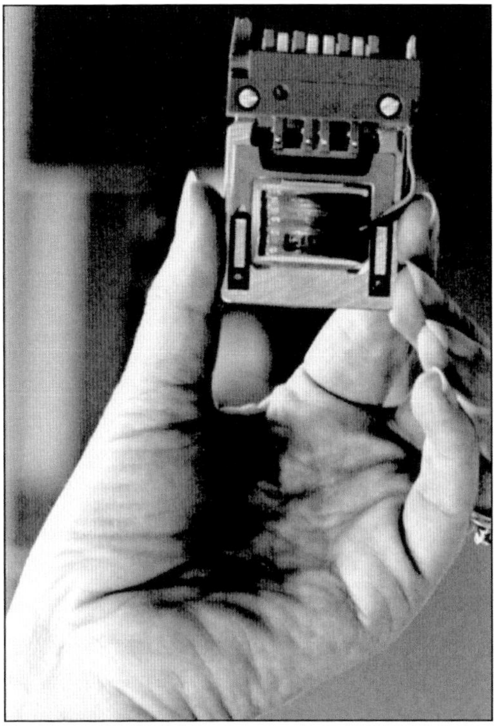

In 1957, the first year of operation, the 40,000-square-foot IBM plant made wire contact relays such as this one, with a work force of several hundred. This electromechanical switch was capable of holding one "bit" of data in early computers. (Courtesy IBM.)

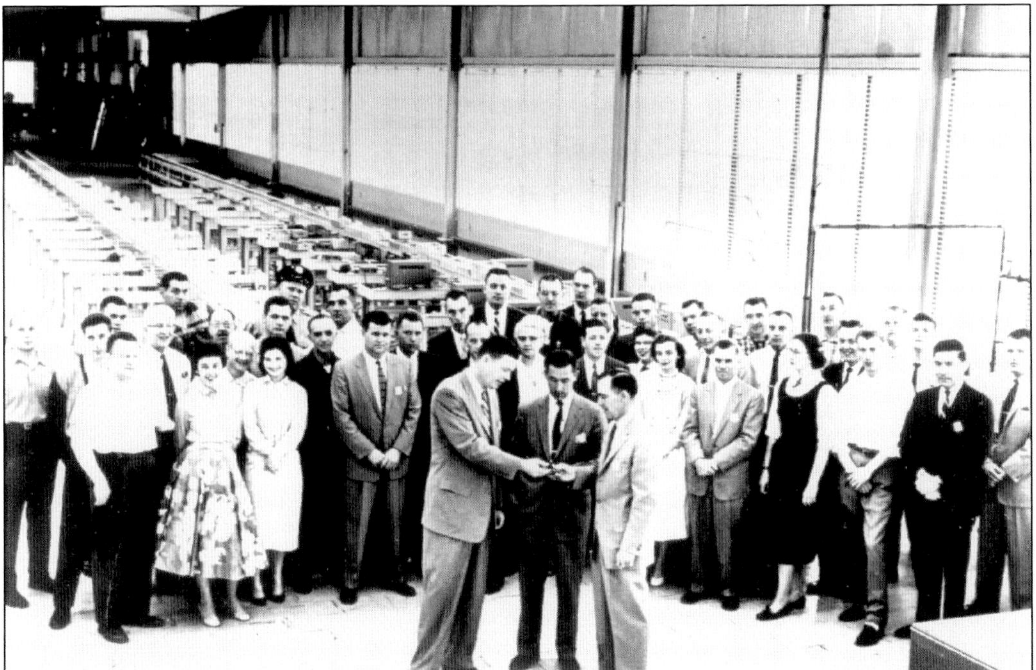

On May 13, 1957, the first wire contact relay came off the line. Almost the whole Essex Junction IBM work force was on hand for this ceremonial photograph. The rapid growth at IBM in the 1960s contributed to an economic boom in the area. By the end of 1969, some 3,900 employees worked in a manufacturing space of about a million square feet. (Courtesy IBM.)

Manufactured in 1983, this 256-kilobyte memory chip, on a fingertip, represents the microelectronics production at the IBM plant that makes computer chips for everything from mainframes to laptops. Employment peaked at 8,500 in 2001, and recent layoffs have made everyone cognizant of the importance of the state's largest private employer. (Courtesy IBM.)

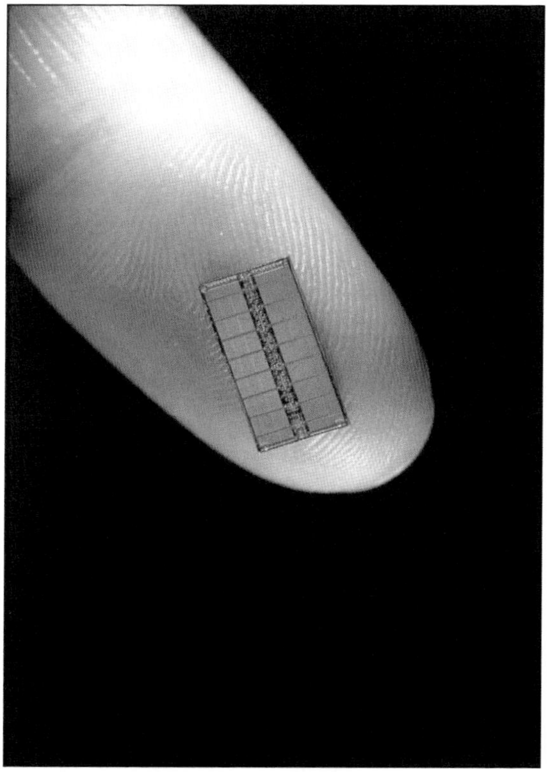

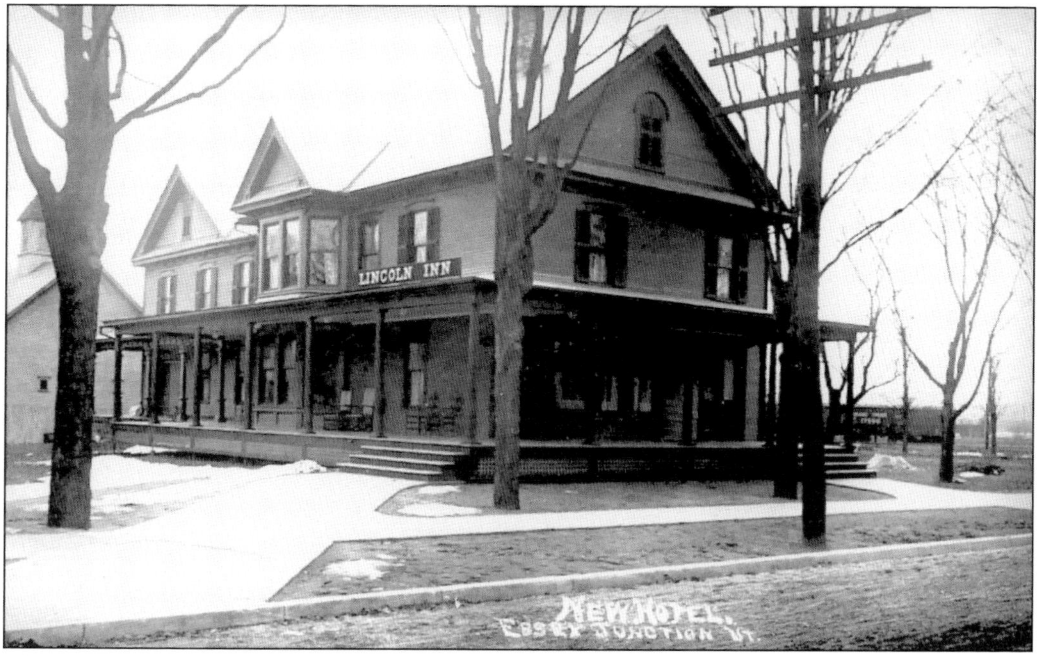

The Lincoln Inn was established in 1914 by a group of prominent Essex Junction residents, under the name of the Essex Junction Hotel Company. Their director was lawyer and town clerk Allen Martin. The Job Bates place, on the corner of Park and Maple Streets, was purchased and turned into a hotel. This photograph dates from the inn's first year.

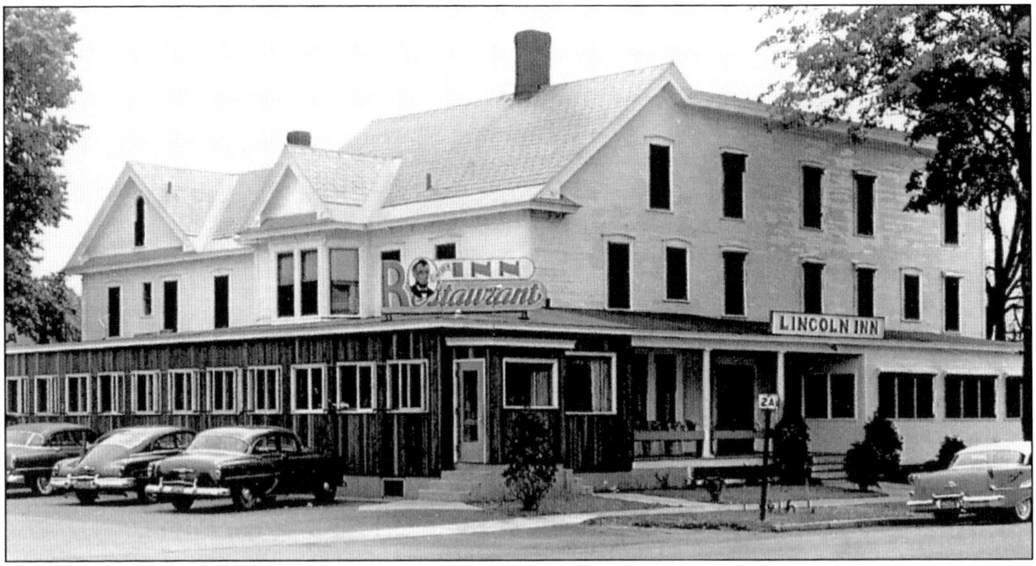

Through the years, the Lincoln Inn has seen various owners and several renovations. Since 1962, the Kourebanas family has been involved with it. By placing it prominently on its menus, the inn has introduced thousands of customers to "The Lay of the Lost Traveler," a poem by Edward J. Phelps that wishes, "I hope in hell his soul may dwell who first invented Essex Junction."

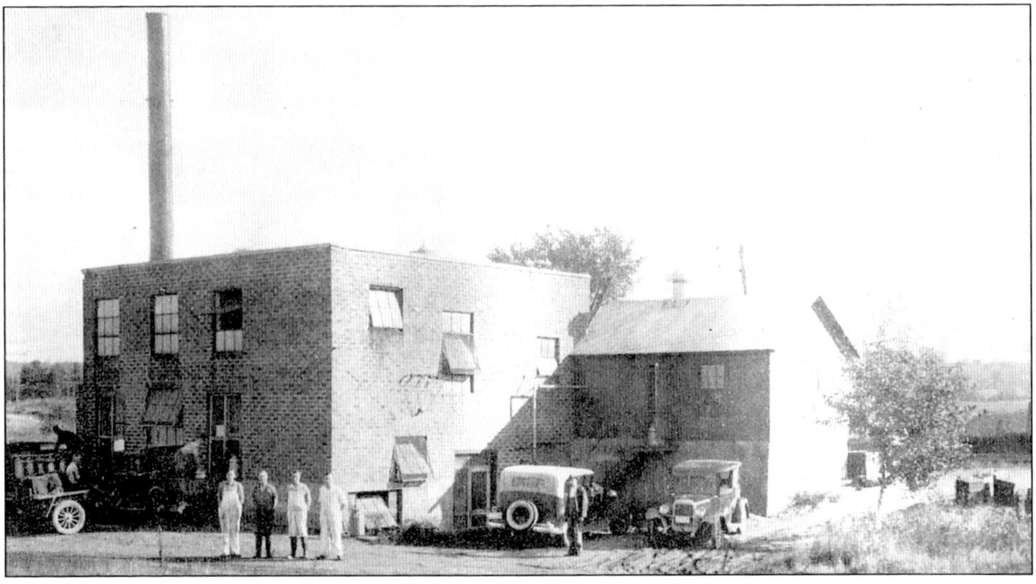

The Milton Co-operative Creamery Corporation was established with major financial backing from the Essex Trust. The group set up receiving stations in several surrounding towns for the convenience of area farmers. The Essex Junction station, seen here *c.* 1935, was built in 1925. Most of the milk in the early years was shipped to the Boston area. The operation continued until 1960–1961. The building still stands at 67 Lincoln Street.

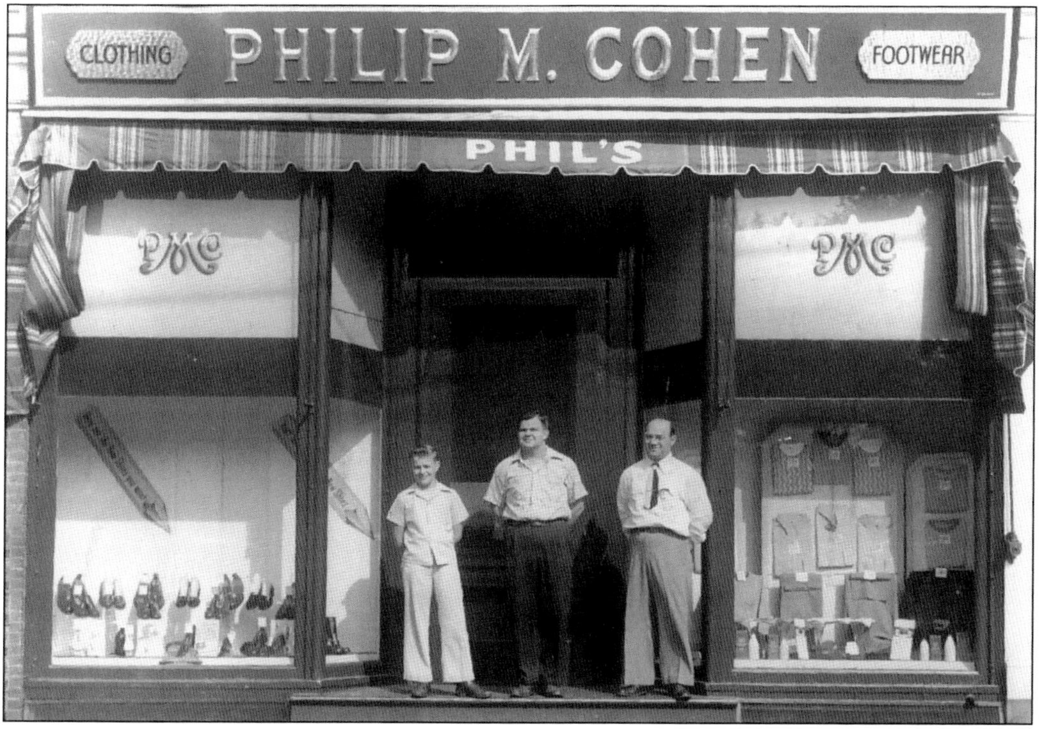

Phil Cohen (right) started an Essex Junction men's clothing store in 1933. In 1942, he bought the A. B. Rugg Company in the Brownell Block and changed the name to Philip M. Cohen Clothing and Footwear. Cohen was active in the community and served in the Vermont House of Representatives. Phil's son Matt took over the business, now called Phil's Trading Post, and moved it to the Essex Outlets in May 2003.

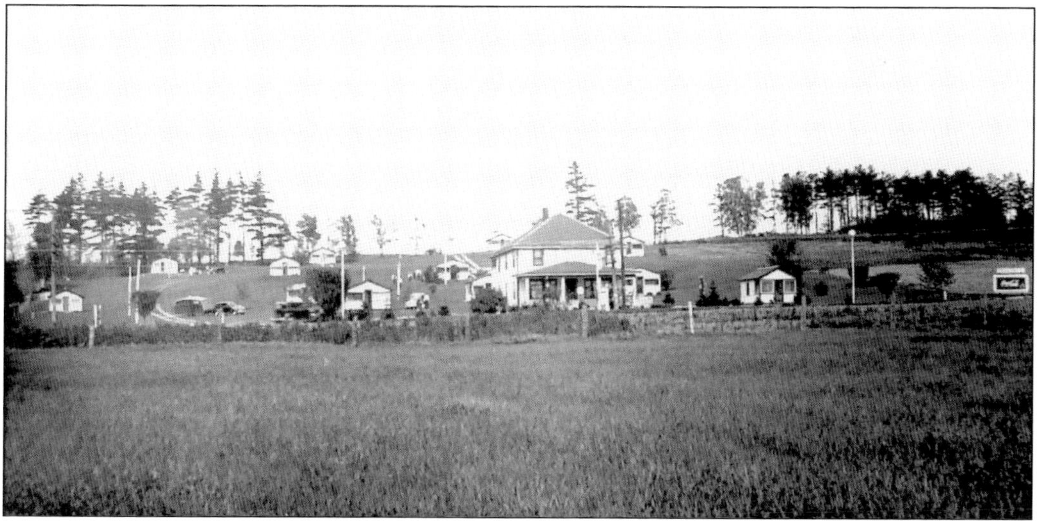

Pictured here c. 1938 is Fairside, east of the fairgrounds in Essex Junction. "On Route 15 direct to Smugglers Notch through Mount Mansfield. 12 large heated, screened-in cabins with running water and flush toilets. Comfortable and quiet. Near Fort Ethan Allen, Winooski, Vt., and Burlington on Lake Champlain." The cabin rental business was started in 1929 by R. A. Perry.

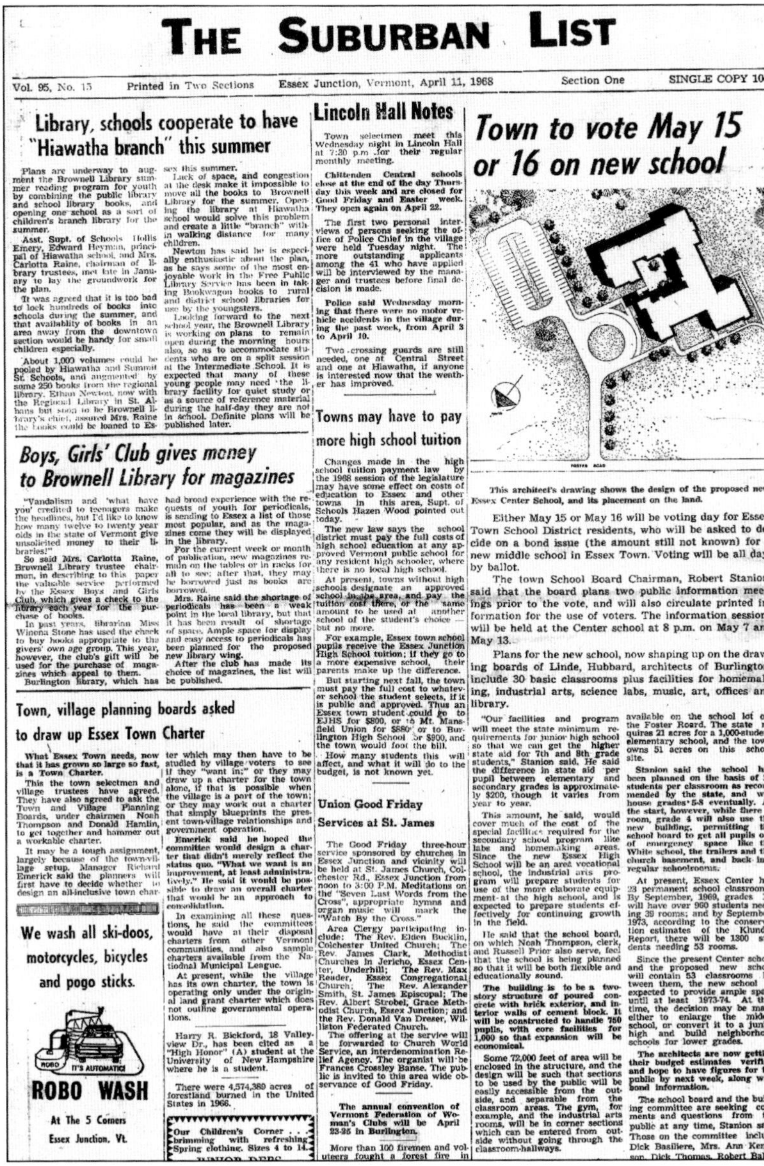

THE SUBURBAN LIST

Vol. 95, No. 15 Printed in Two Sections Essex Junction, Vermont, April 11, 1968 Section One SINGLE COPY 10c

Library, schools cooperate to have "Hiawatha branch" this summer

Plans are underway to augment the Brownell Library summer reading program for youth by combining the public library and school library books, and opening one school as a sort of children's branch library for the summer.

Asst. Supt. of Schools Hollis Emery, Edward Heyman, principal of Hiawatha school, and Mrs. Carlotta Raine, chairman of library trustees, met late in January to lay the groundwork for the plan.

It was agreed that it is too bad to lock hundreds of books into schools during the summer, and that availablity of books in an area away from the downtown section would be handy for small children especially.

About 1,000 volumes could be pooled by Hiawatha and Summit St. Schools, and augmented by some 250 books from the regional library. Ethan Newton, now with the Regional Library in St. Albans but soon to be Brownell library's chief, assured Mrs. Raine the books could be loaned to Essex this summer.

Lack of space, and congestion at the desk make it impossible to move all the books to Brownell Library for the summer. Opening the library at Hiawatha school would solve this problem and create a little "branch" within walking distance for many children.

Newton has said he is especially enthusiastic about the plan, as he says some of the most enjoyable work in the Free Public Library Service has been in taking Bookwagon books to rural and district school libraries for use by the youngsters.

Looking forward to the next school year, the Brownell Library is working on plans to remain open during the morning hours also, so as to accommodate students who are on a split session at the Intermediate School. It is expected that many of these young people may need the library facility for quiet study or as a source of reference material during the half-day they are not in school. Definite plans will be published later.

Boys, Girls' Club gives money to Brownell Library for magazines

"Vandalism and 'what have you' credited to teenagers make the headlines, but I'd like to know how many twelve to twenty year olds in the state of Vermont give unsolicited money to their libraries!"

So said Mrs. Carlotta Raine, Brownell Library trustee chairman, in describing to this paper the valuable service performed by the Essex Boys and Girls Club, which gives a check to the library each year for the purchase of books.

In past years, librarian Miss Winona Stone has used the check to buy books appropriate to the givers' own age group. This year, however, the club's gift will be used for the purchase of magazines which appeal to them.

Burlington library, which has had broad experience with the requests of youth for periodicals, is sending to Essex a list of those most popular, and as the magazines come they will be displayed in the library.

For the current week or month of publication, new magazines remain on the tables or in racks for all to see; after that, they may be borrowed just as books are borrowed.

Mrs. Raine said the shortage of periodicals has been a weak point in the local library, but that it has been result of shortage of space. Ample space for display and easy access to periodicals has been planned for the proposed new library wing.

After the club has made its choice of magazines, the list will be published.

Town, village planning boards asked to draw up Essex Town Charter

What Essex Town needs, now that it has grown so large so fast, is a Town Charter.

This the town selectmen and village trustees have agreed. They have also agreed to ask the Town and Village Planning Boards, under chairmen Noah Thompson and Donald Hamlin, to get together and hammer out a workable charter.

It may be a tough assignment, largely because of the town-village setup. Manager Richard Emerick said the planners will first have to decide whether to design an all-inclusive town charter which may then have to be studied by village voters to see if they "want in;" or they may draw up a charter for the town alone, if that is possible when the village is a part of the town; or they may work out a charter that simply blueprints the present town-village relationships and government operation.

Emerick said he hoped the committee would design a charter that didn't merely reflect the status quo. "What we want is an improvement, at least administratively." He said it would be possible to draw an overall charter that would be an approach to consolidation.

In examining all these questions, he said the committees would have at their disposal charters from other Vermont communities, and also sample charters available from the National Municipal League.

At present, while the village has its own charter, the town is operating only under the original land grant charter which does not outline governmental operations.

Harry R. Bickford, 18 Valleyview Dr., has been cited as a "High Honor" (A) student at the University of New Hampshire where he is a student.

There were 4,574,389 acres of forestland burned in the United States in 1966.

Our Children's Corner . . . brimming with refreshing Spring clothing. Sizes 4 to 14.

We wash all ski-doos, motorcycles, bicycles and pogo sticks.

ROBO IT'S AUTOMATIC!

ROBO WASH

At The 5 Corners

Essex Junction, Vt.

Lincoln Hall Notes

Town selectmen meet this Wednesday night in Lincoln Hall at 7:30 p.m. for their regular monthly meeting.

Chittenden Central schools close at the end of the day Thursday this week and are closed for Good Friday and Easter week. They open again on April 22.

The first two personal interviews of persons seeking the office of Police Chief in the village were held Tuesday night. The more outstanding applicants among the 41 who have applied will be interviewed by the manager and trustees before final decision is made.

Police said Wednesday morning that there were no motor vehicle accidents in the village during the past week, from April 3 to April 10.

Two crossing guards are still needed, one at Central Street and one at Hiawatha, if anyone is interested now that the weather has improved.

Towns may have to pay more high school tuition

Changes made in the high school tuition payment law by the 1968 session of the legislature may have some effect on costs of education to Essex and other towns in this area, Supt. of Schools Hazen Wood pointed out today.

The new law says the school district must pay the full costs of high school education at any approved Vermont public school for any resident high schooler, where there is no local high school.

At present, towns without high schools designate an approved school in the area, and pay the tuition cost there, or the same amount to be used at another school of the student's choice — but no more.

For example, Essex town school pupils receive the Essex Junction High School tuition; if they go to a more expensive school, their parents make up the difference.

But starting next fall, the town must pay the full cost to whatever school the student selects, if it is public and approved. Thus an Essex town student could go to EJHS for $800, or to Mt. Mansfield Union for $880 or to Burlington High School for $900, and the town would foot the bill.

How many students this will affect, and what it will do to the budget, is not known yet.

Union Good Friday Services at St. James

The Good Friday three-hour service sponsored by churches in Essex Junction and vicinity will be held at St. James Church, Colchester Rd., Essex Junction from noon to 3:00 P.M. Meditations on the "Seven Last Words from the Cross", appropriate hymns and organ music will mark the "Watch By the Cross."

Area Clergy participating include: The Rev. Elden Bucklin, Colchester United Church; The Rev. James Clark, Methodist Churches in Jericho, Essex Center, Underhill; The Rev. Max Reader, Essex Congregational Church; The Rev. Alexander Smith, St. James Episcopal; The Rev. Albert Strobel, Grace Methodist Church, Essex Junction; and the Rev. Donald Van Dreser, Williston Federated Church.

The offering at the service will be forwarded to Church World Service, an interdenomination Relief Agency. The organist will be Frances Crossley Banse. The public is invited to this area wide observance of Good Friday.

The annual convention of Vermont Federation of Woman's Clubs will be April 23-25 in Burlington.

More than 100 firemen and volunteers fought a forest fire in

Town to vote May 15 or 16 on new school

FOSTER ROAD

This architect's drawing shows the design of the proposed new Essex Center School, and its placement on the land.

Either May 15 or May 16 will be voting day for Essex Town School District residents, who will be asked to decide on a bond issue (the amount still not known) for a new middle school in Essex Town. Voting will be all day, by ballot.

The town School Board Chairman, Robert Stanion, said that the board plans two public information meetings prior to the vote, and will also circulate printed information for the use of voters. The information sessions will be held at the Center school at 8 p.m. on May 7 and May 13.

Plans for the new school, now shaping up on the drawing boards of Linde, Hubbard, architects of Burlington, include 30 basic classrooms plus facilities for homemaking, industrial arts, science labs, music, art, offices and library.

"Our facilities and program will meet the state minimum requirements for junior high school so that we can get the higher state aid for 7th and 8th grade students," Stanion said. He said the difference in state aid per pupil between elementary and secondary grades is approximately $200, though it varies from year to year.

This amount, he said, would cover much of the cost of the special facilities required for the secondary school program like labs and homemaking areas. Since the new Essex High School will be an area vocational school, the industrial arts program will prepare students for use of the more elaborate equipment at the high school, and is expected to prepare students effectively for continuing growth in the field.

He said that the school board, on which Noah Thompson, clerk, and Russell Prior also serve, feel that the school is being planned so that it will be both flexible and educationally sound.

The building is to be a two-story structure of poured concrete with brick exterior, and interior walls of cement block. It will be constructed to handle 750 pupils, with core facilities for 1,000 so that expansion will be economical.

Some 72,000 feet of area will be enclosed in the structure, and the design will be such that sections to be used by the public will be easily accessible from the outside, and separable from the classroom areas. The gym, for example, and the industrial arts rooms, will be in corner sections which can be entered from outside without going through the classroom-hallways.

available on the school lot off the Foster Roard. The state requires 21 acres for a 1,000-student elementary school, and the town owns 51 acres on this school site.

Stanion said the school has been planned on the basis of 25 students per classroom as recommended by the state, and will house grades 5-8 eventually. At the start, however, while there is room, grade 4 will also use the new building, permitting the school board to get all pupils out of emergency space like the White school, the trailers and the church basement, and back into regular schoolrooms.

At present, Essex Center has 23 permanent school classrooms. By September, 1969, grades 1-8 will have over 960 students needing 39 rooms; and by September, 1973, according to the conservation estimates of the Klunder Report, there will be 1300 students needing 53 rooms.

Since the present Center school and the proposed new school will contain 53 classrooms between them, the new school is expected to provide ample space until at least 1973-74. At that time, the decision may be made either to enlarge the middle school, or convert it to a junior high and build neighborhood schools for lower grades.

The architects are now getting their budget estimates verified, and hope to have figures for the public by next week, along with bond information.

The school board and the building committee are seeking comments and questions from the public at any time, Stanion said. Those on the committee include Dick Basiliere, Mrs. Ann Kennison, Dick Thomas, Robert Baker

The *Burlington Clipper* was established in Burlington in 1874. In 1898, Lewis Thayer moved the paper to Essex Junction, and until 1920, 13 weekly newspapers were printed by the Essex Publishing Company. Eventually, in 1940, the number was reduced to one, the *Suburban List*. Milo Reynolds joined the business in 1904 as the advertising manager and soon became a partner with Lewis Thayer. From 1920 to 1957, he ran the firm with Lewis Thayer's son Harrison. Reynolds was noted for his two full-size pages of strong editorials. In 1957, Reynolds sold the Essex Publishing Company and the newspaper to Ruth and Proctor Page. At that time, the paper covered most of the small towns in Chittenden and Grand Isle Counties. As Essex grew, the Pages spent more time covering the happenings in the town and village. The tradition of two pages of editorials continued, and the news items covered bigger issues. Indicative of its closer-to-home coverage, it was renamed the *Essex Record* in 1969. The Pages sold the newspaper in 1977. In 1981, the newly named *Essex Reporter* continued the legacy of local coverage. It now distributes 8,500 copies weekly in Essex and surrounding towns.

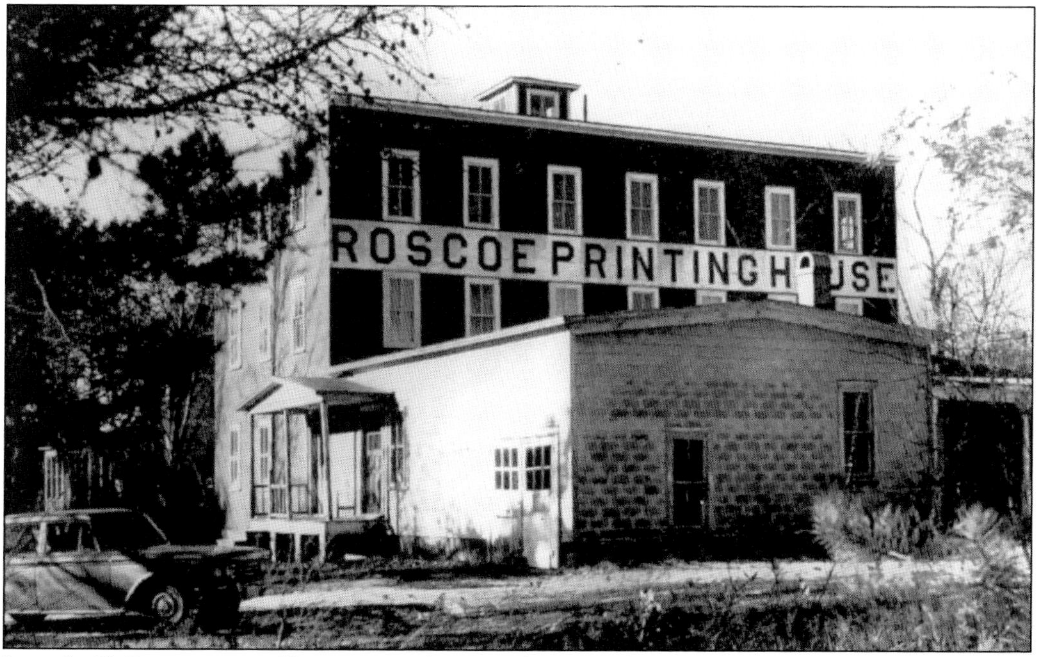

Lincoln H. Roscoe moved his printing business from Jericho to Roscoe Court in Essex Junction in 1904. Roscoe Printing produced calendars, annual reports, advertisements, and ruled paper, among other things. In 1982, Lincoln's son Lester, age 77, was still using the "hot type" printing press, with lead melted down to form raised letters that were inked and applied directly to paper. The building has since been torn down.

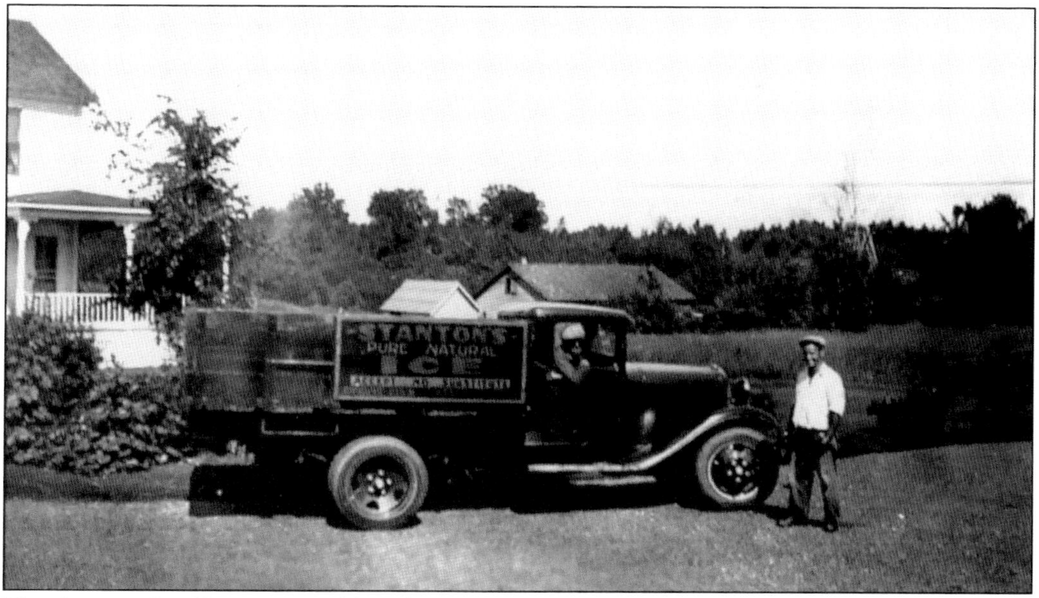

The Stanton Ice House, owned by Thomas Stanton, was located in the Silver Bow area of the Winooski River above the dam. Ice from the river was stored in the icehouse and insulated with sawdust. The sawdust was washed off at the water tank, and the load was weighed at a scale house. Stanton delivered in a truck like this to businesses and residences in Essex Junction from 1921 to c. 1946.

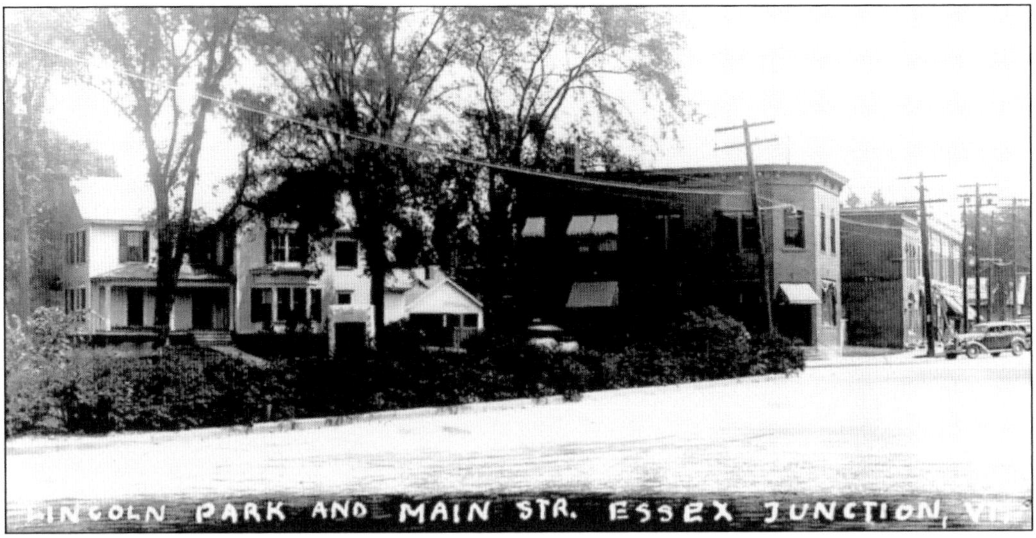

In 1872, a group of area businessmen received a charter for a banking institution in Essex Junction. But it was not until 1913 that the Essex Trust Company on Main Street opened for business. The first officers were president Samuel A. Brownell, vice president Dr. David Marvin, treasurer Merl B. Clark, and counsel Allen Martin. Brownell's residence is to the left of the bank building in this view. The trust is now Banknorth.

ESSEX TRUST COMPANY

Essex Junction, Vermont.

There are six good reasons why you should make this bank your depository:

The rule of Safety first, Profit second.

A reserve in excess of the legal requirement.

Directors having the respect of the community.

Strength promoting the stability of a customer's busi-ness.

Local experience enabling us to assist you in the right way.

A bank not too large to give every consideration to the interests of every customer.

These are the inducements we offer to make you a SAT-ISFIED DEPOSITOR of this worthy Institution.

An early newspaper advertisement promotes the Essex Trust Company. A March 26, 1914, article in the *Essex Record* lauds the Essex Trust Company as a "model of suburban banking construction" with "a massive burglar proof vault." Other details such as heavy glass counters, letters in gold leaf, and an interior finish in natural oak "were planned with a view to substantial service and endurance."

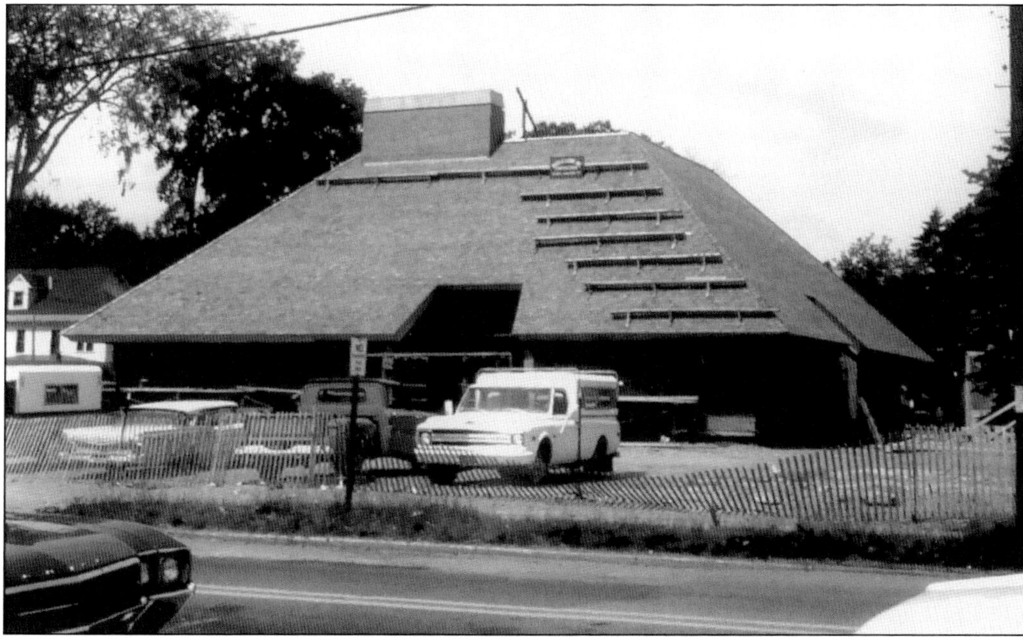

The Chittenden Trust Company opened its branch office in Essex Junction on October 27, 1970, at the corner of Pearl and Park Streets. Here, the building is under construction. The William Bennett Johnson house, constructed in 1901 and last used by Robinson's Fuel as a service station, was taken down to make room for the new construction.

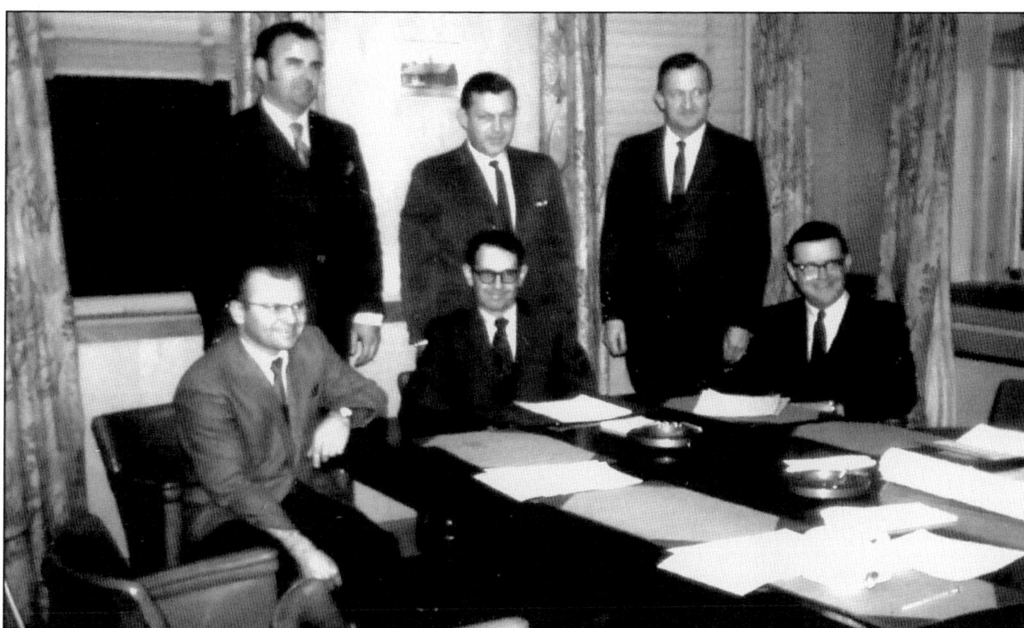

Board members congregate for the first executive meeting of the Essex Junction office of the Chittenden Trust Company on January 8, 1970. Pictured here, from left to right, are the following: (first row) Herbert G. Prakelt, M.D.; Steele Griswold, chairman; and Philip A. Kolvoord, Esq.; (second row) Conrad P. Flynn, the first manager; William D. Flanders Jr.; and James E. Reed.

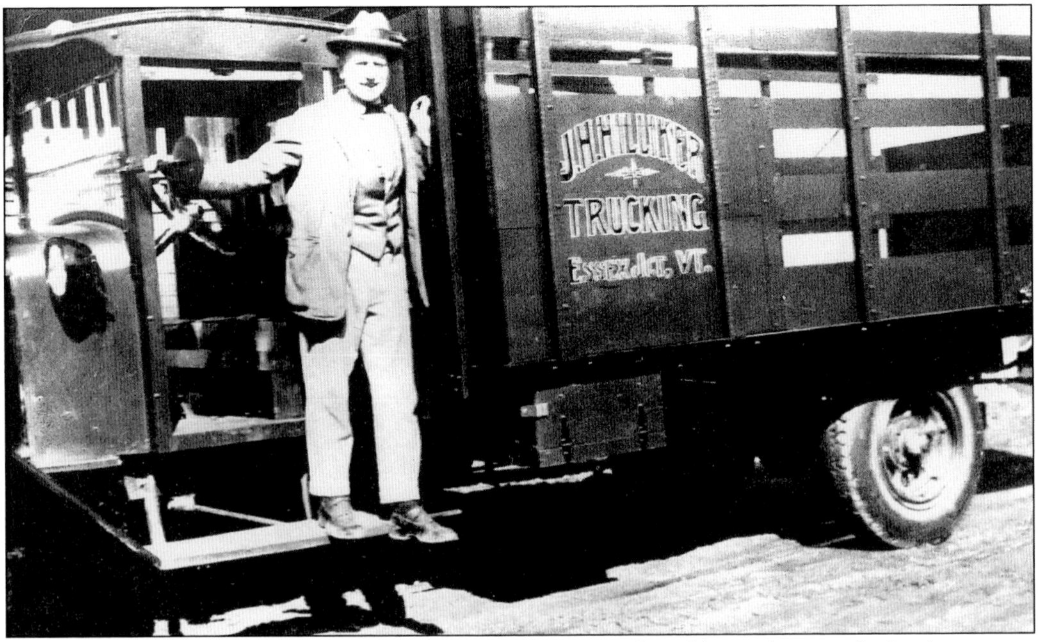

Judson H. Hilliker converted an old car into a moving van by adding a box on the back, starting Hilliker's Van Service in 1915. His new truck appears here c. 1916. In 1946, his son-in-law Clifford McLure joined the firm, which became Hilliker and McLure Van Service. It was located at 23 Pearl Street and later at 6 Central Street. In 1980, Peder Marcussen, son-in-law of McLure, took over McLure Moving and Storage.

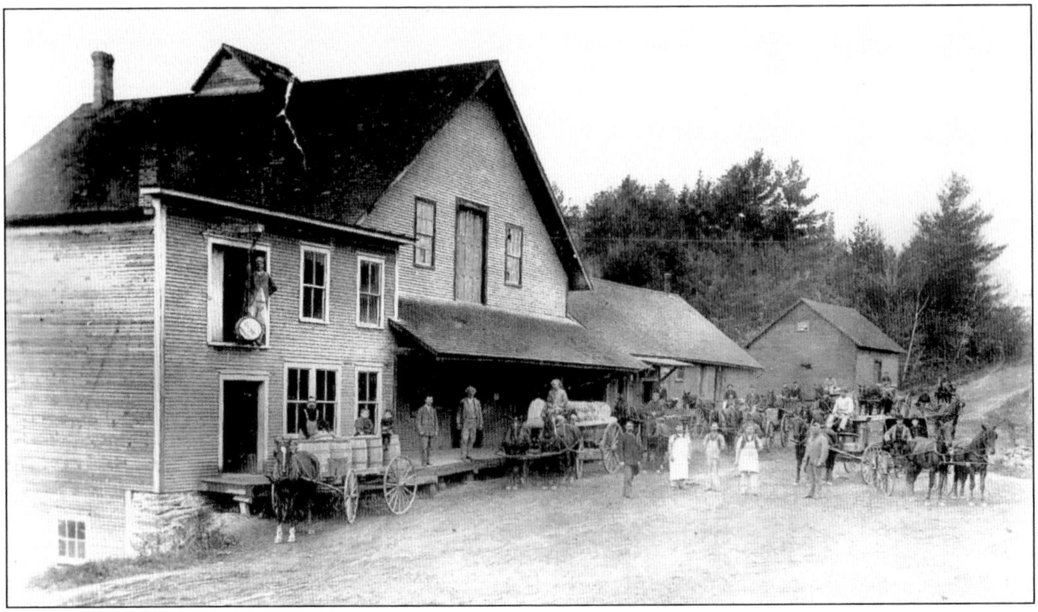

William B. Johnson moved from Williston after having purchased an existing gristmill on the Winooski River in the late 1800s, upstream from the present dam. He then started his career as a custom miller and a wholesaler and retailer in flour and feed. Johnson purchased the Essex Creamery and was active with both the Essex Co-operative Savings and Loan Association and the People's Light and Power Company.

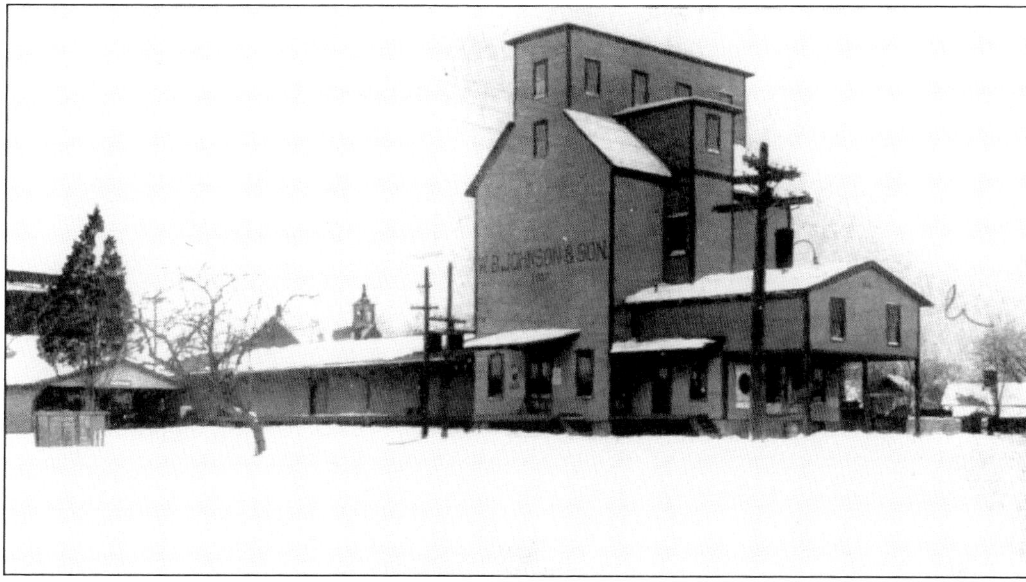

William B. Johnson moved his plant to 10 acres by the Central Vermont Railway when the mill water rights were sold to the power company, which proposed the construction of a new dam. The new site had a private siding that could receive flour and grain from the Midwest. Shortly after 1906, a coal business was added. Over the years, two of Johnson's sons joined the business. Maynard Auto Supply now occupies the site.

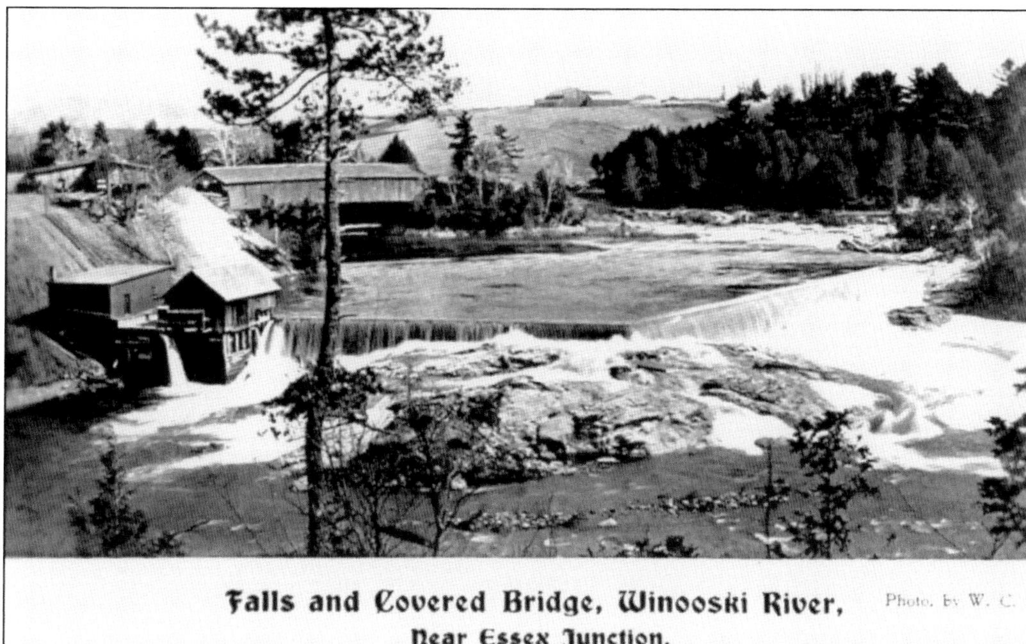

Hubbel's Falls (named for Elnathan Hubbel, one of the area's first settlers), on the Winooski River, was exploited early for its waterpower. Over the years, sawmills, a carding mill, a gristmill, and a hemp mill all operated at the falls. This 1899 view shows the Brownell dam, a lumbermill, and the power plant at the left. The present Green Mountain Power plant is located just above this site.

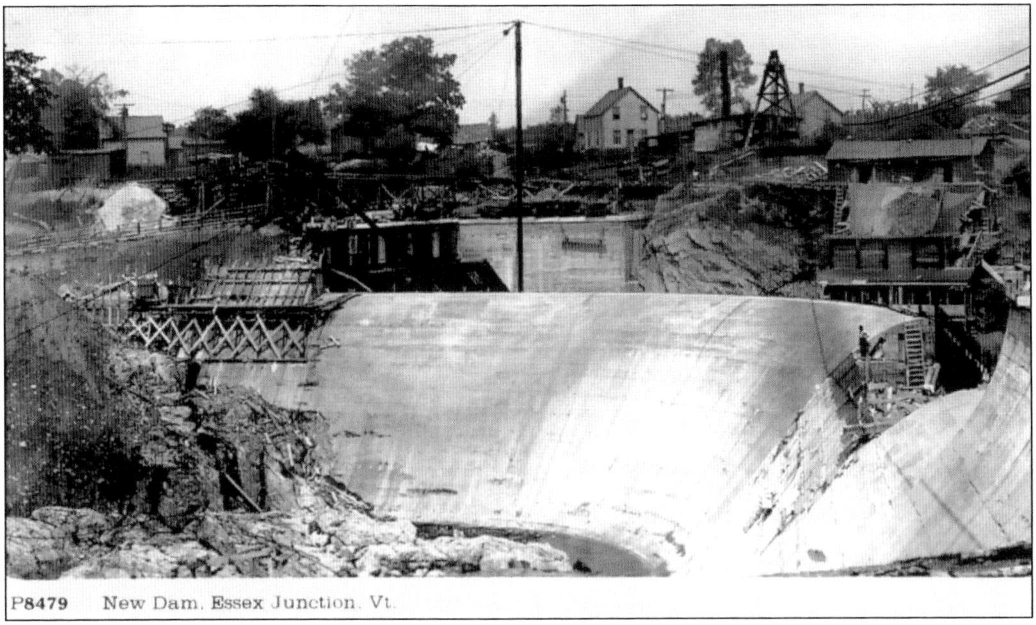

In May 1917, a 10,000-horsepower hydroelectric plant (now Green Mountain Power Plant 19) opened, at that time the largest in the state. It furnished electricity for Burlington, Winooski, Essex Junction, and the surrounding communities. The concrete dam was built in stages, since the flow of the river could not be stopped. Water was diverted to go over sections not yet built.

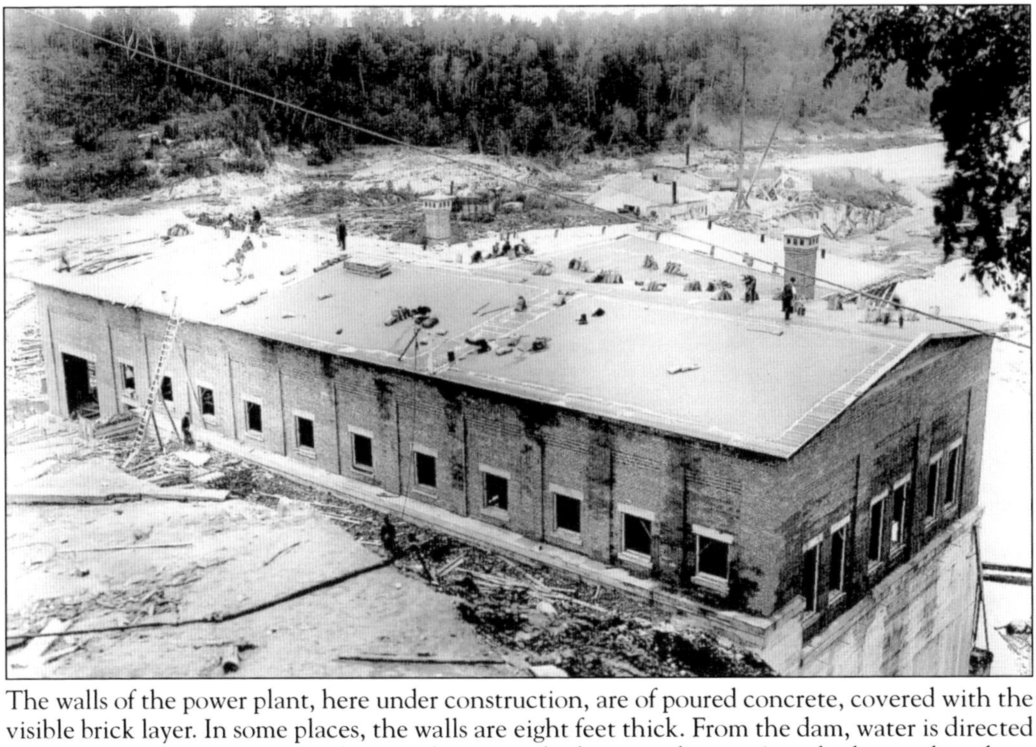

The walls of the power plant, here under construction, are of poured concrete, covered with the visible brick layer. In some places, the walls are eight feet thick. From the dam, water is directed through four penstocks to four huge turbines inside the powerhouse. Attached to each turbine is a generator that produces electricity.

Dean Bailey, one of 13 people who worked at the plant, was a switchboard operator at the powerhouse. Now there is just one worker, as a computer monitors and controls the system. It can turn the turbines off and on in response to power needs, safety considerations, and water levels. More than 4,000 homes in Essex Junction are lighted by the output from this plant.

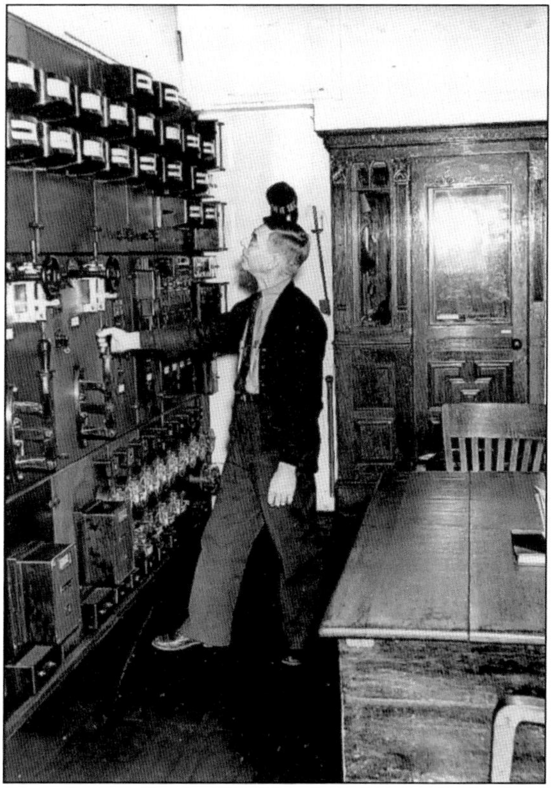

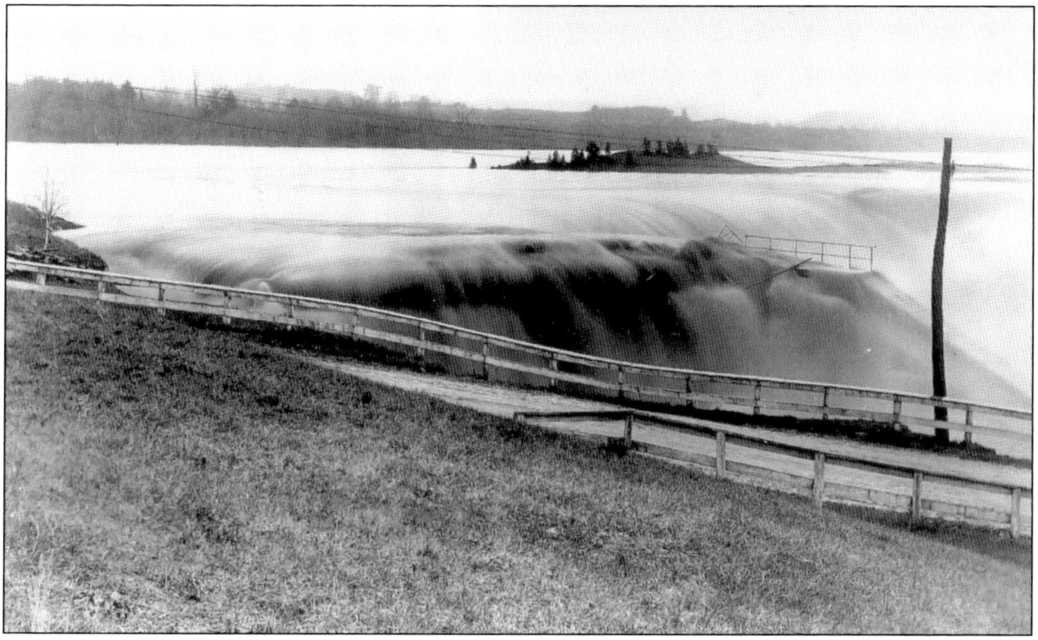

The inscription on this photograph reads, "Nov. 4, 1927. . . . Looking East from side of hill in front of power house of Essex Junction. Water rising over Intake and Head gates." The flood of 1927 will long be remembered as one of Vermont's worst natural disasters. After a very wet October, several days of heavy rain in early November gave the water no place to go but downstream.

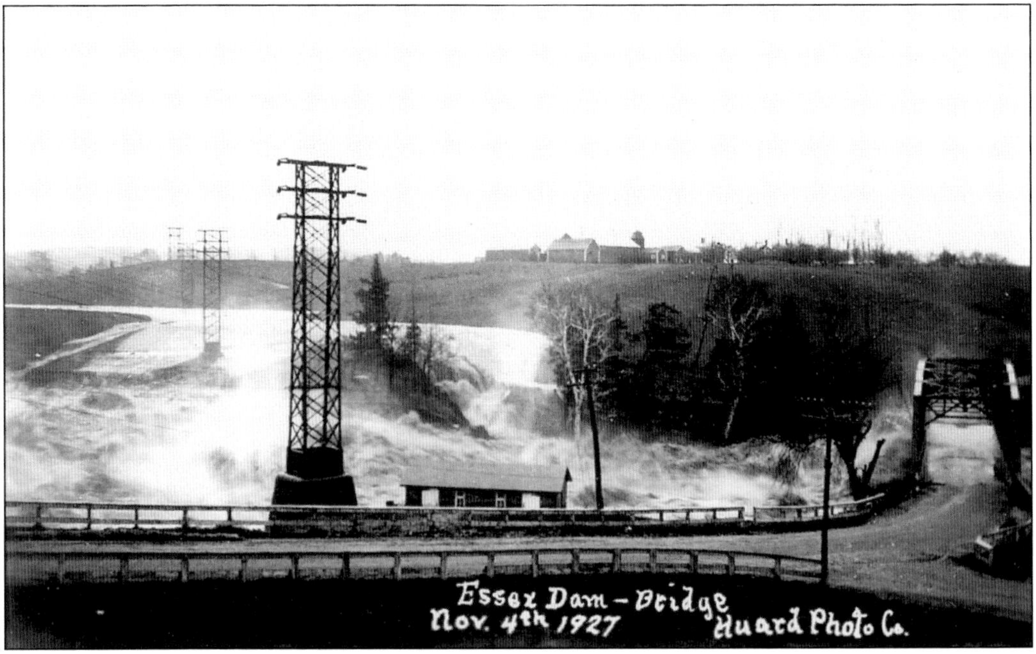

The river gauge one and a half miles downstream of the Route 2A bridge showed the water cresting at 50.4 feet, well over the flood stage of 15 feet. The iron bridge held, but the powerhouse was filled with debris. The flood damage on the downstream Whitcomb farm was extensive. The water rose to the second floor in the farmhouse, and the three-story barn was moved off its concrete foundation.

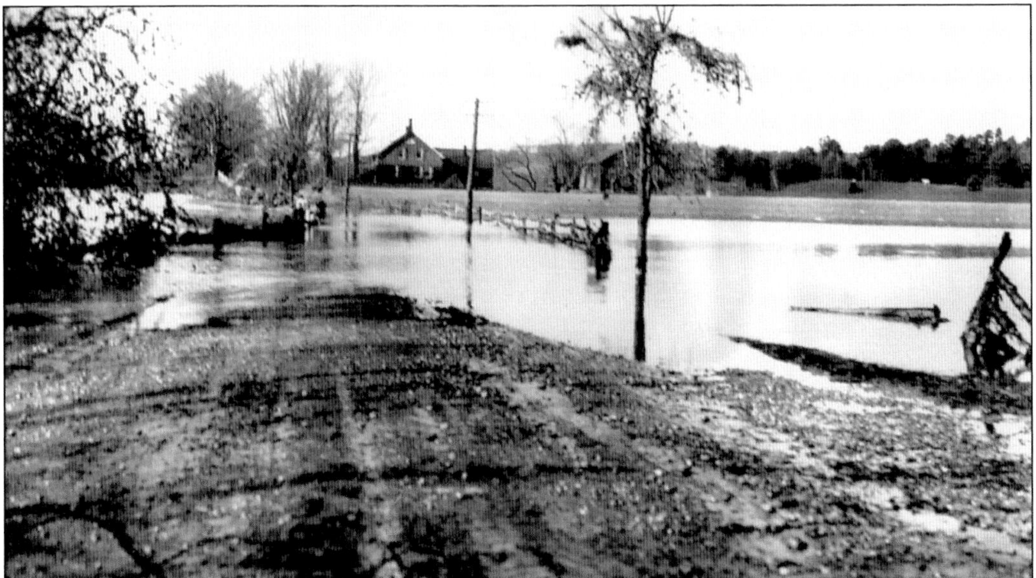
The Drury family on River Road was awakened by a phone call and told the flood was coming. Relatives from Essex Junction provided shelter for the family. The next day, the Drurys learned their brick house was still standing. The man in the fire tower on Saxon Hill could see the chimneys of their house, as the water had only reached the second story. The mud mark is clear in this 1927 photograph.

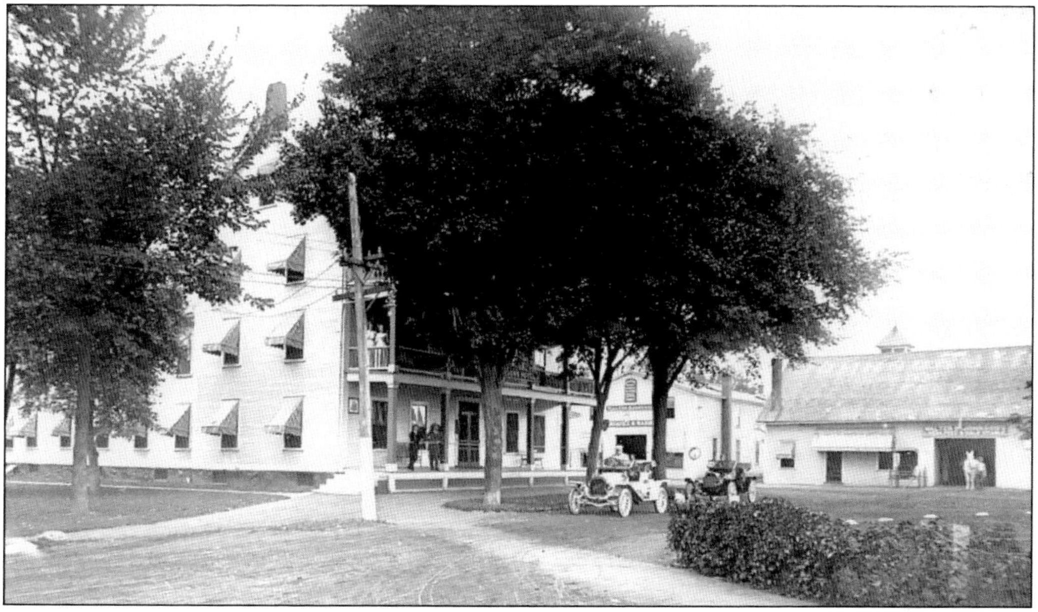

Walter B. Johnson bought the Central House in Essex Junction *c.* 1891 and changed the name to Johnson's Hotel. He ran the hotel in conjunction with his railroad restaurant business (a café in the station) in Essex Junction. The hotel, located on the corner of Central and Railroad Streets, burned down in 1912. Johnson also ran a livery stable and, in his last 12 years, was a car salesman.

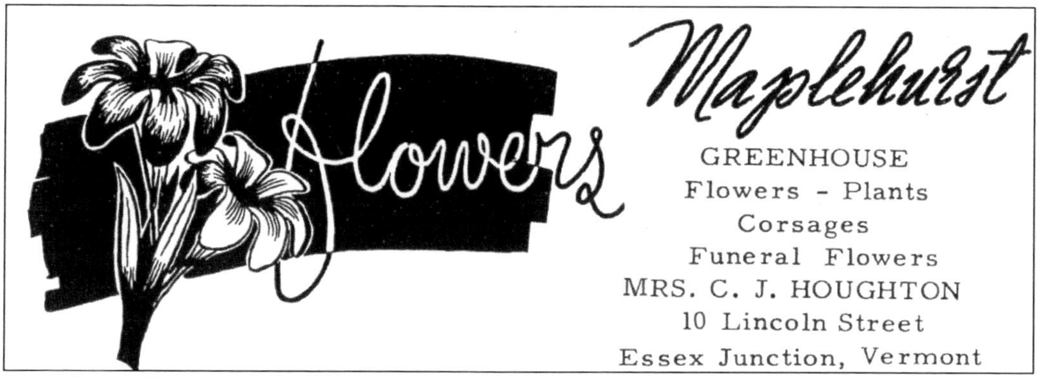

Maplehurst Florist began in 1943, when Charles and Phyllis Houghton purchased property on Lincoln Street from the McNalls. The Houghtons expanded the business from spring seedlings to fresh-cut flowers offered year-round. The business was passed down to son Carlton and daughter Christina in 1981. Carlton's son Jon joined the firm in 1993. This advertisement appeared in the 1953 Essex Junction High School yearbook.

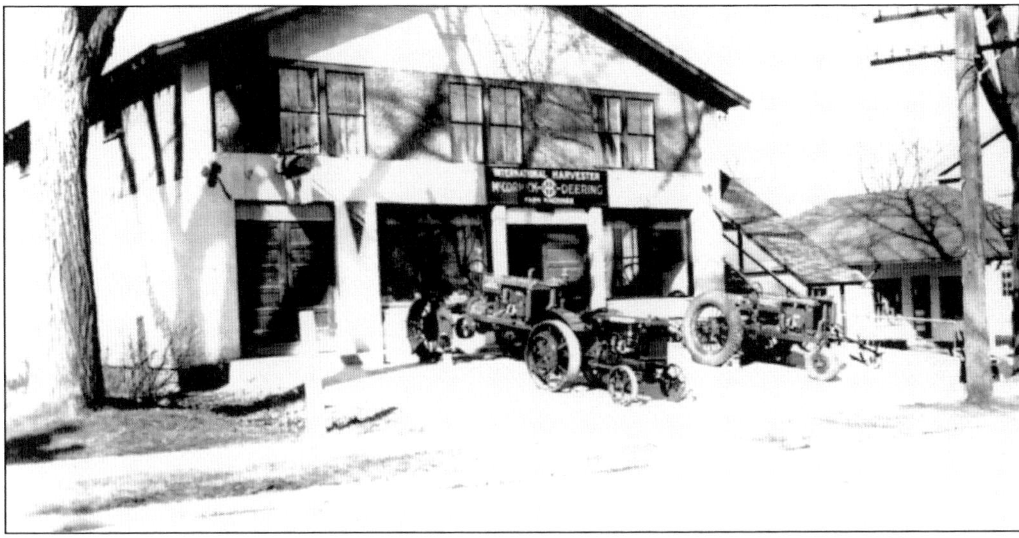

C. E. Brown started Clayton Brown's Tractor Sales on Pearl Street in 1936, also selling mowers, plows, spreaders, refrigerators, and freezers. The equipment was repaired in the basement. Brown had a storage building for more farm equipment off the east side of Park Street near the tracks. The Colonial Theatre was located in the back of this building. The business closed in 1983.

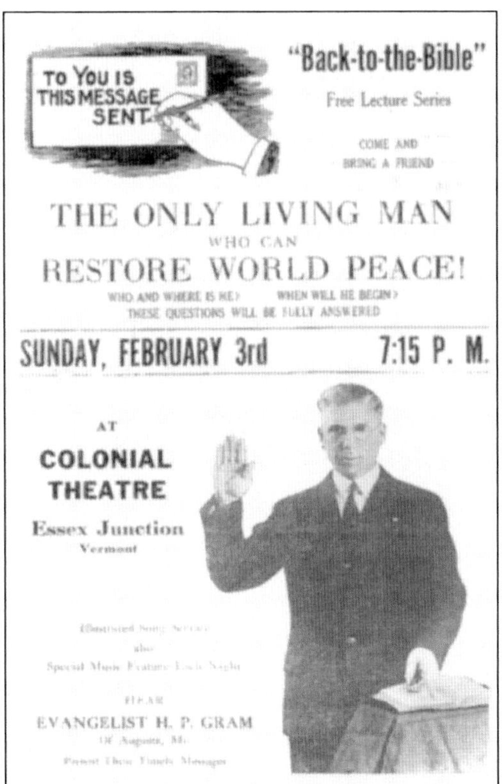

The Colonial Theatre was home to movies, high school plays, and musical revues. Evangelist H. P. Gram promised to answer such questions as "What and Where is Hell? What is its temperature? population? management? and duration?" When the building was renovated in 1984 and turned into the Colonial Office Complex, old movie posters were found behind the walls of the projection room.

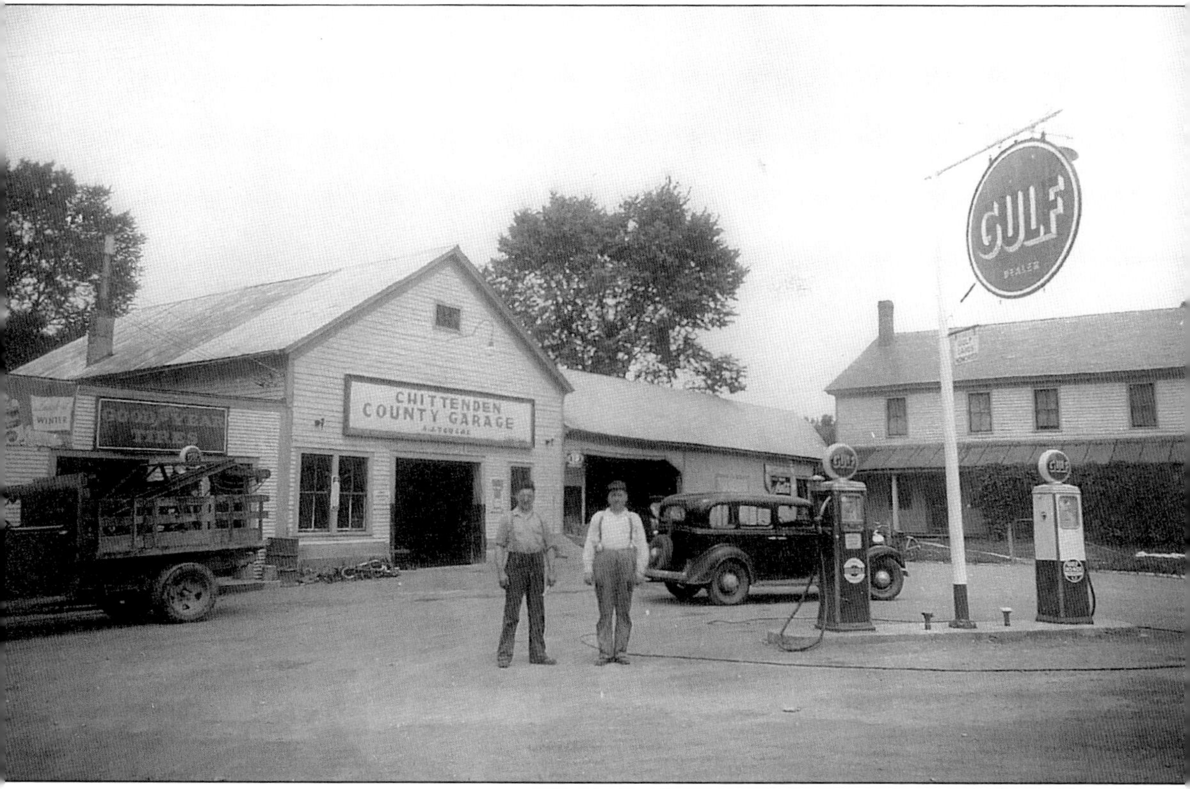

The Chittenden County Garage, seen here in 1934, was located on the corner in Essex Center. George Tougas's uncle Lucien Cote (left) and his father, Alpherie "Joe" Tougas, appear here. The buildings are, from left to right, Joe's office, the main garage, the shed, and the Tougas home, with apartments upstairs and a grocery store downstairs. Joe Tougas ran this business from 1929 to 1944. George Tougas remembers the garage was open six days a week, with his father doing all kinds of auto repairs. He also did welding for area farmers. He had a high-speed grinder to sharpen corn-blower knives used to cut cornstalks for cattle feed. Joe Tougas also had a 24-hour wrecker service. George's mother, Rita, ran the store, and he helped after school. One of his jobs was to keep the coolers filled with ice from the icehouse. Weekends were very busy since they were the only store around that sold beer and wine. The store was closed on Sundays, but if someone needed something, they would open up to provide the service.

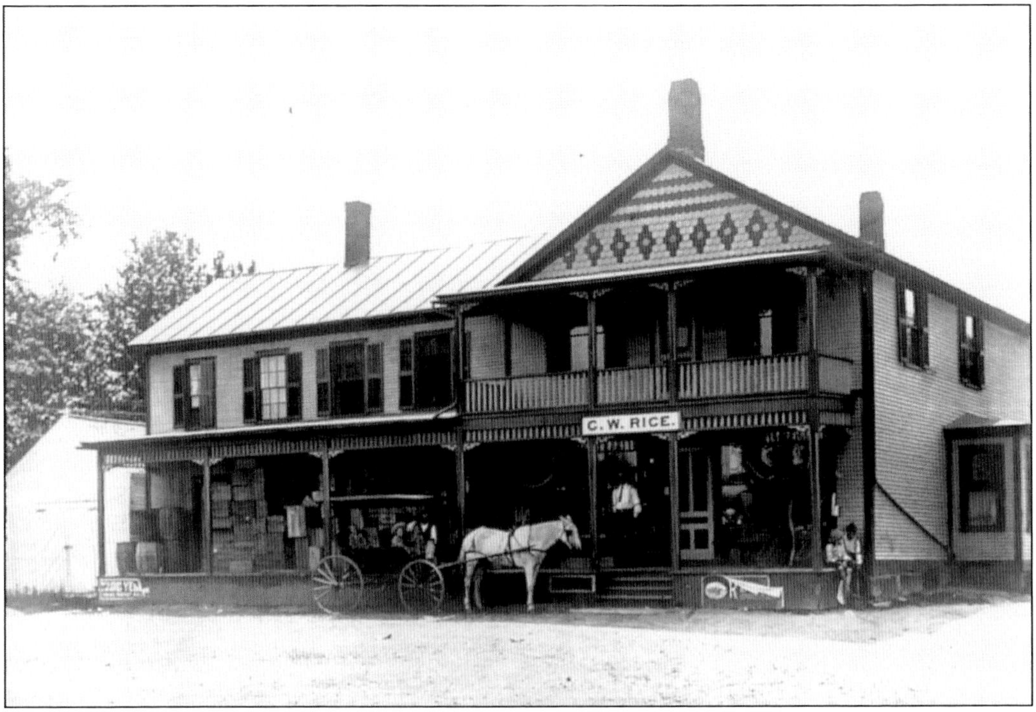

The C. W. Rice Store building on the common in Essex Center dates from *c.* 1819. For many years, it was the home of a general store originally leased by Thaddeus Fletcher. Fletcher prospered and became an active member of the community. Later, he and his daughter Mary lent financial support to institutions in Essex and Burlington. This postcard is from the early 1900s.

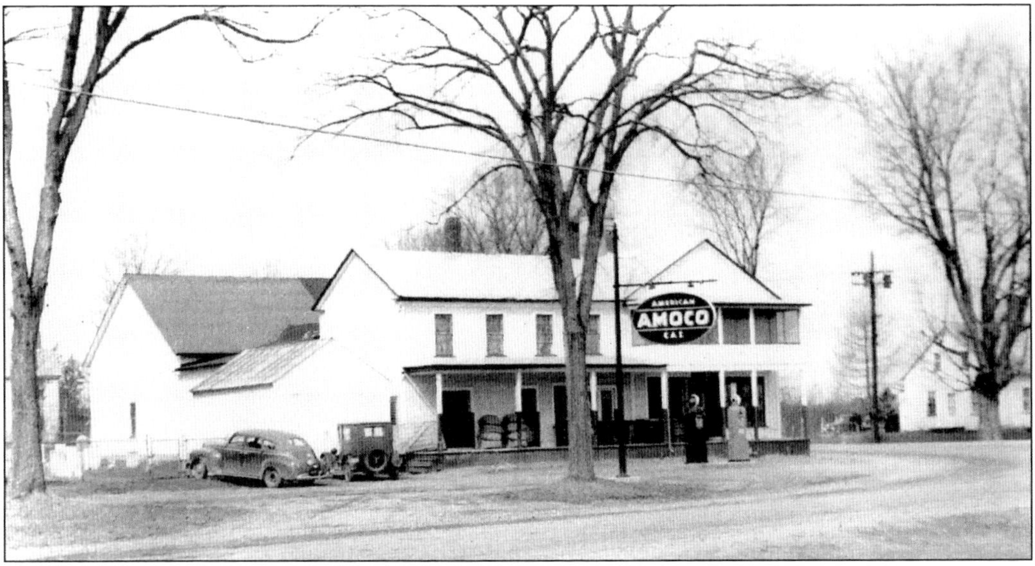

The store in Essex Center, seen here *c.* 1950, passed from C. W. Rice to the Goddette brothers in 1915, and to Stanley Fiske in 1947, who added a grain business. This building has also served as the Essex Post Office. Later, the Vermont Conservatory of Ballet had its home here for a number of years. (Photograph by Evans Knapp.)

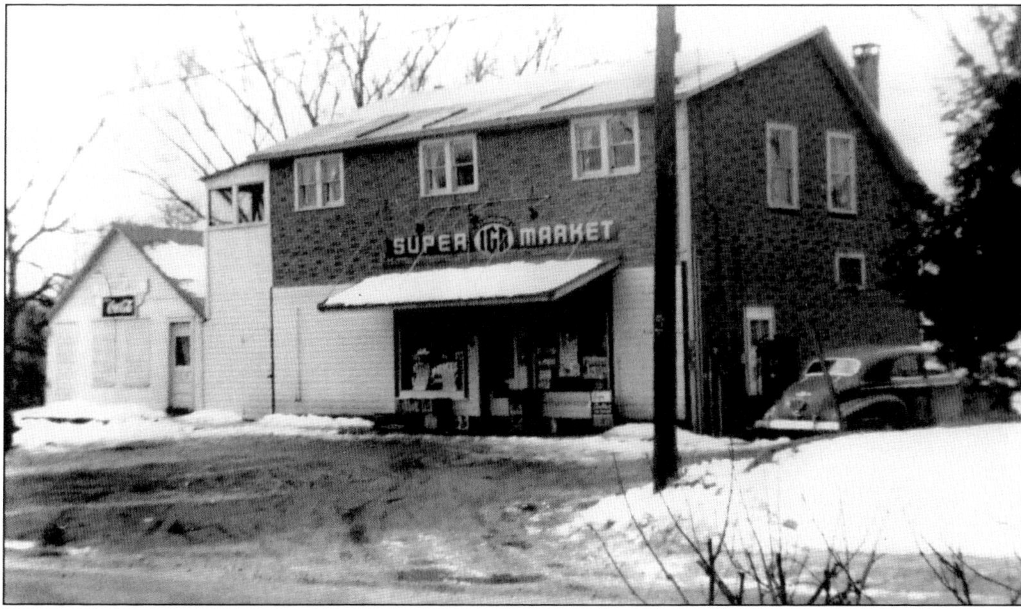

Fred Ortstein ran the IGA Supermarket on Jericho Road in Essex Center behind the library. A 1958 *Burlington Sunday News* article said the store "provides a modern check-out counter and a full line of 'sundries.' But the 'Supermarket' has a rural flavor that is actually more typical of Vermont than that of the 'Country Store.' " Evans Knapp took this photograph in 1949. The building is now the home of All About Hair. (Photograph by Evans Knapp.)

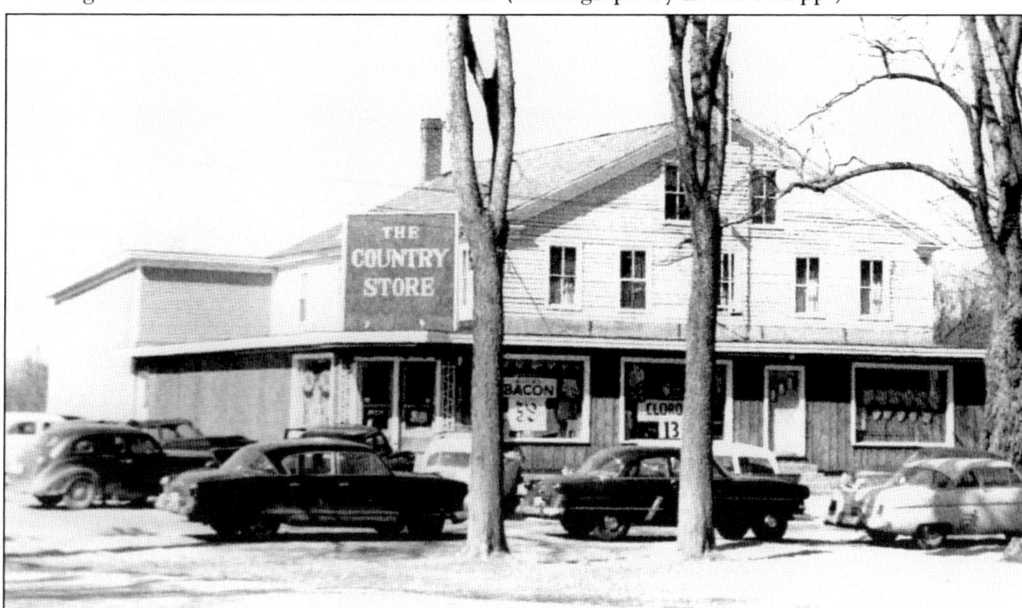

In 1958, the Country Store in Essex Center was described as "citified" since it was open on Sundays and evenings and was supported by a great deal of advertising in newspapers, on the radio, and on television. It provided employment for many area residents who would have otherwise had to look to Essex Junction. This photograph is dated 1957. (Photograph by Evans Knapp.)

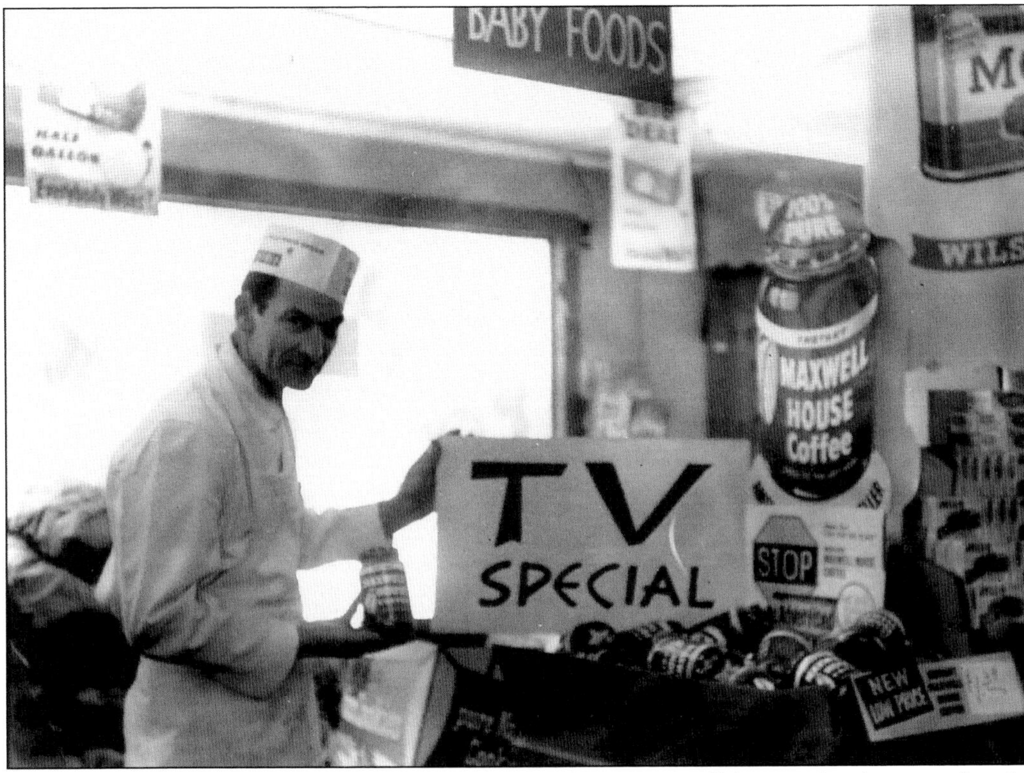

The proprietor of the Country Store, Merle Wood, became a well-known local personality for his sales acumen and dedication to his business. Betsy (Thrasher) Melvin recalls, "He was a real fore-runner of the supermarket. He would sell ten loaves of bread for a dollar. He always had a loss leader to get you into his store." (Photograph by Evans Knapp.)

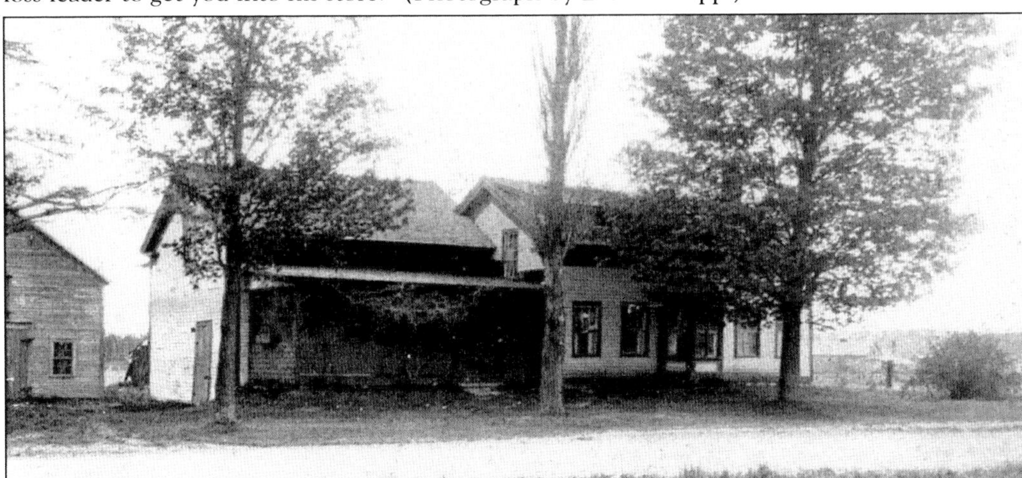

The Twin Maples tourist home was run by Walter and Eileen Westcott in the 1940s and 1950s. In summers, Nancy Bartlett washed dishes, waited tables, and changed linen there from 1948 to 1952. She remembers a clientele of mostly professional people from the New York City area, who were happy to stay put once they got there. The home was located just east of the present Essex Discount Beverage.

TWIN MAPLES

THIS IS A HOMELIKE PLACE on the outskirts of a small village, 9 miles from Burlington and on direct road to Mt. Mansfield, Newport and Montreal. Bus service several times daily. The house has a large screened porch. Comfortable rooms, electric lights and bath. Garage. Jersey milk, fresh eggs and home cooking. Waffles and Vermont maple syrup a specialty.

RATES

Overnight Tourists—Lodging, Supper and Breakfast, $2.00
Boarders by the Week—$2.00 per Day, $12.00 per Week

Route 15 · On Hard Surface Road · Telephone 17-22

MR. & MRS. W. G. WESCOTT, ESSEX, VERMONT

It is interesting to note what amenities were emphasized in this advertisement for the Twin Maples tourist home "on a hard surfaced road" in Essex Center.

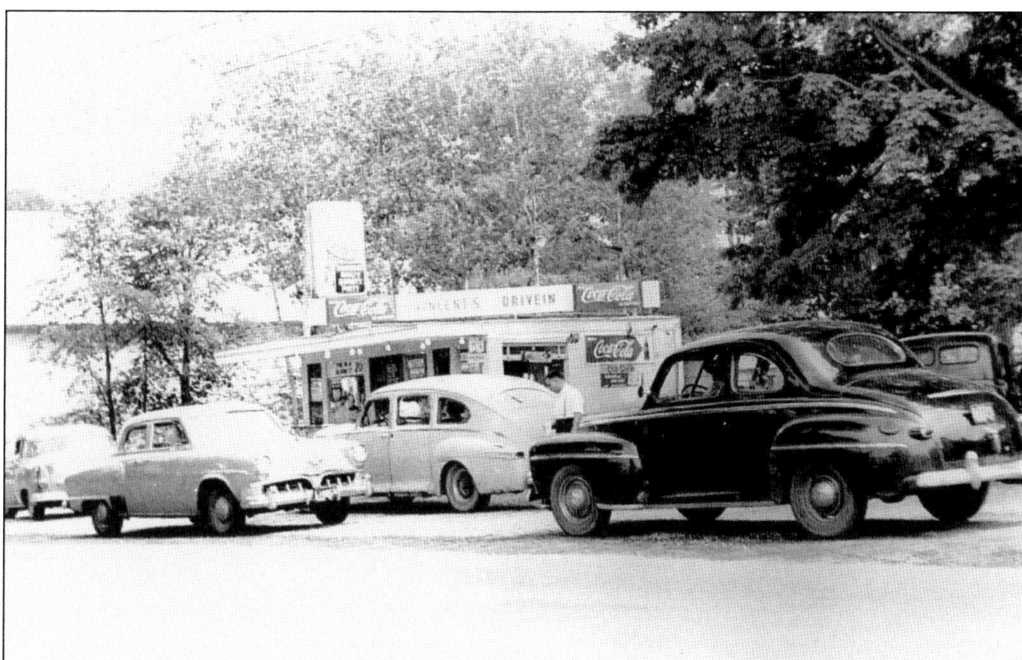

Vincent's, seen here in a mid-1950s photograph, was located where Powell's Place currently stands in Essex Center. It was run by Joe and Eleanor Vincent. It had a range of food offerings including creemees, malts, French fries, pepper steaks, and fried clams. It was also a popular hangout for local youth. Since this was a seasonal business, Joe worked as a janitor in the local schools. (Photograph by Evans Knapp.)

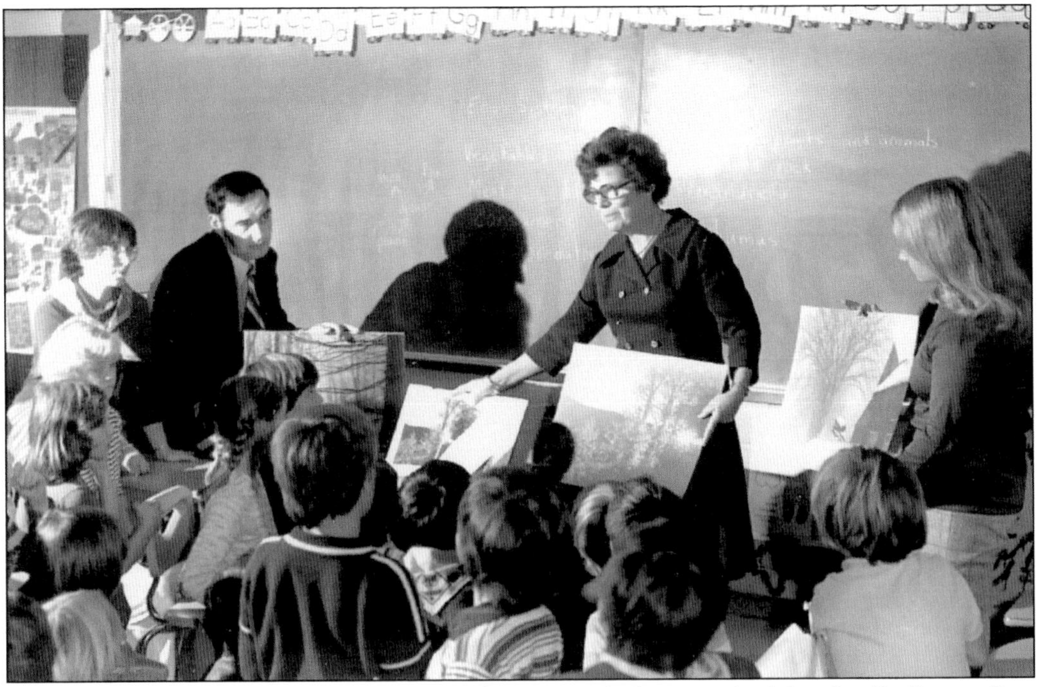

Betsy Thrasher came to Essex in 1955 and wrote and photographed for the *Burlington Free Press* and the *Suburban List*. Betsy married Tom Melvin, and in 1971, they formed the Artistic Alliance, a photographic studio and gallery. Two books of their photographs and Robert Frost poetry have been published. Here, Melvin shares *Robert Frost Country* with third-graders and principal Howard Magnant at Essex Elementary School in 1977. A second book, *Robert Frost's New England*, was published in 2000. (Courtesy Tom Melvin.)

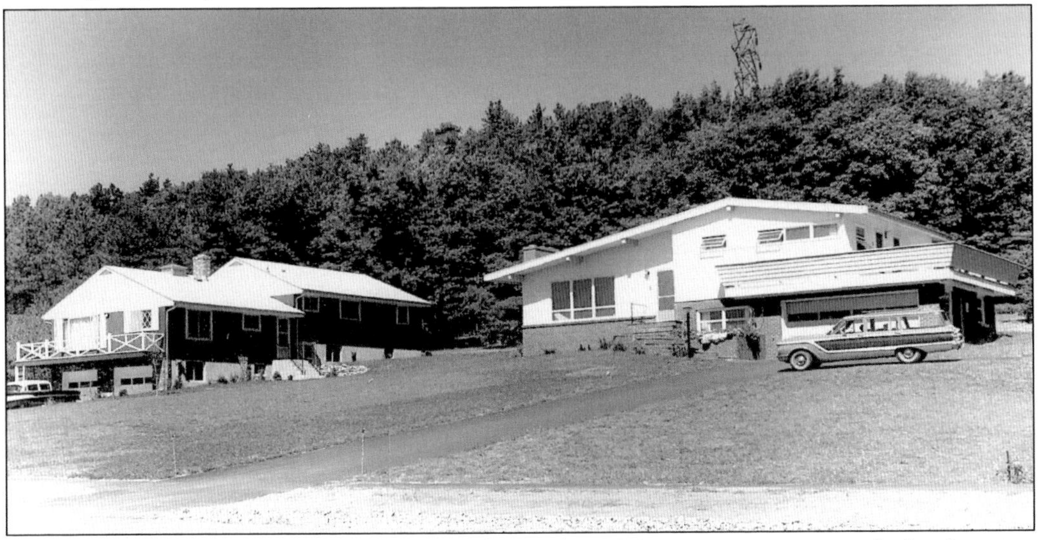

Pinewood Manor Inc., started in 1959 by Robert Marcotte, was one of the housing developments that resulted from the economic boom created by IBM locating in Essex. There are now about 250 homes on large wooded lots, with plans for 100 more. The accompanying Pinewood Shopping Center on River Road opened in 1970 and initially included a grocery store, pharmacy, and Seward's Restaurant. It is now mostly commercial and office space.

Four

People, Farms, and Families

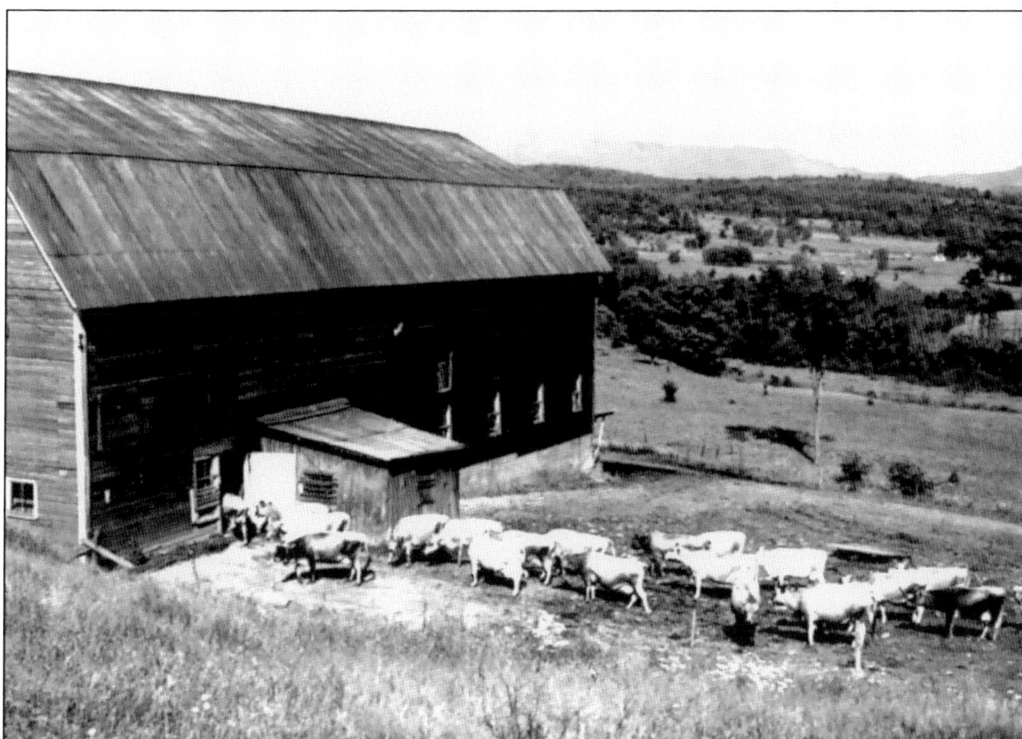

The 1913 barn on the Noah Thompson farm on Bixby Hill Road is depicted here on June 9, 1953. It was a three-story structure, 100 feet long by 40 feet wide. Horse-drawn wagons, and later trucks, would drive in the top level and roll the hay off to the mows below. The stable was on the lower level. The barn was flattened by a windstorm on May 3, 1983.

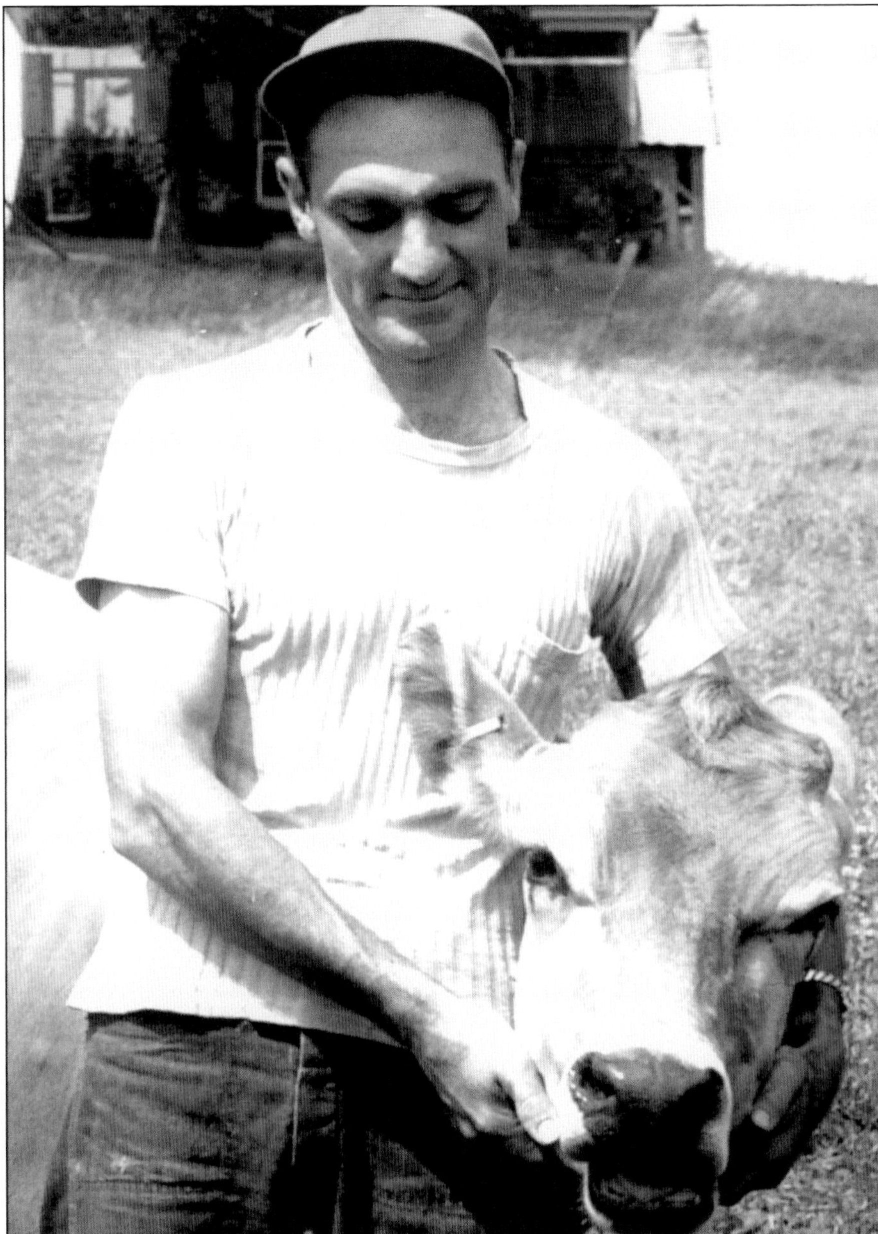

Noah Thompson appears with one of his Jersey calves *c.* 1952. After a varied military flying career, including combat over Germany and the Berlin Airlift, Noah, along with his wife, Betty, settled on a dairy farm in Essex Center in 1950 "with the best view in town." The 185-acre Thompson farm included a herd of 35 registered Jerseys, two horses, machinery, a sugarhouse and maple grove, and a tenant house at the foot of Bixby Hill. Much of the land in the present Birchwood neighborhood (Tanglewood Drive) was their 30-acre wood lot. Both Thompsons were active in the community—Noah with the school board and planning commission, and Betty with the Women's Club and PTA. By 1962, the Jersey herd had grown to about 90 head, but in 1964, the Thompsons retired from farming. They maintain their ties to the community by summering in Essex Center.

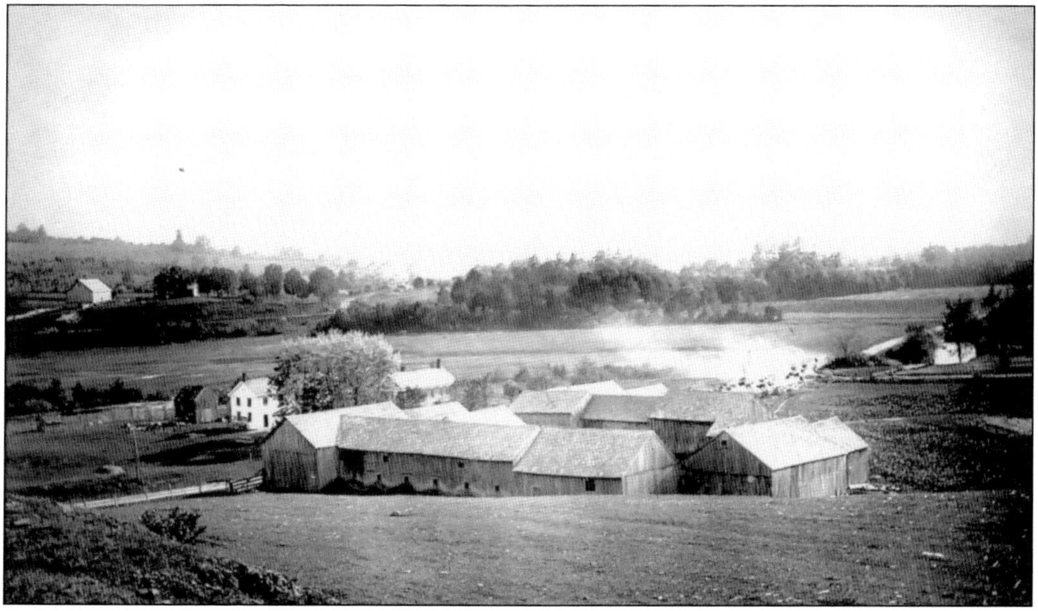

Green Meadow Farm, on Route 15 near the Jericho line, has been in the Whitcomb family since 1848. This 1910 photograph shows the herd kicking up dust while crossing the Browns River. The cow barn and horse barn were rebuilt after a 1915 fire, and today the well-kept buildings are an Essex landmark. It was last farmed by John Whitcomb and his brother George in 1988.

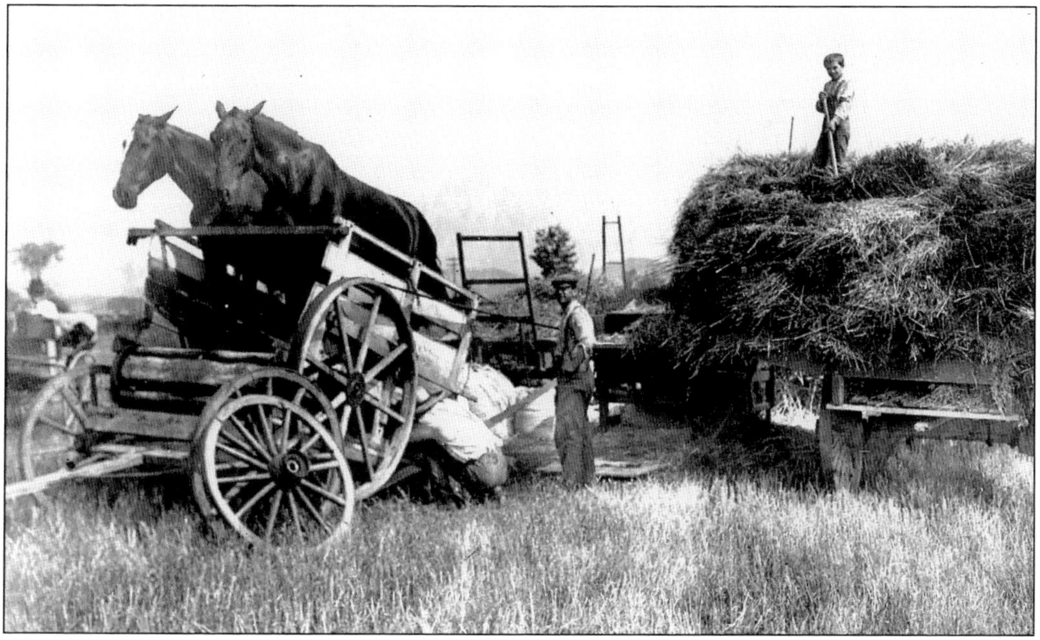

Albert and Sarah Chapin moved to Essex Center from Jericho in the 1860s. With land on Old Stage Road and Chapin Road, they established a dairy farm. Albert's son Willis and his wife, Ellen, raised Morgan horses, which were used for many chores. Here, they help thresh oats. Willis Chapin's son Claude, bending near the equipment, appears to be fixing something in this photograph from the early 1900s.

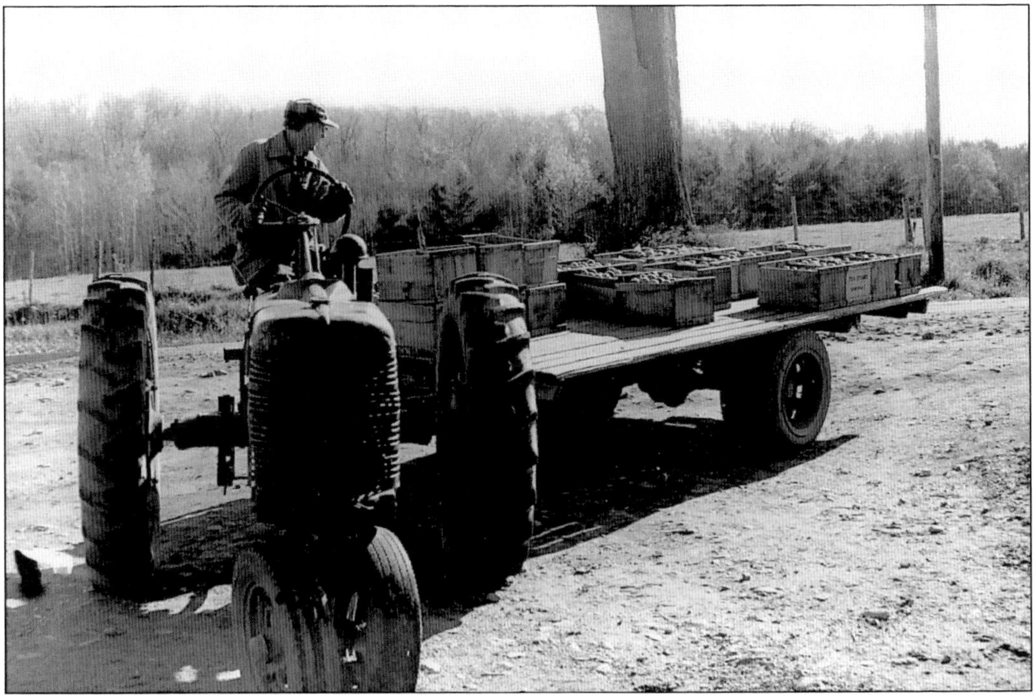

Claude Chapin, the third generation on the farm, started the apple orchard in 1929. Graton and Jesse Chapin were the fourth generation to continue on the farm. Dairying continued as the main source of income, along with making maple syrup, selling apples, and raising bees to make honey. Graton carries a load of picked apples *c.* 1979. Chapin Orchard is now owned by Phillip and Helen Murdock.

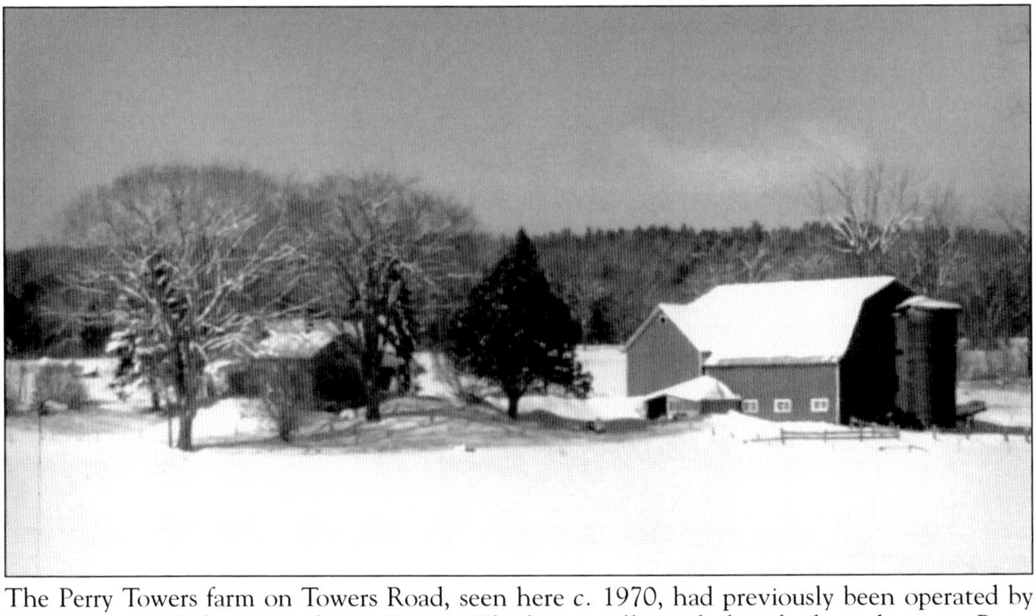

The Perry Towers farm on Towers Road, seen here *c.* 1970, had previously been operated by Perry's parents, Robert S. and Mae Towers. The house still stands, but the barn does not. Perry served in the navy in World War II and was active in town affairs. Perry's wife, Mildred, was a teacher at Williston Central School from 1959 to 1971. (Courtesy Betsy [Thrasher] Melvin.)

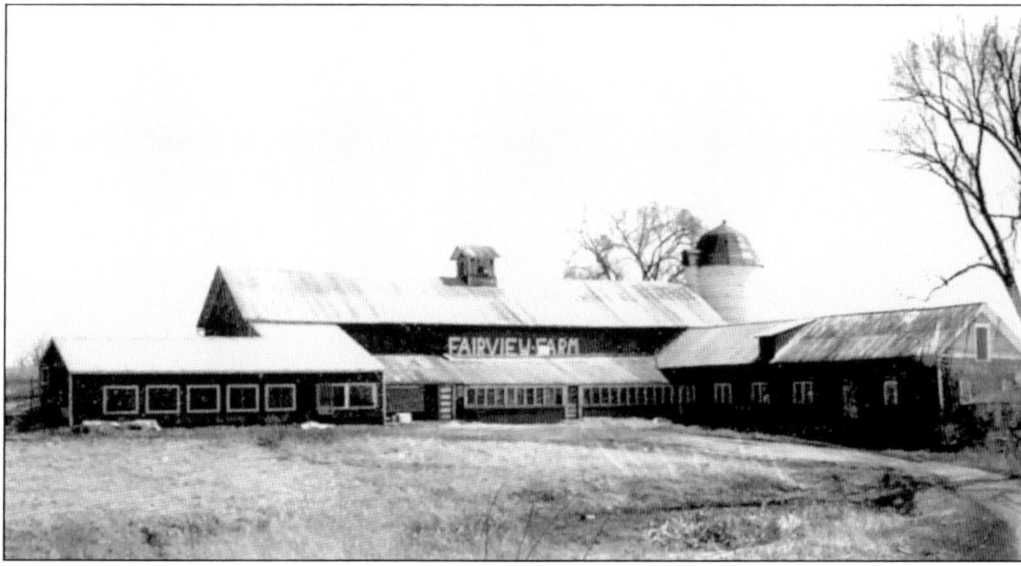

The barns of the Yandow Fairview Farm were located off Route 15 near the village line. It was an operating farm up until 1964. In the late 1960s, Larry Yandow Sr. kept the house but sold the rest of the farm property, including the land where Athens Drive is now. The silo, the last remaining evidence of the farm, was taken down in 1995.

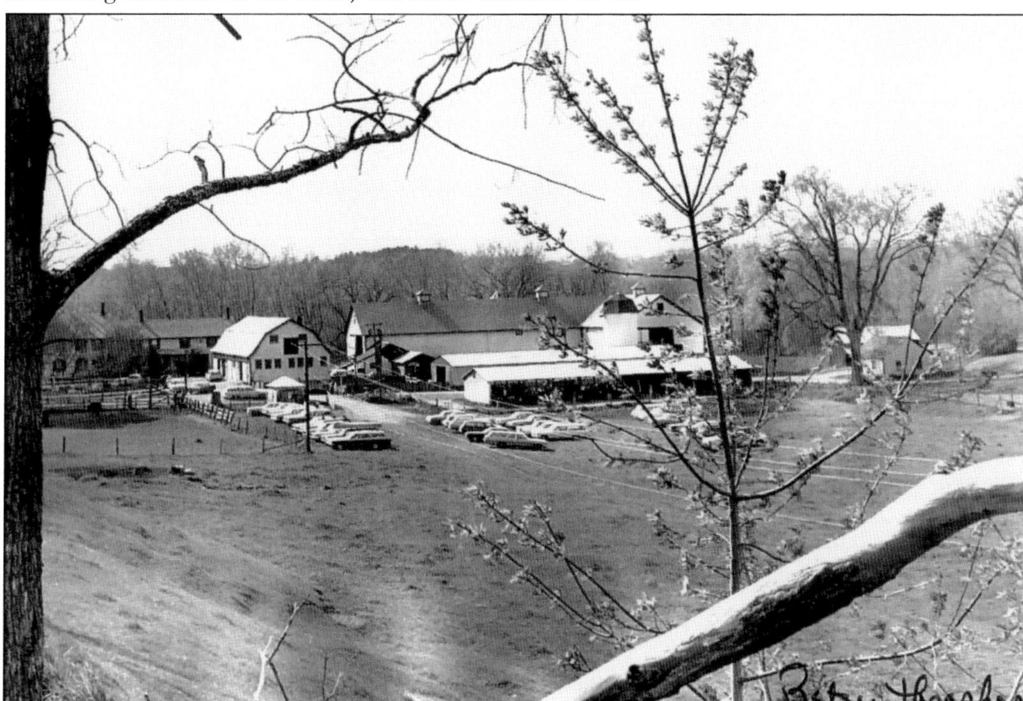

The Whitcomb farm celebrates its centennial. The farm was established by Lorenzo Dow Whitcomb and his wife, Cornelia (Goodrich), when they purchased the land and existing buildings in 1867. It is located along the Winooski River in the village of Essex Junction. A 1971 fire destroyed the brick house and many of the family records and photographs. (Courtesy Betsy [Thrasher] Melvin.)

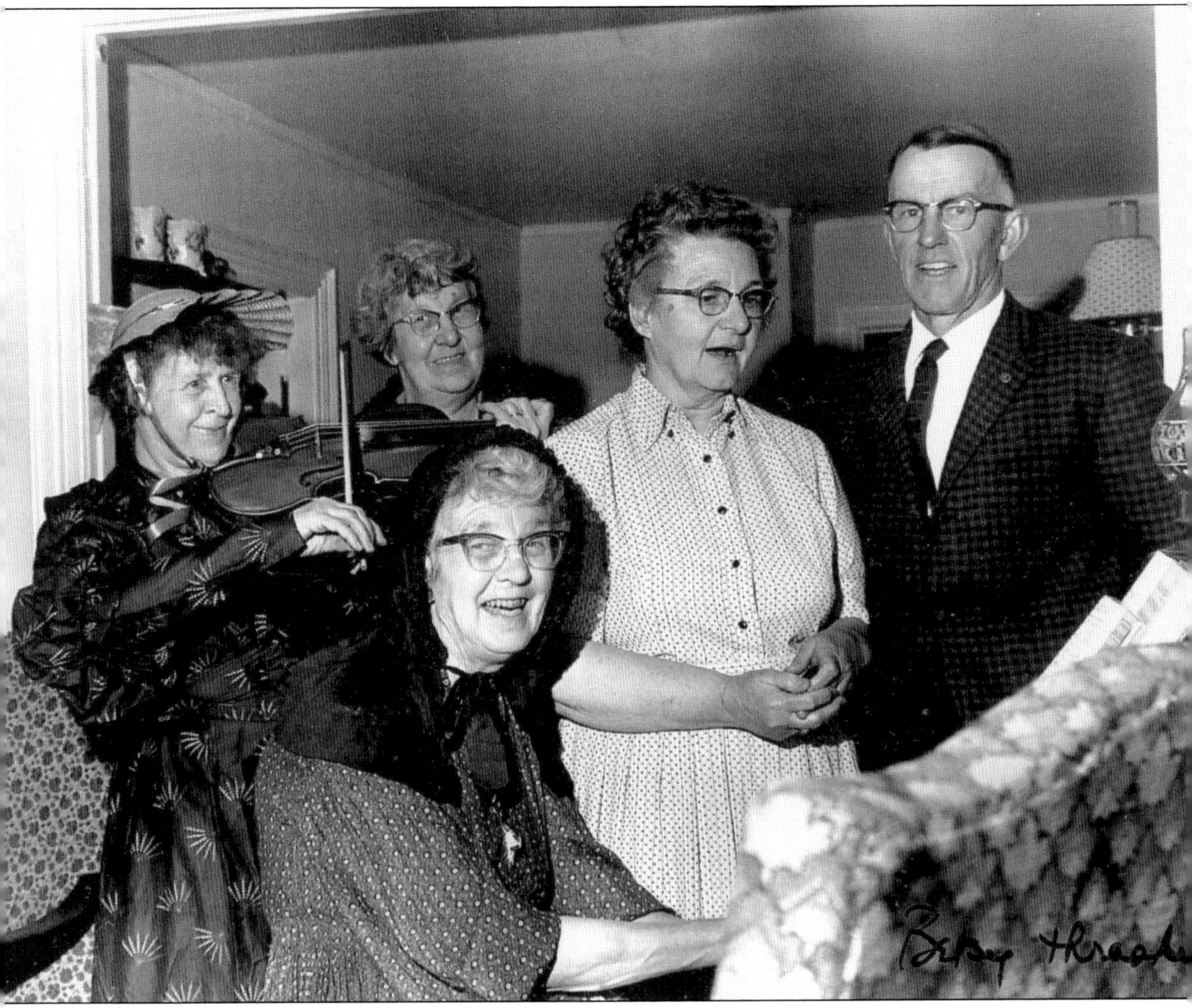

In 1967, the Whitcomb farm in Essex Junction celebrated its centennial with 600 people in attendance. Standing, from left to right, are Virginia Anderson (on violin), Gladys Estabrook, Kathryn "Tommy" Whitcomb, and Robert Whitcomb. Rosetta Estabrook is at the organ. The farm was enlarged over the years, eventually totaling about 640 acres of mostly fertile river bottom land. Run by successive Whitcomb generations, the farm operations have included dairying and growing sweet corn for the H. C. Baxter & Brother corn-canning plant. The farm also grew potatoes, with plenty going to soldiers at Fort Ethan Allen. Robert began breeding harness horses that raced at Saratoga, producing several winners. A 1956 *Vermont Life* article detailed Robert's logging on 200 acres, the construction of a corn-picking device, and the 90 milkers that sent milk to the Milton Co-operative Creamery on Lincoln Street. (Courtesy Betsy [Thrasher] Melvin.)

The Wool family gathers for a photograph c. 1909. Pictured here, from left to right, are the following: (first row) Ruth Catherine, Glenn Allen, and Louis Paine; (second row) Lewis Michael and his wife, Kate (Paine) Wool. "Lou" Michael Wool was born on February 24, 1859, at Butler's Corners. He lost his lower left arm in a hunting accident but became an accomplished painter who studied under Vermont landscape artist Charles L. Heyde.

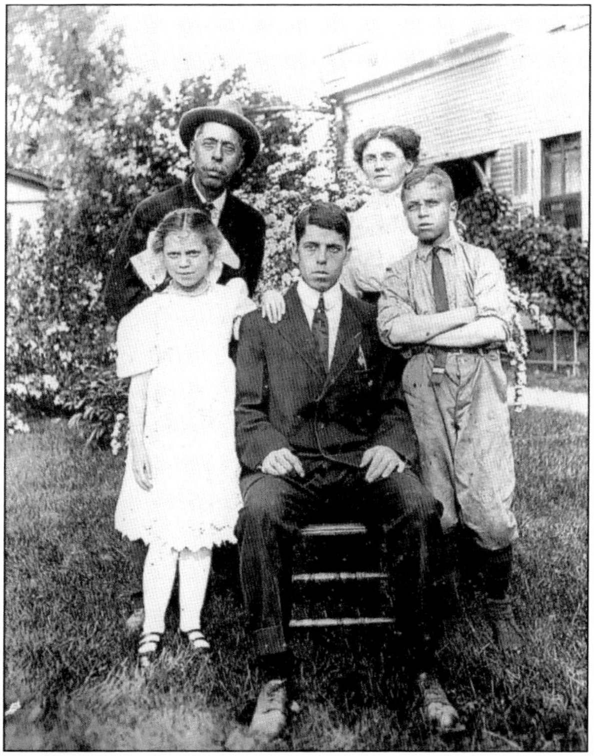

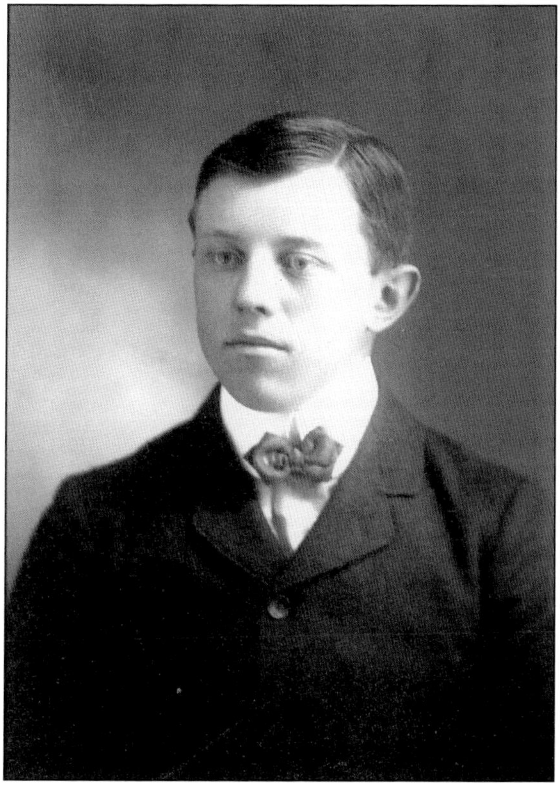

William Henry Wool appears here as a young man. He was most notably remembered as a director of the Champlain Valley Fair and "host" of the horticulture building. Because he served as a town lister for 26 years, he had an encyclopedic knowledge of local people and property. He served on the town school board and as a trustee of the Essex Classical Institute for more than 50 years.

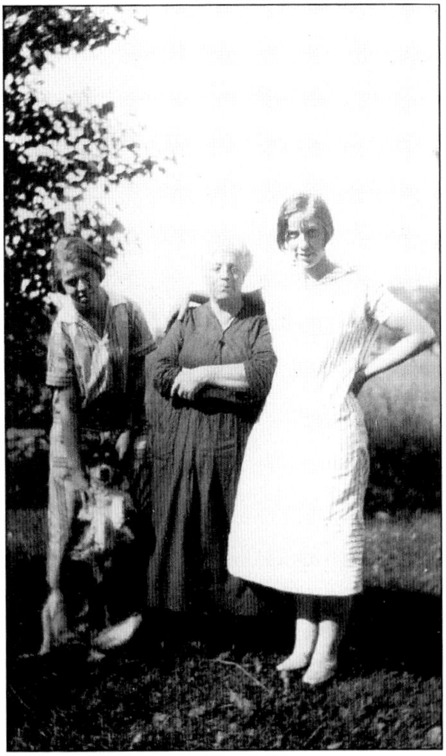

Shown here are Ruth (Wool) Blood (left), Alice (Wool) Pilon (center), and Mary Monihan c. 1925. Mary was born in Underhill in 1905 and graduated from the Essex Classical Institute. Married to Joseph Laliberte, the operator at the Ethan Allen Creamery, she became an accomplished rug maker, using a loom that her mother, Alice Pilon, had used for 50 years. She would sell the rugs or give them to friends.

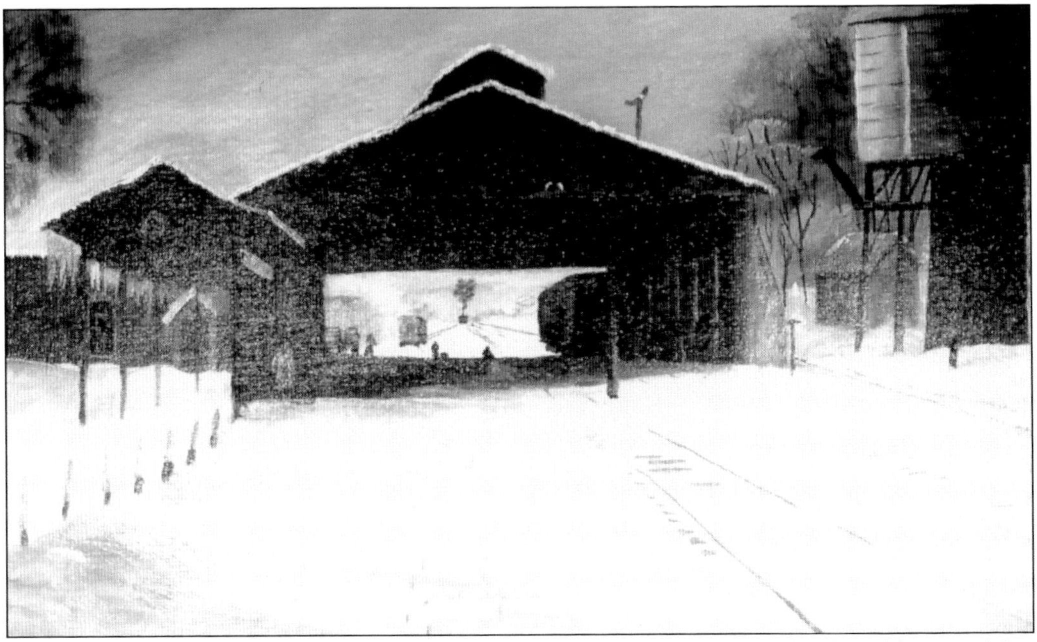

This oil painting of the train station was created by Mary (Monihan) Laliberte. After weaving rugs for about 10 years, Laliberte turned to painting. She received instruction and encouragement in oil painting from her uncle Lewis Michael Wool. She became well known for her paintings of local scenes, many of which are displayed in Essex Junction businesses. (Courtesy S. Henry Lampert, D.D.S.)

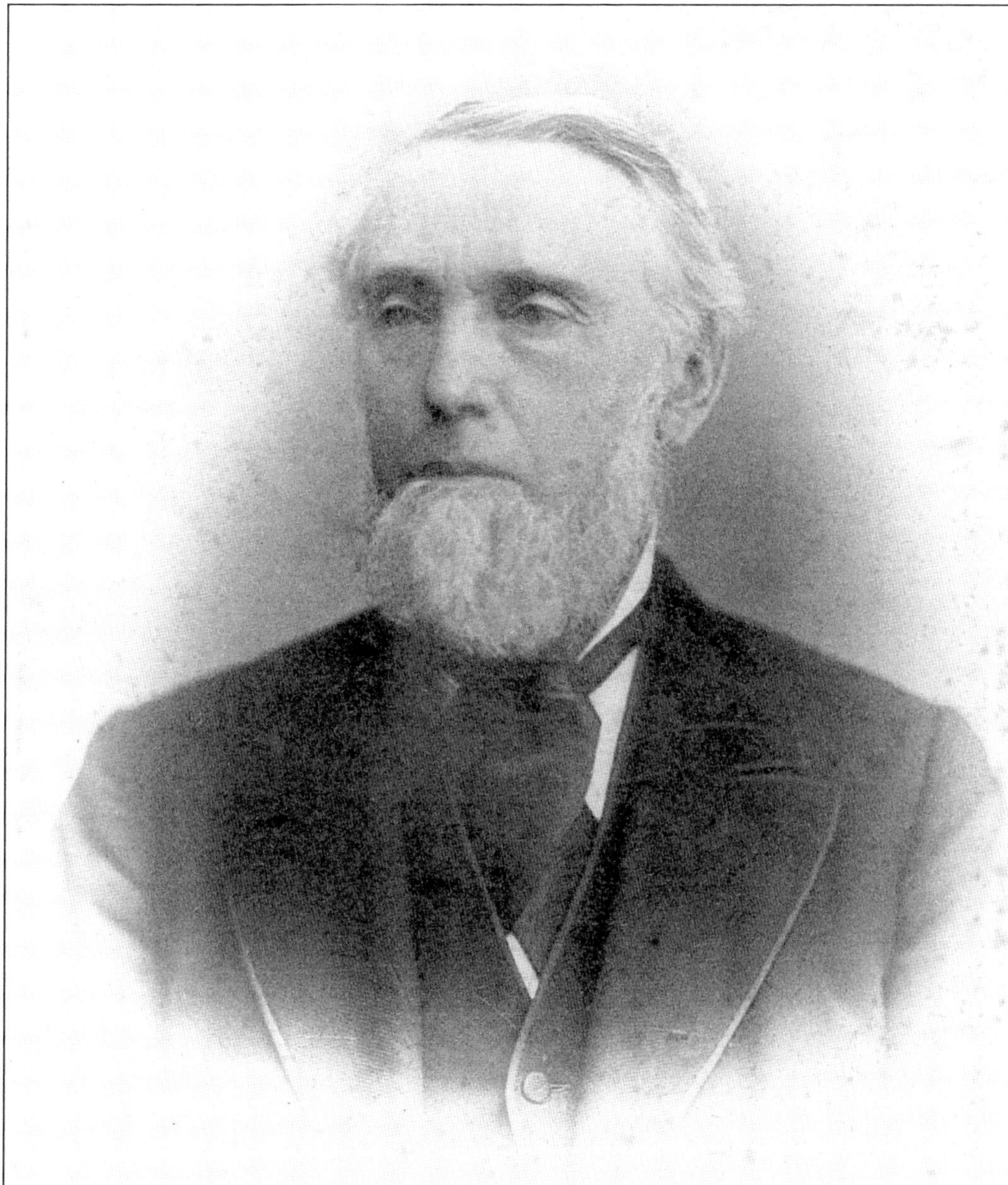

Lucius Castle Butler was born in Essex in 1820. Today, he is remembered for his history of the town and the memorial record of Essex residents who fought in the Civil War. He served in the legislature, as superintendent of schools, and as president of the Essex Classical Institute. He married Hannah Drury Page, the daughter of Col. Samuel Page. Dr. Butler learned medicine under the guidance of several local doctors and received his degree from Woodstock Medical College in 1843. Combining his medical knowledge and writing talents, he became the associate editor of the *Medical and Surgical Reporter* in Philadelphia for several years. A laudatory 19th-century biography stated, "Dr. Butler is a public-spirited and influential citizen; a prominent, leading, and beneficent member of his noble profession; a medical practicioner [*sic*] of the foremost class in his native State, and a keen and practical observer, whose worth is realized not only in Vermont and contiguous states, but throughout the land."

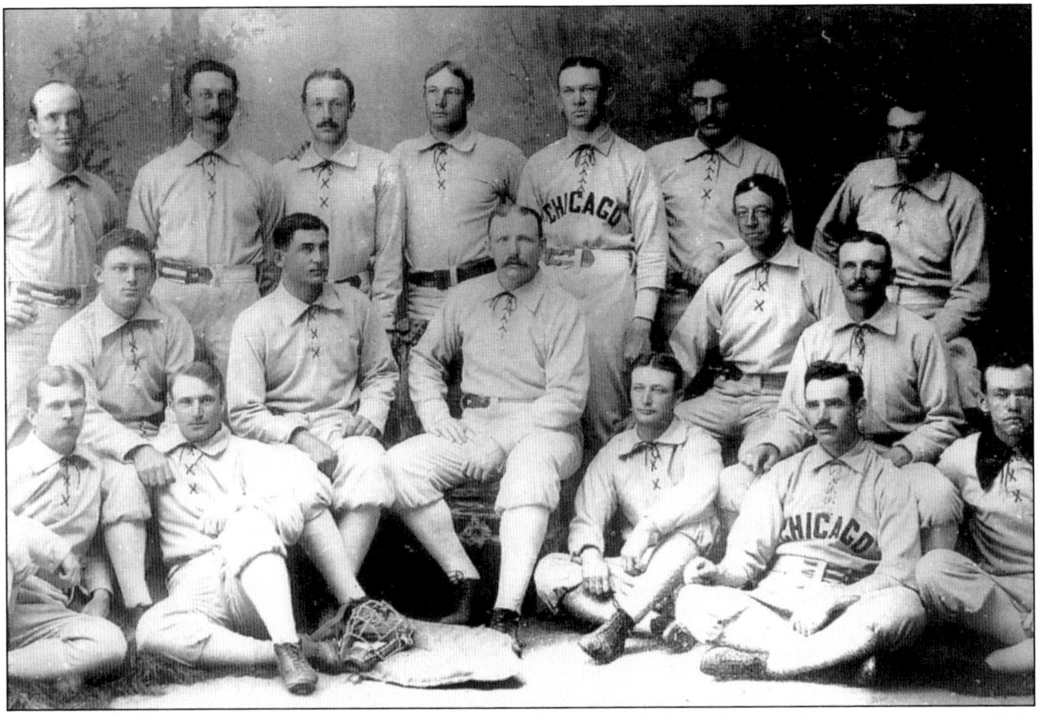

Bert Abbey, also known as "the Dazzler," stands third from left with the Chicago Colts c. 1893. He was born in 1869 on the family farm on Browns River Road in Essex. While attending the University of Vermont, he helped bring its baseball program to prominence. In his major-league career (1892–1896), Abbey compiled a pitching record of 22-40 with such teams as the Washington Senators and the Brooklyn Bridegrooms.

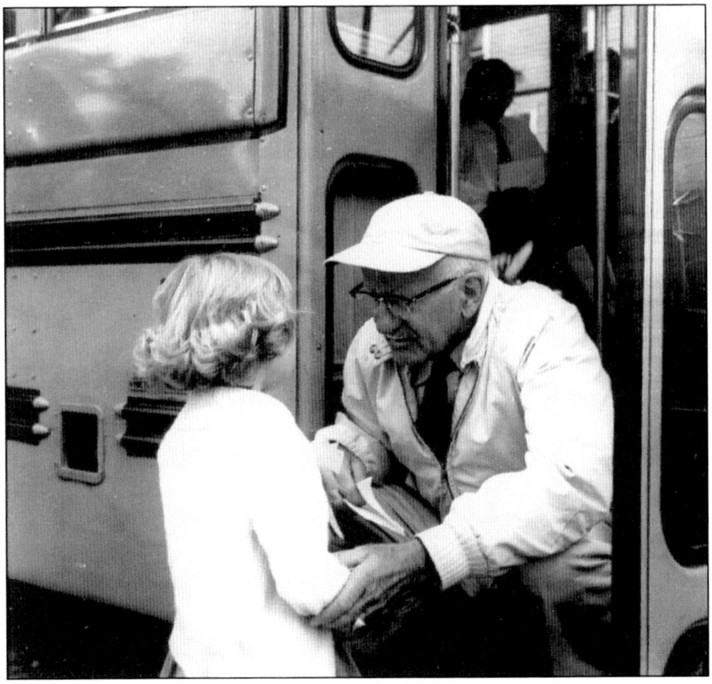

On the first day of school in September 1962, bus driver Ray Nichols greets a young student. Nichols, a longtime resident of Essex Center, was a school bus driver for more than 20 years. He was president of the Village of Essex Center in its first year, 1952. The village was set up to establish a water supply for Essex Center. One of his duties was to check the chlorine level every day. (Courtesy Betsy [Thrasher] Melvin.)

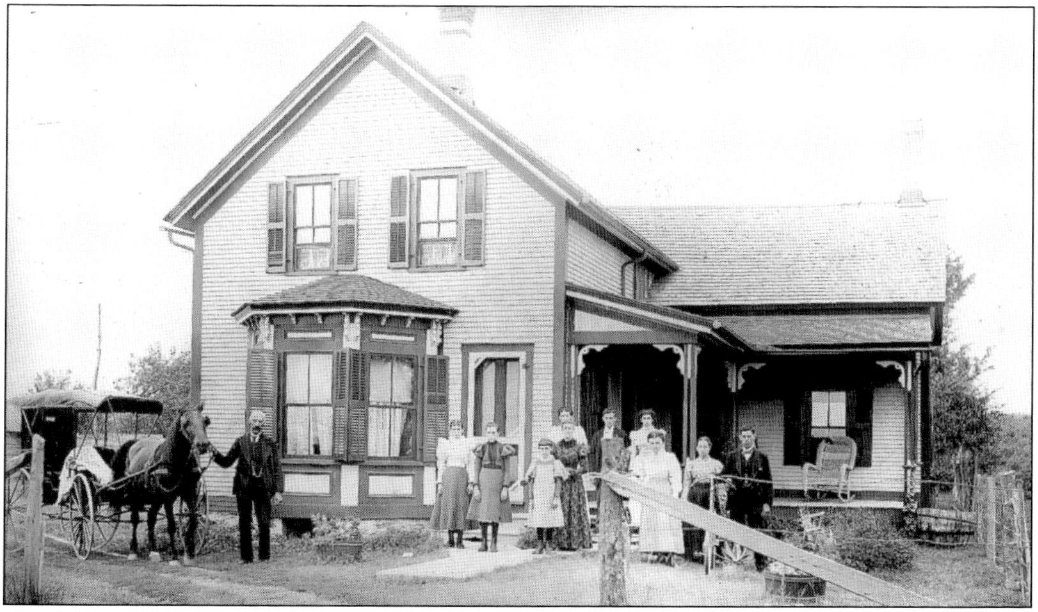

The Valyou house on Willeys Court appears here in 1895. Frank Valyou (left) also owned property across from the fairgrounds on Pearl Street, which he bought for 50¢ an acre. He worked at the Shelburne Shipyards and was also a carpenter. His son George (right) was a carpenter, as was George's son Harry. Several houses on West, Park, and South Streets were built by the Valyous.

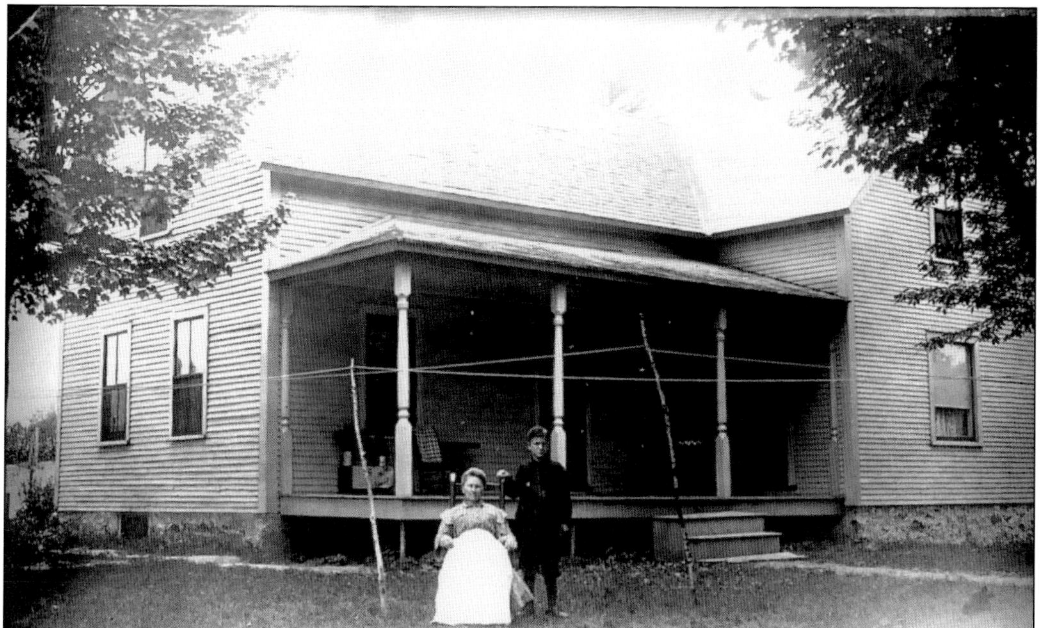

Philomena "Phoebe" Paro and her son George Oscar Paro are in front of their house on the corner of Camp and Maple Streets c. 1904. Phoebe's husband, also named George, ran a basement-level shoe store on Railroad Avenue.

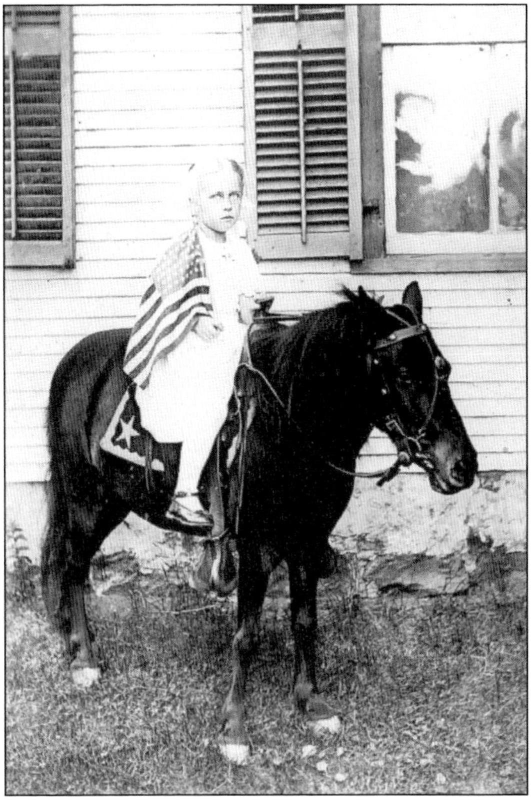

Florence Remington is pictured here c. 1915. A longtime resident of Essex Junction, she owned and operated Remington's Store, at 12 Main Street, for more than 30 years. Remington's sold dry goods, glassware, gift items, and greeting cards. She graduated from Essex Junction High School and lived all her life in the family home on North Street.

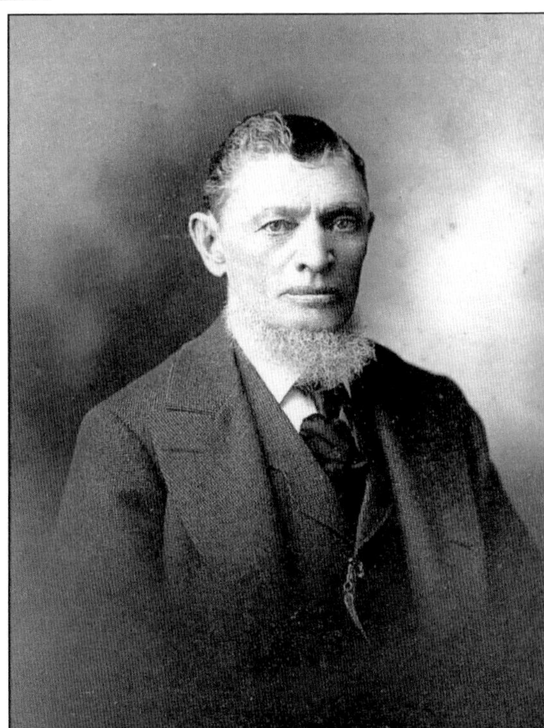

George Beecher arrived from Germany in 1848 and settled on a farm in Essex on Osgood Hill Road. He married Rebecca Fletcher in 1859 and had three children. A Civil War veteran serving with Company I, 6th Vermont Regiment, he participated in the battles of Winchester, Fisher's Hill, and Cedar Creek and in the Richmond Campaign. He was on the select board and the Essex Classical Institute board and was overseer of the poor in 1892.

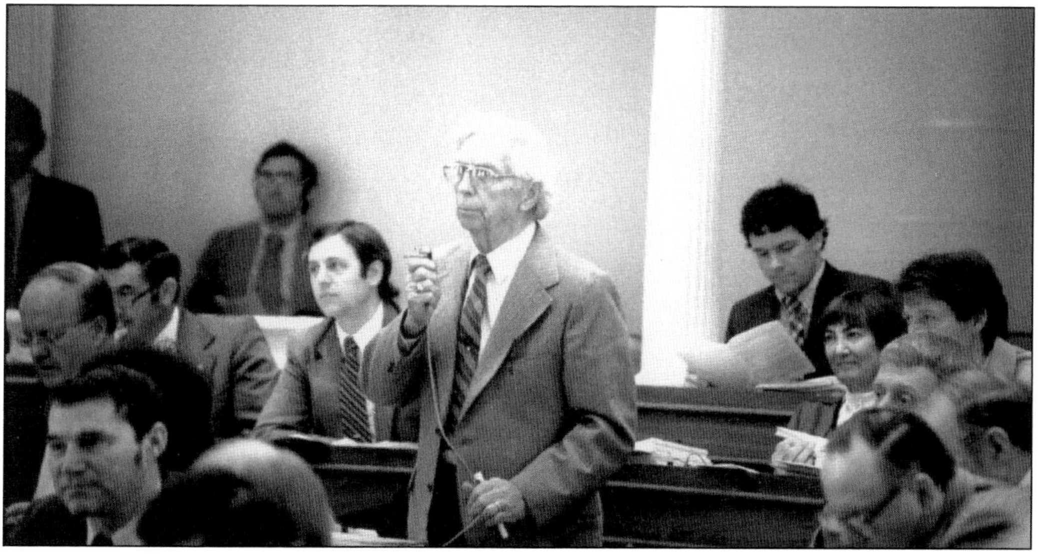

Martin Powell Sr. was an educator and an active member of the community. Graduating from the University of Vermont in 1930, he taught for many years and was the school principal in Essex from 1954 to 1962. He also served as the town moderator from 1959 to 1983. Here, Powell addresses the legislature in Montpelier, where he served as Essex representative from 1969 to 1984.

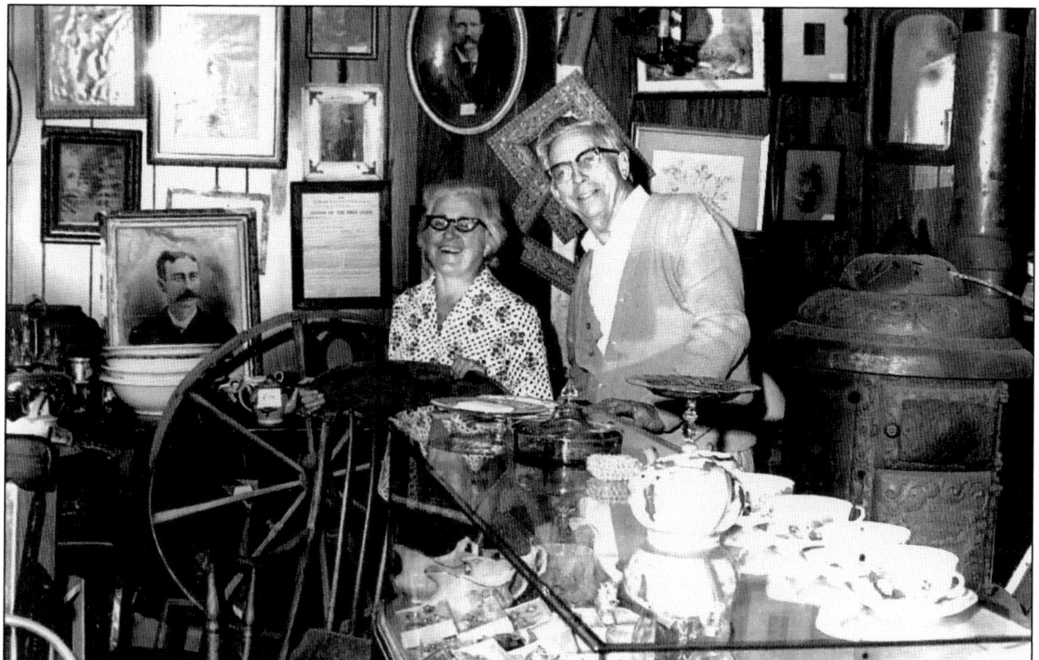

Martin Powell Sr. and his wife, Orilla, appear in their antique shop in Essex Center. They advertised "antiques, primitives, and other goodies—old dishes, chairs, tables, pictures, and picture frames. Also—all types of caning, reed work, rush work, furniture repair." Powell's Place, a snack bar started by the couple in 1971 next to the antique shop, is still a familiar gathering spot in town.

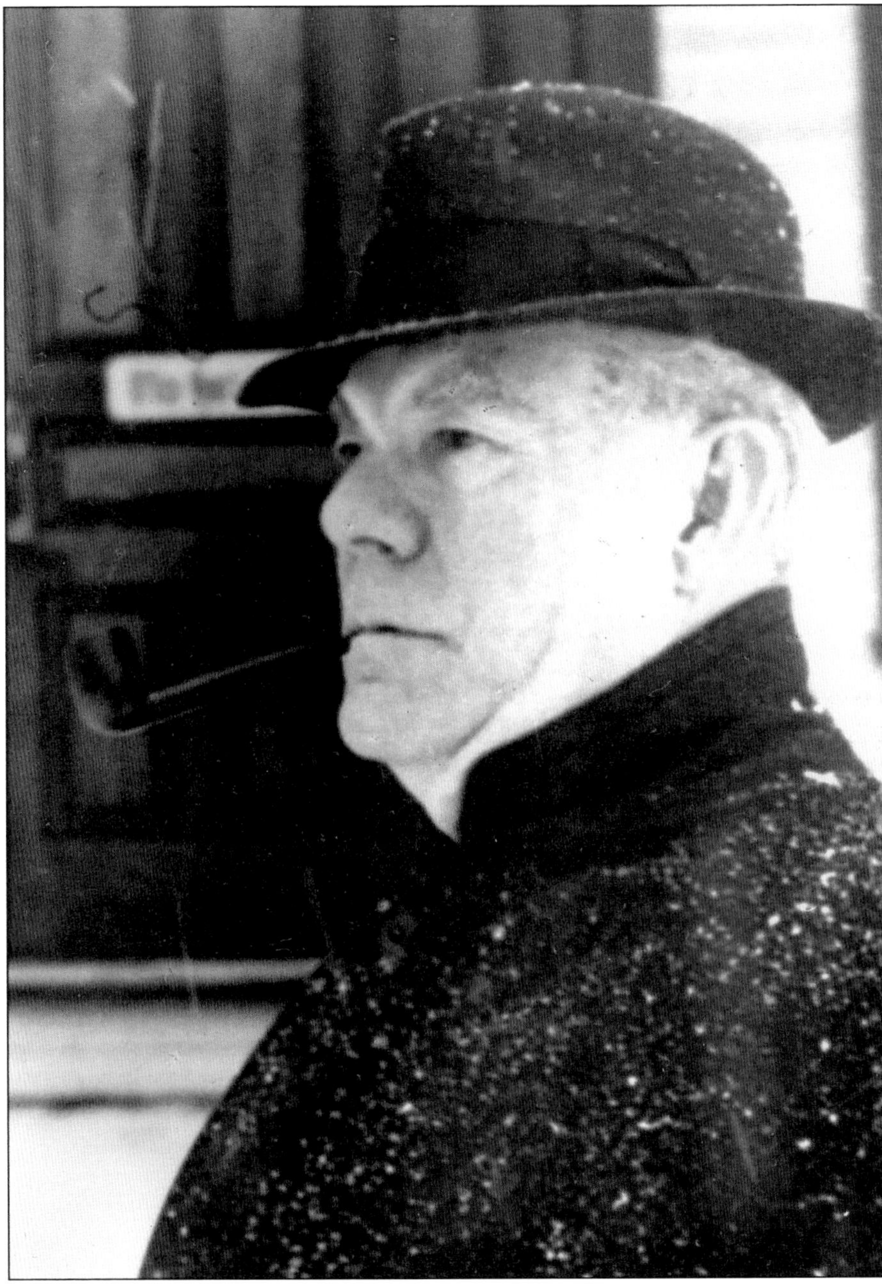

Allen Martin was born in Williamstown on August 14, 1875. Educated at St. Johnsbury Academy, he was admitted to the bar on October 14, 1898. His list of public offices includes town clerk for 50 years, village clerk, and member of the board of water commissioners. He was instrumental in the establishment of the Saxon Hill Forest as a water resource for the village of Essex Junction. Martin also served as state's attorney for Chittenden County and assistant U.S. attorney. He was the Vermont state liquor administrator just after Prohibition was repealed. He practiced law in an office on Park Terrace; his home was also on Park Terrace. Allen Martin married Kizzie Bates, a member of the Job Bates family, on January 14, 1903, in Essex Junction. They had seven children. After Kizzie died, Martin married Helen Keir Snyder.

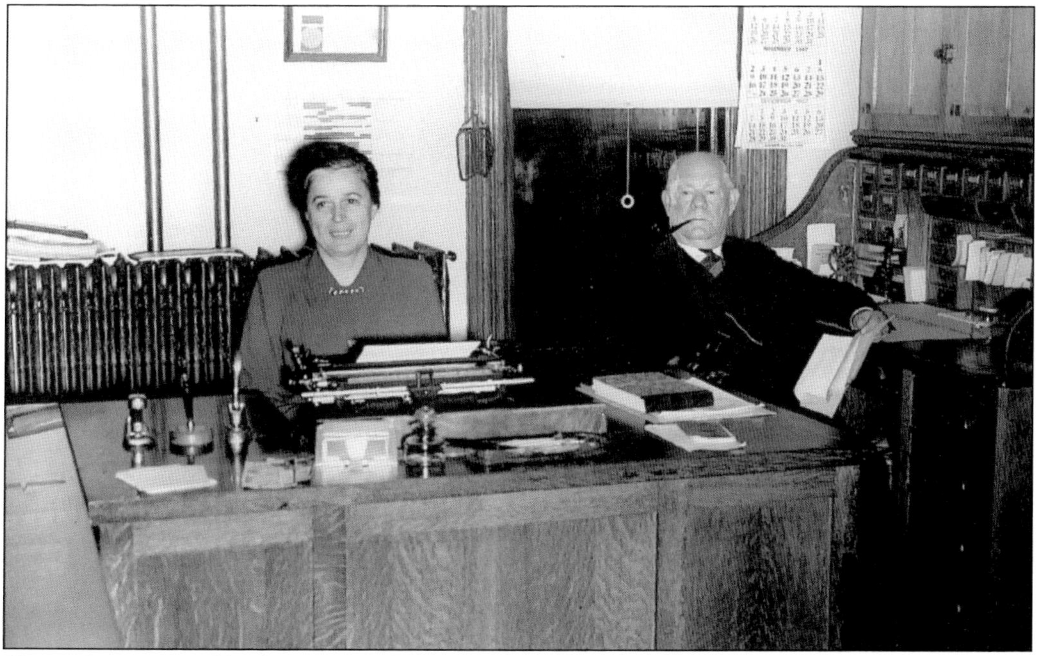

Shown here are Mildred Barnes and Allen Martin in 1947. Barnes moved to Essex Junction in 1919 to a house on Pearl Street and lived there for 70 years. Her first job, in 1921, was helping town clerk Allen Martin. Over the years, she served as assistant town clerk, town clerk, and Essex town treasurer, among other offices. With her honesty and patience, she set an example for Vermont town clerks.

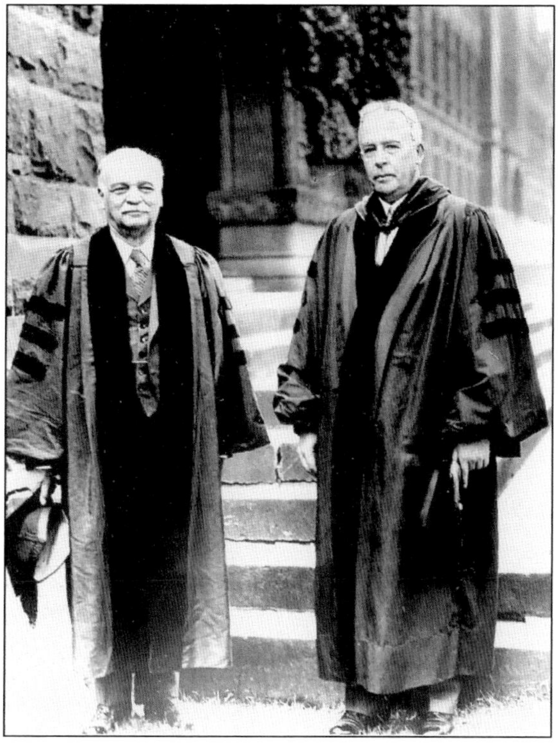

Guy Bailey (right) grew up in Essex Junction and attended the University of Vermont. He served in the legislature and was Vermont secretary of state from 1908 until 1917. He was the 13th president of the University of Vermont, serving from 1920 to 1940. Charles Curtis (left), vice president of the United States, received an honorary degree from the university and gave the commencement address in 1932. (Courtesy Vermont Historical Society.)

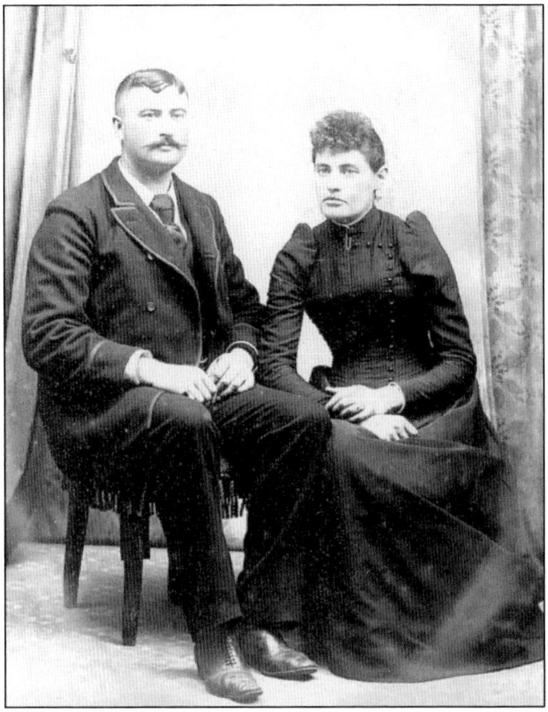

As a young man, Edgar W. Drury delivered ice in Burlington and met Daisy I. Town. This photograph was taken on their wedding day, June 24, 1891. They had one son and three daughters. Daisy died in 1900 at 32 years of age. Edgar's sister Beulah Drury, a dressmaker who never married, came to raise the four children. Edgar worked the Drury farm on River Road until 1927.

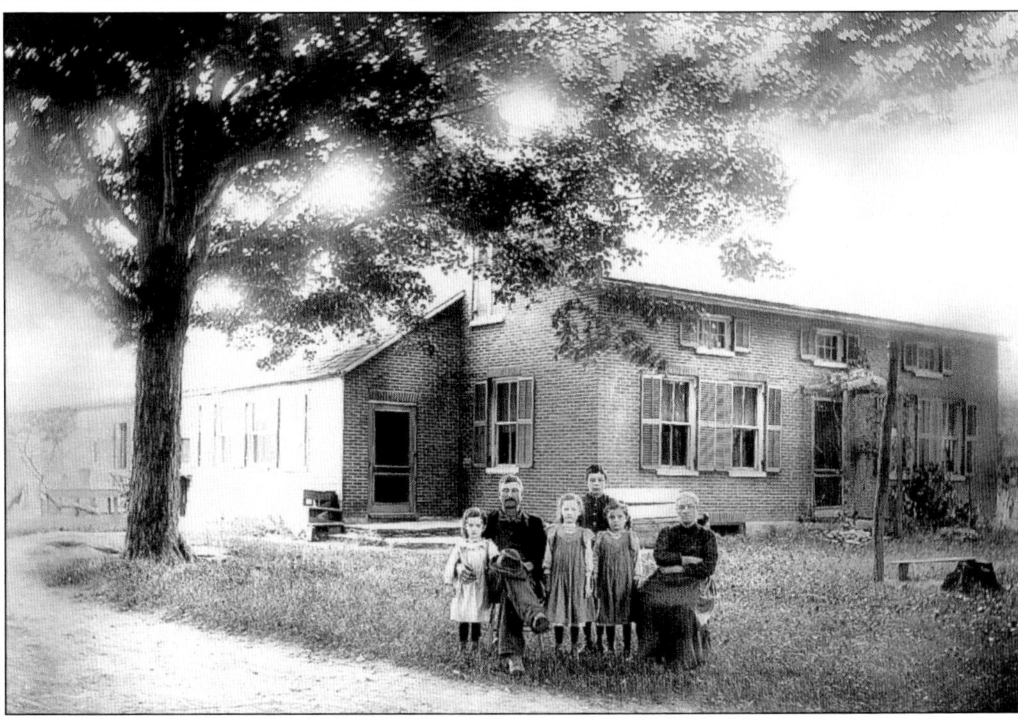

This photograph of the Drury farmhouse was taken by a traveling photographer who stopped by in 1903. Pictured here are, from left to right, Helen Drury; her father, Edgar; Anna; Leon; Gladys; and aunt Beulah. Before the impromptu image was taken, Helen had fetched her father, and they had all posed in front of the house, which still stands at 159 River Road.

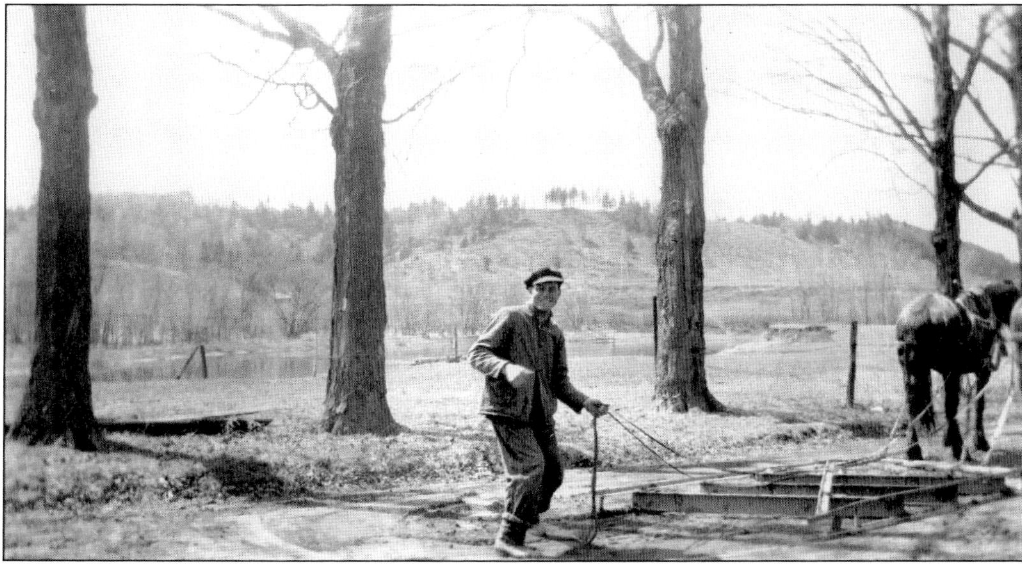

Leon Drury does road work on River Road with a team of horses. He always lived on the family farm. After the 1927 flood, he and his wife, Carrie (Pettingill) Drury, bought the property from his father, Edgar. Leon sold the farm in 1950. Carrie Drury had two daughters from a previous marriage, Ruby and Bertha Story. Leon did not have any children.

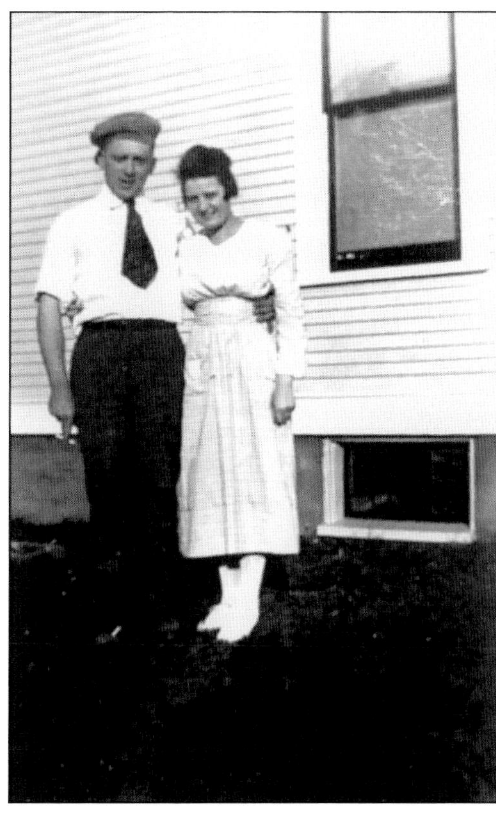

Warner and Gladys (Drury) Gregory are pictured here *c.* 1919. Gladys ran the pharmacy in the Yandow Block until her death in 1935. Warner remarried and was active in village government, serving as president from 1950 to 1951. He owned a dry goods store and the Northland Glove Company on Pearl Street, which started *c.* 1943. The business made ski mittens with innovative metal clips to connect them together, and gloves for utility workers.

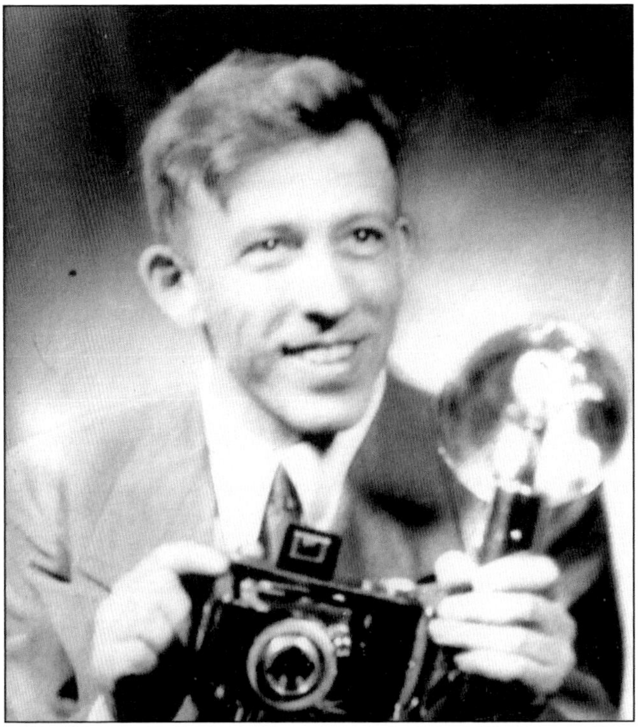

Evans Knapp, a longtime resident of Essex Center, became locally known for his photographs and paintings. He loved country music and the Champlain Valley Fair. He lived with his mother at 22 Jericho Road, at the intersection with Sand Hill Road. Many of his photographs of Essex Center in the 1950s have survived and give us a glimpse into the past.

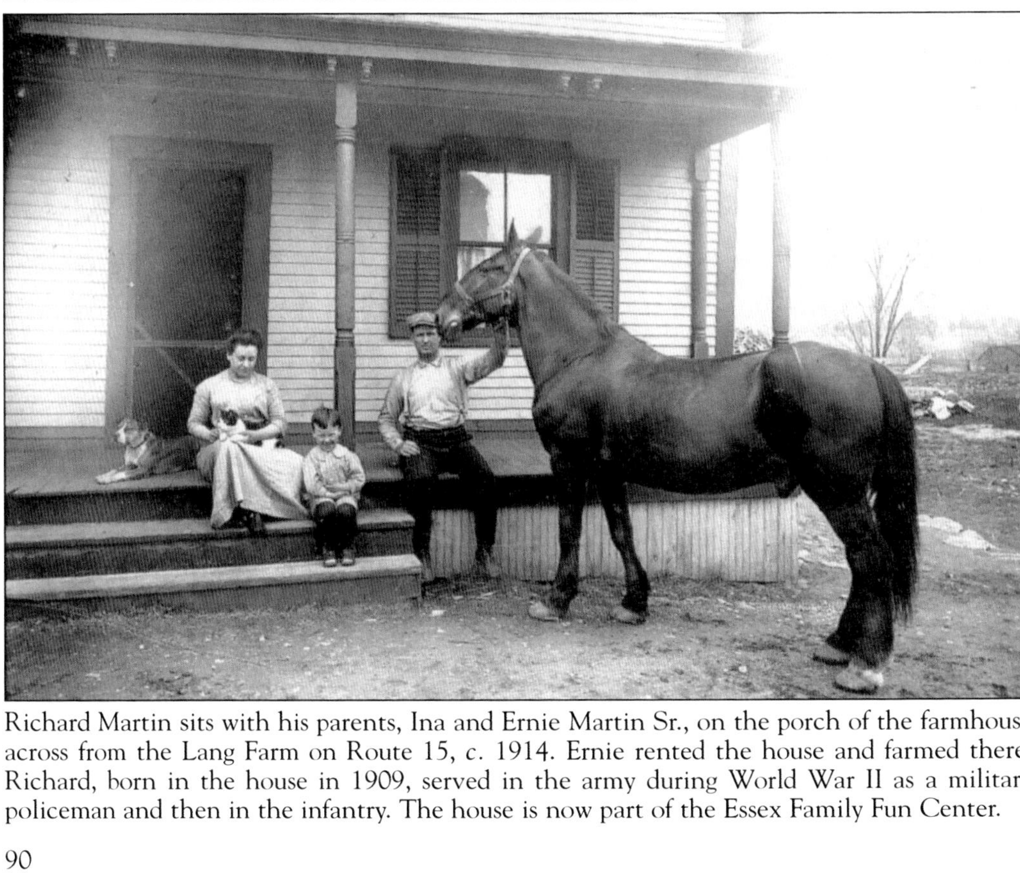

Richard Martin sits with his parents, Ina and Ernie Martin Sr., on the porch of the farmhouse across from the Lang Farm on Route 15, c. 1914. Ernie rented the house and farmed there. Richard, born in the house in 1909, served in the army during World War II as a military policeman and then in the infantry. The house is now part of the Essex Family Fun Center.

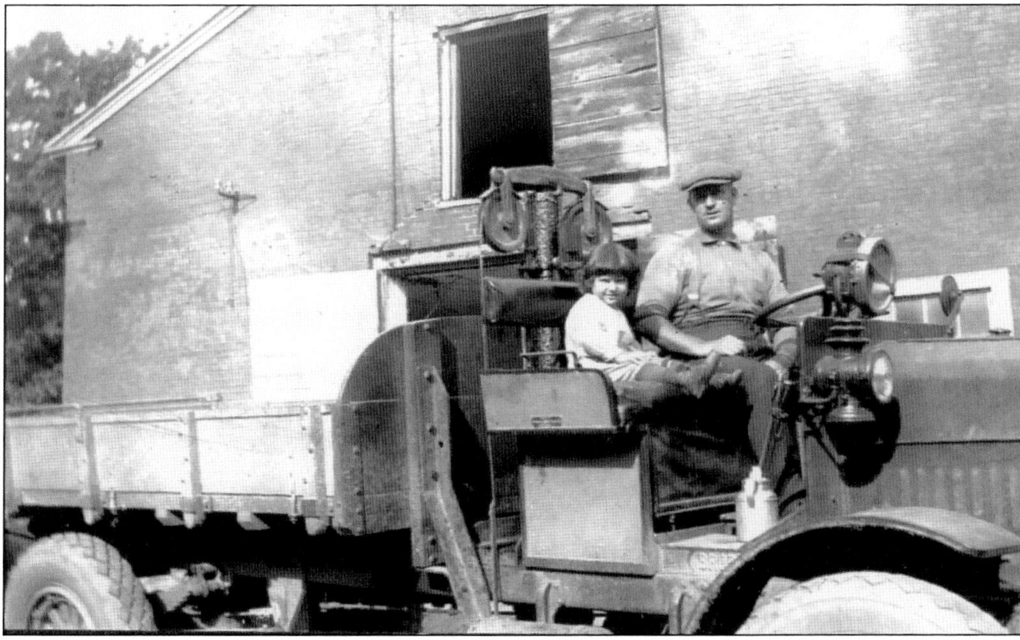

Ernie Martin Sr. and his son Richard pose with the first truck purchased for the Essex Junction Street Department. Ernie went to Cortland, New York, to pick up this Brockway dump truck. As superintendent of the street department for many years, one of his duties was to sand the trolley tracks after an ice storm so the trolleys could get back to Burlington.

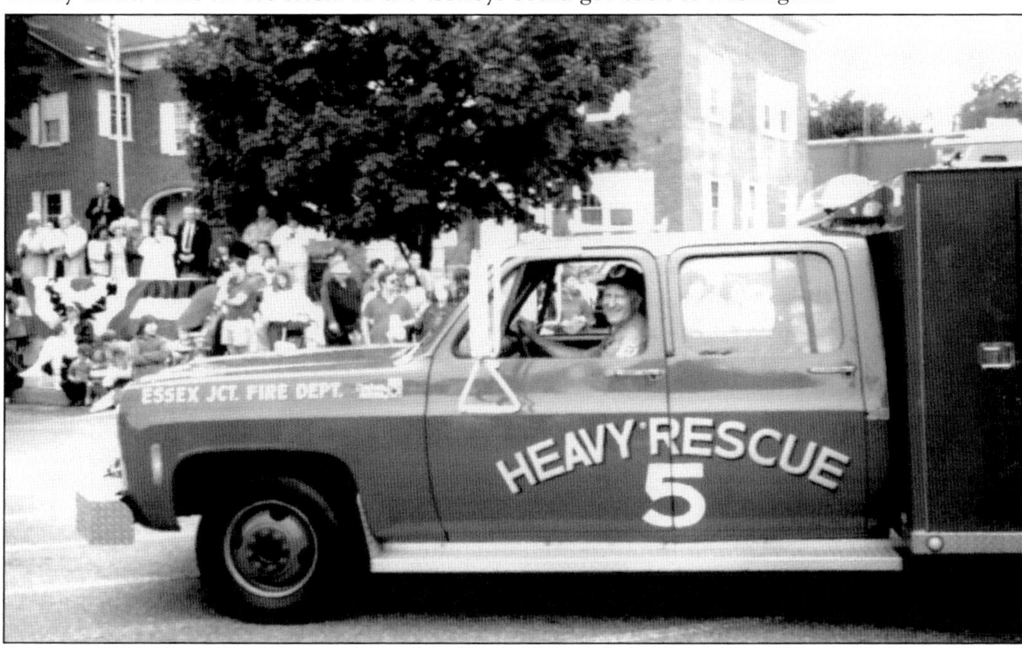

Ernie Martin Jr. drives the heavy rescue truck in the 1989 Memorial Day parade. Joining the fire department in January 1940, he has been a life member. While Martin was a high school student, Richard Nichols would pick him up at the high school and take him along to a fire. At that time, the department had one engine, a 1927 Childs pumper, kept in Lincoln Hall on the Pearl Street side.

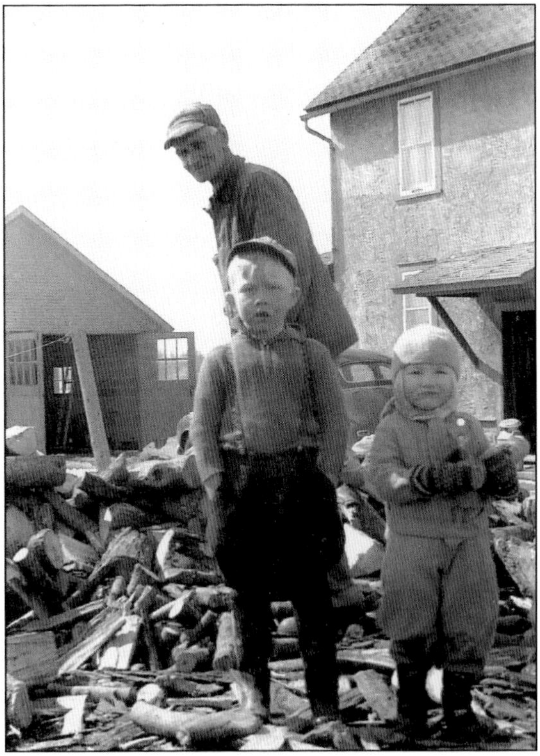

Carlton Houghton and his sister Christina help with grandfather Percival W. Holland's woodpile at his farm on Pearl Street in the early 1940s. The farmhouse was located about where Merchant's Bank is today. Carlton remembers helping to drive his grandfather's cows through the Five Corners to Cascade Street in the summer.

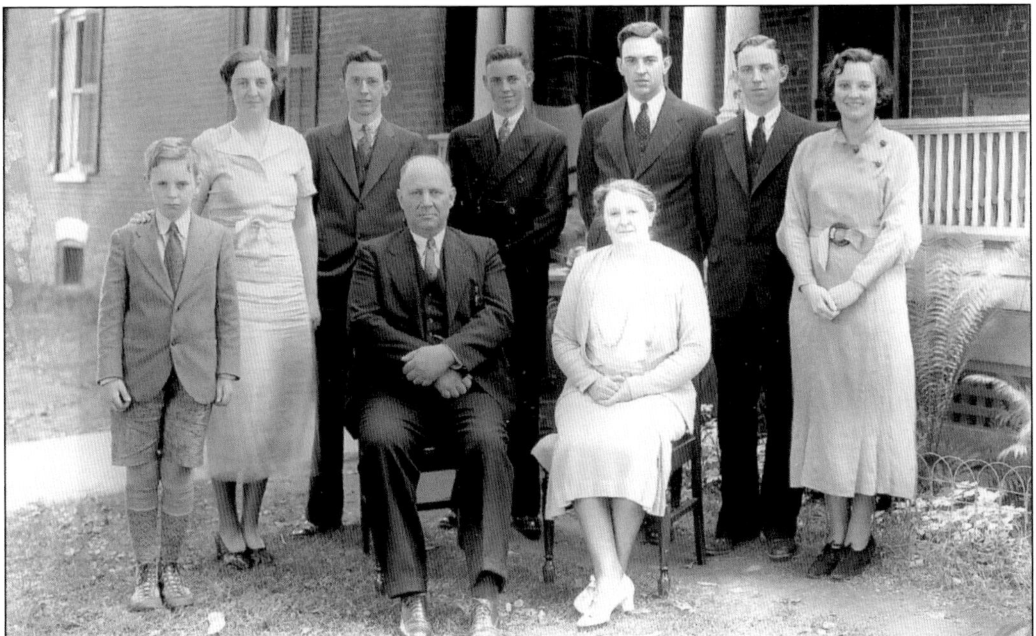

Arthur J. Crandall and wife, Nellie (MacKenzie) Crandall, both seated, moved from Bolton and bought this house at 23 Maple Street in 1917. Arthur was the postmaster in Essex Junction from September 24, 1943, to May 7, 1945. Standing, from left to right, are their children Paul, Dorothy, Jim, Walter, Albert, Robert, and Helen. This photograph was taken *c.* 1930.

Albert Crandall graduated first in his medical school class at the University of Vermont in 1933. In 1942, he enlisted in the 101st Airborne. Arriving by glider before D-Day forces, he set up the first Allied hospital in France on the front lines. He practiced general medicine from his office at 20 Maple Street from 1946 to 1963, performed surgery at the Fanny Allen Hospital, and taught clinical surgery at the university.

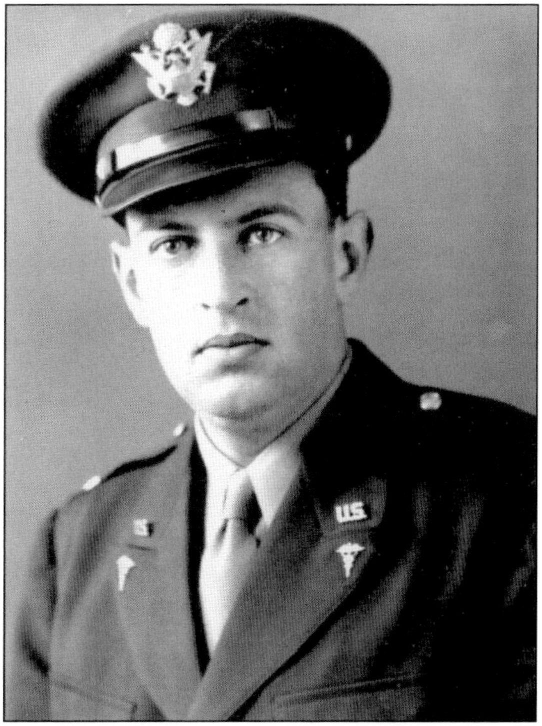

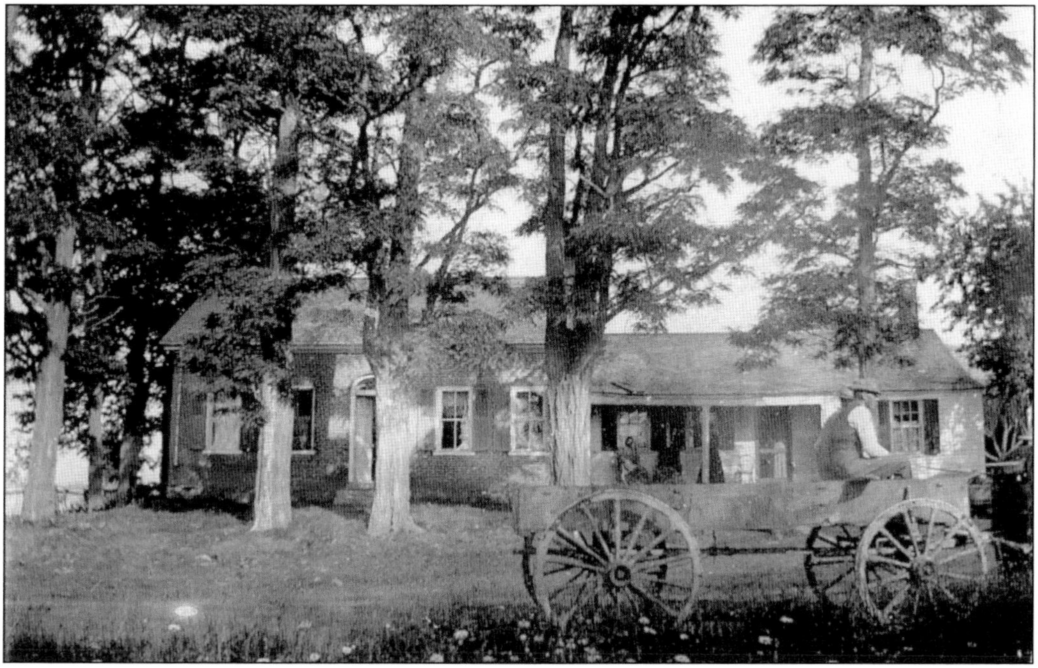

James S. Parker and his wagon appear in front of his brick house at the corner of Old Stage and Lost Nation Roads *c.* 1900. James attended the Essex Classical Institute and Maple Lawn Academy. He was then schooled at the Montpelier Seminary, where he was a prominent baseball player. He returned to Essex to farm with his father, Martin B. Parker. James's daughter Mary still lives in the house.

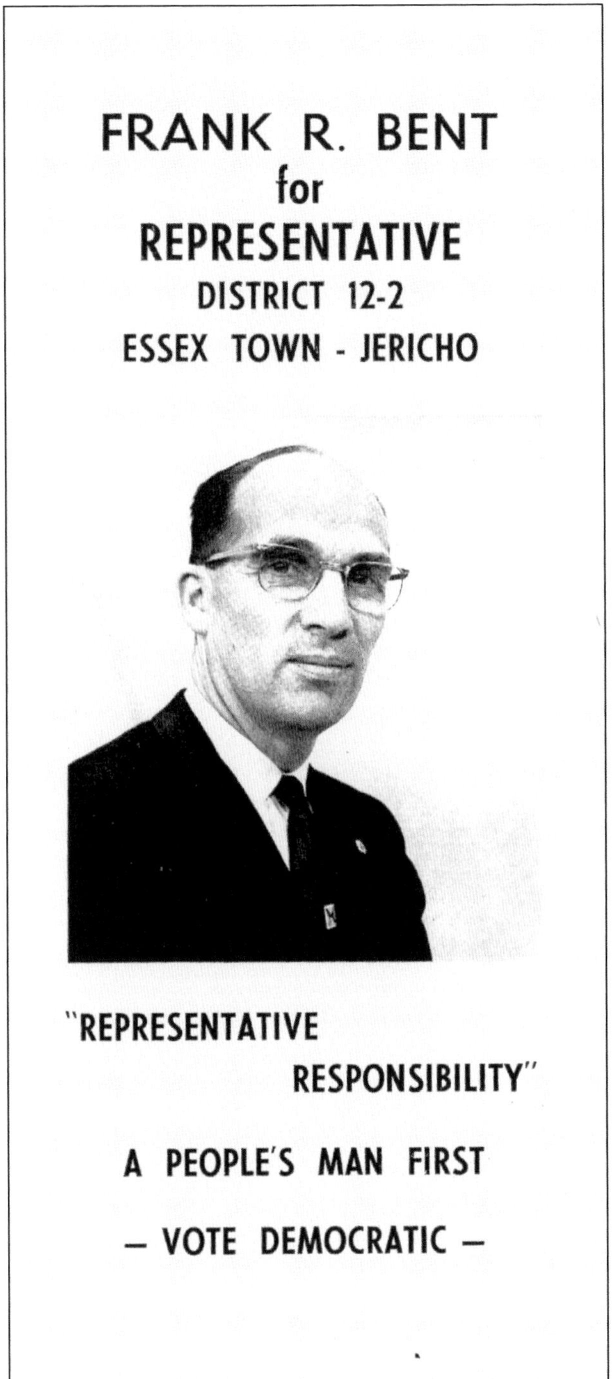

Frank Bent was very active in many aspects of Essex affairs but is perhaps best remembered for his role in researching and publishing a town history to coincide with the bicentennial celebration in 1963. He chaired the Essex Junction Lions Club Horse Show for years and was an officer in the Chittenden County Historical Society. His professional training was in accounting and public relations. This campaign brochure is from 1968.

Five

Schools and Churches

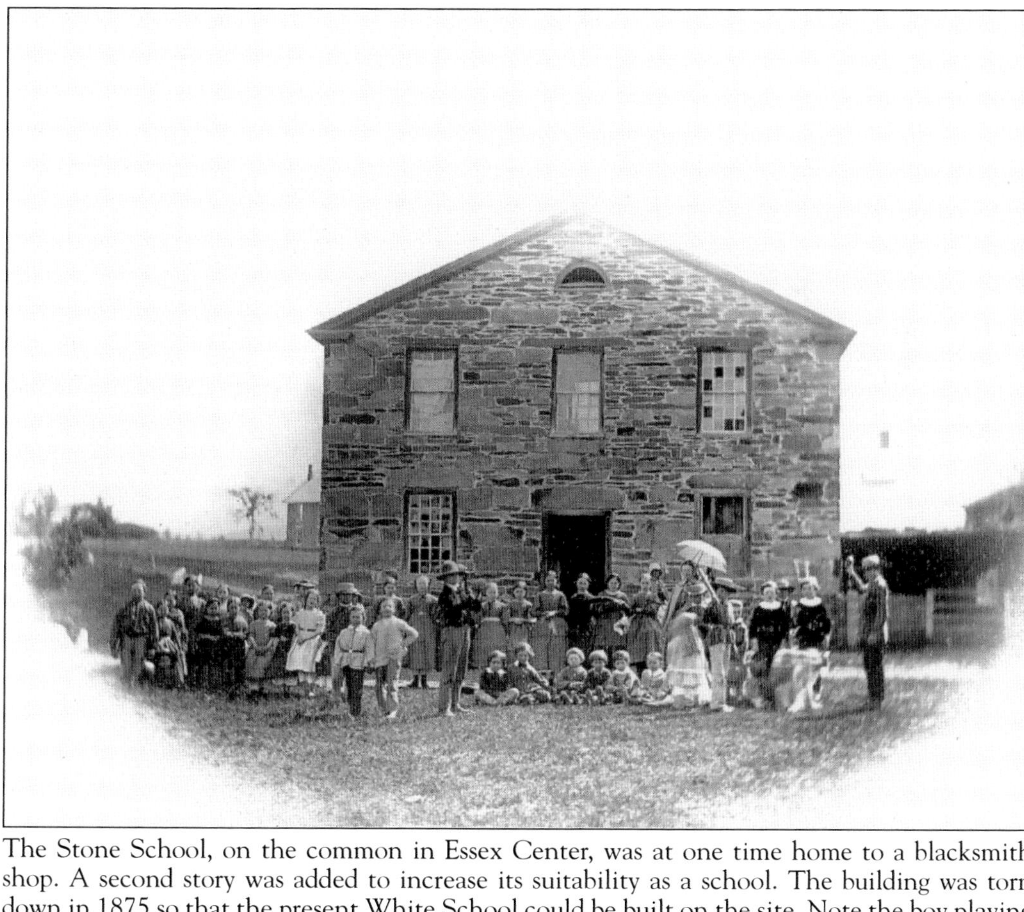

The Stone School, on the common in Essex Center, was at one time home to a blacksmith shop. A second story was added to increase its suitability as a school. The building was torn down in 1875 so that the present White School could be built on the site. Note the boy playing soldier in the first row. This photograph was taken c. 1868.

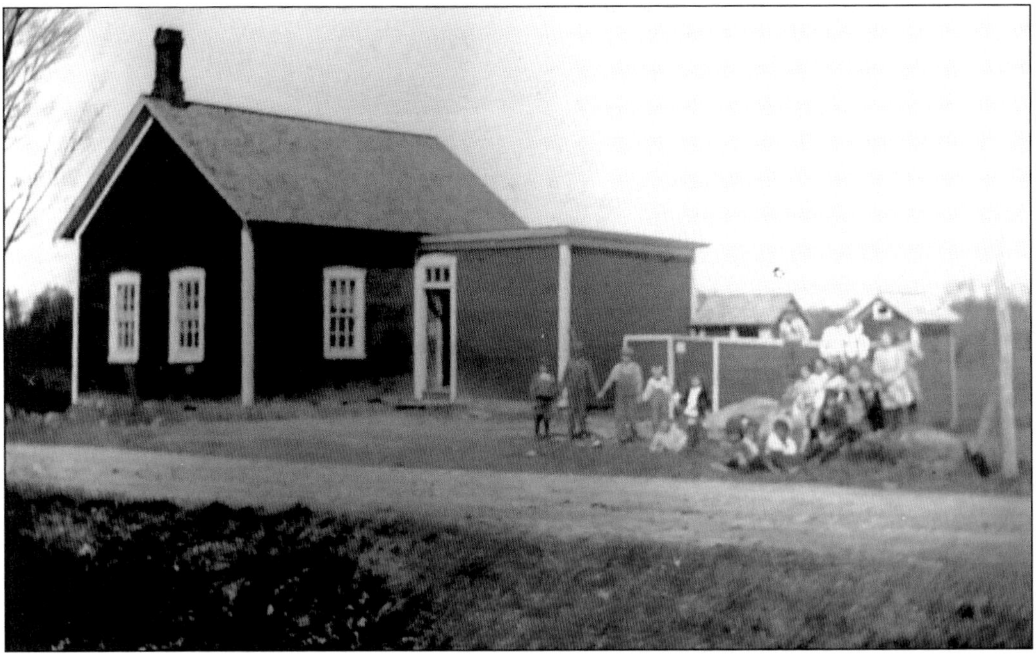

Record exists of a school located on the northeast corner of Page's Corners as early as 1838. At that time, this was the center of the town. Several businesses and the town's first post office were located here. This building was used as a school until 1923, then sold and likely moved to 213 Pearl Street in Essex Junction.

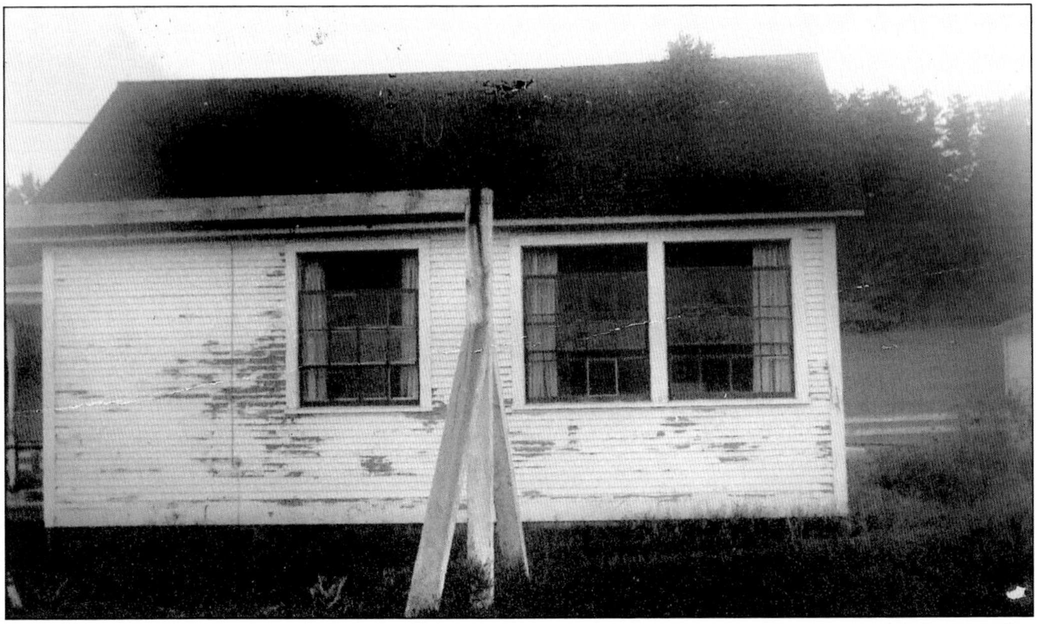

The Griffin School was the last one-room school in operation in Essex. It was established in the 1840s and was closed in 1958. Philip Kolvoord bought it for $2,500, including swings, teeter-totter, a kerosene stove, and a well, and used it as his residence for two years. It still stands at the intersection of Route 2A and Gardenside Lane. With its large windows, it retains the look of a schoolhouse.

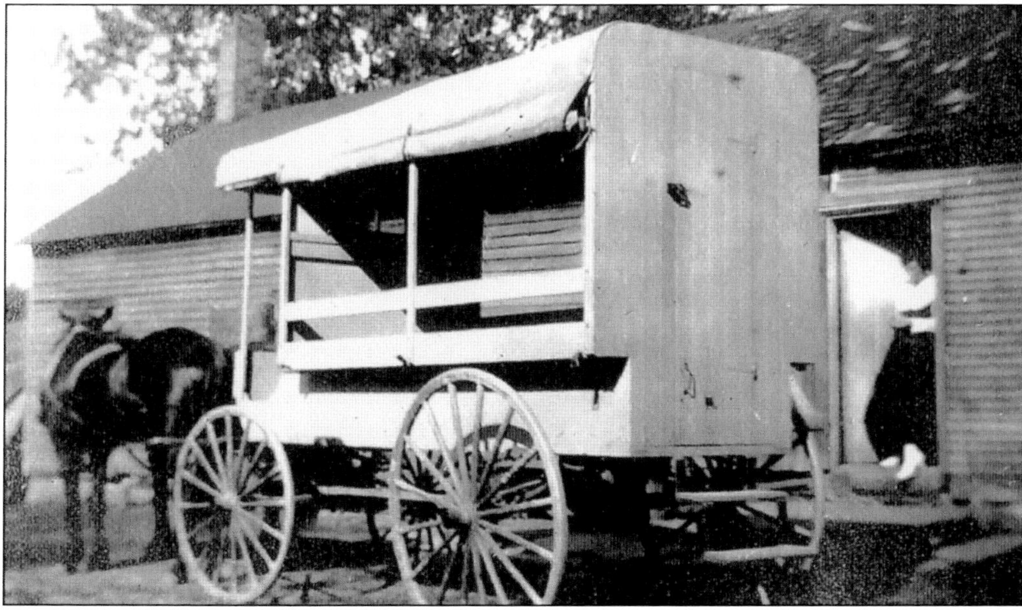

This is David Robinson's school barge at the Drury farm on River Road. The barge had seats on both sides, and in warm weather, curtains could be rolled up to let the air in. There were steps at the back of the wagon. The driver had a rope so that he could open and shut the door. Anna Dury stands in the doorway of the house.

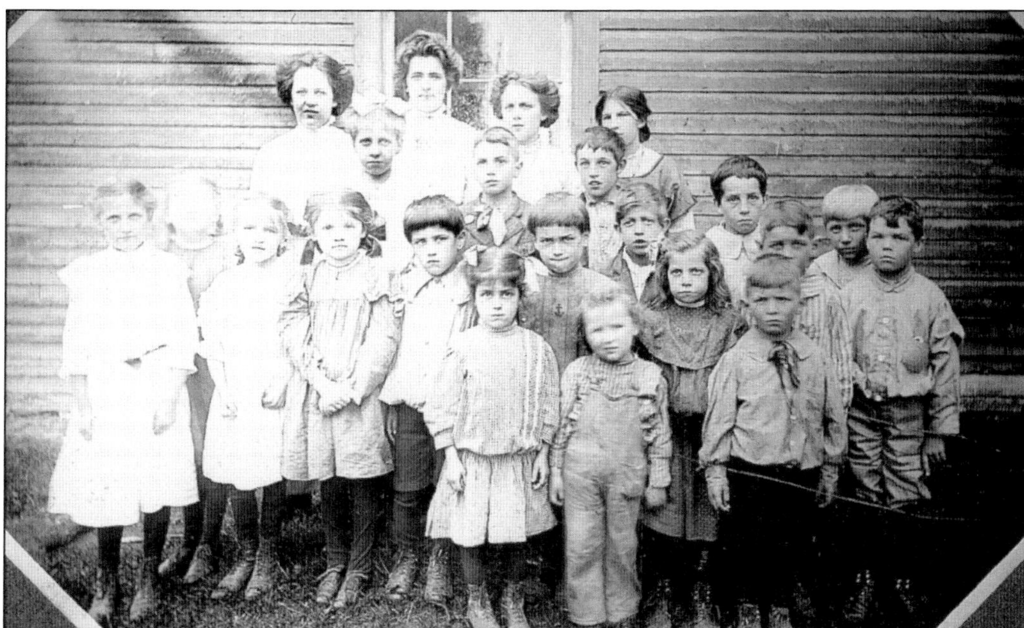

The Butler's Corners School was located on the west side of Old Stage Road, near the intersection of Lost Nation Road. Alice Smith, the teacher of this group, is the tallest person in the back row. She came to Essex from Underhill to teach, boarding with the Martin Parker family near the school. She married Martin's son James S. Parker. This photograph was taken in 1908.

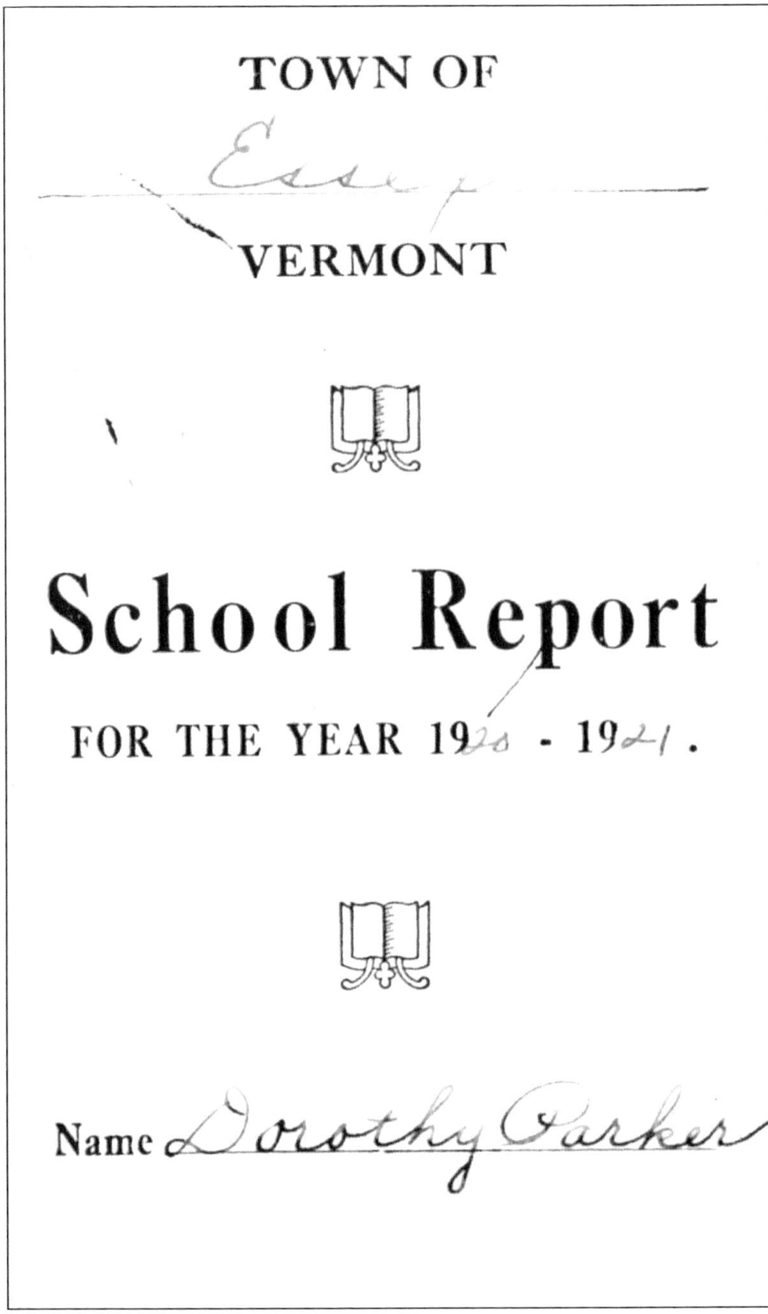

TOWN OF

Essex

VERMONT

School Report

FOR THE YEAR 1920 - 1921.

Name Dorothy Parker

Shown here is Dorothy Parker's 1920–1921 first-grade report for Butler's Corners School from her teacher, Sadie M. Barter. Graded monthly, she received all As in reading, writing, and arithmetic, as well as industry, behavior, and care of school property. The report also contained four pages of the school laws of Vermont, outlining the ages of mandatory schooling—8 to 16—and the role of a truant officer. The child labor laws forbid a child under 16 to be "employed in work connected to railroading, mining, manufacturing, or quarrying, or be employed in a hotel or bowling alley, or in delivering messages, except during vacation and before and after school." Corporal punishment was also addressed and condoned.

The Chittenden County Institute, chartered in 1853, opened on August 29, 1855, with 125 pupils. An 1856 catalog is filled with penciled notes on classmates, such as "tolerable," "pretty good looking," and "sprightly and intelligent." Course offerings included French, music, and art. The 1858–1859 catalog describes its location in "Essex Centre, . . . a pleasant, quiet, healthy village, easy of access by Railroad, to Essex Junction, and thence by Daily Stages."

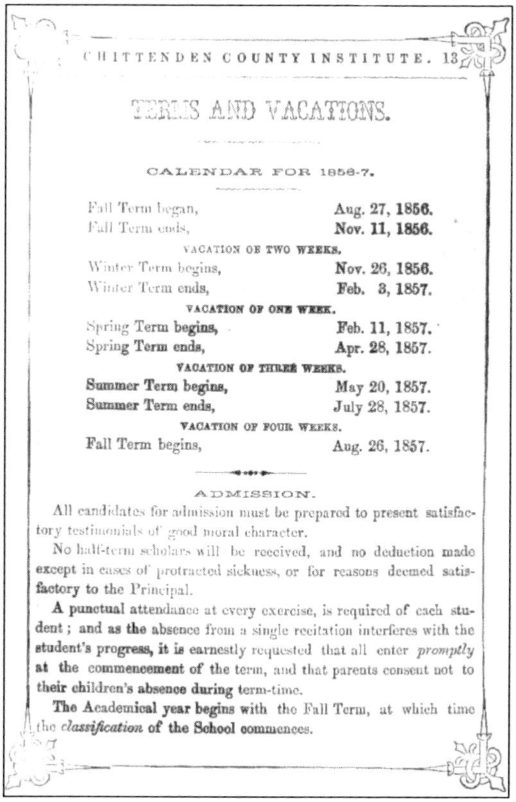

CHITTENDEN COUNTY INSTITUTE. 13

TERMS AND VACATIONS.

CALENDAR FOR 1856-7.

Fall Term began,	Aug. 27, 1856.
Fall Term ends,	Nov. 11, 1856.
VACATION OF TWO WEEKS.	
Winter Term begins,	Nov. 26, 1856.
Winter Term ends,	Feb. 3, 1857.
VACATION OF ONE WEEK.	
Spring Term begins,	Feb. 11, 1857.
Spring Term ends,	Apr. 28, 1857.
VACATION OF THREE WEEKS.	
Summer Term begins,	May 20, 1857.
Summer Term ends,	July 28, 1857.
VACATION OF FOUR WEEKS.	
Fall Term begins,	Aug. 26, 1857.

ADMISSION.

All candidates for admission must be prepared to present satisfactory testimonials of good moral character.

No half-term scholars will be received, and no deduction made except in cases of protracted sickness, or for reasons deemed satisfactory to the Principal.

A punctual attendance at every exercise, is required of each student; and as the absence from a single recitation interferes with the student's progress, it is earnestly requested that all enter *promptly* at the commencement of the term, and that parents consent not to their children's absence during term-time.

The Academical year begins with the Fall Term, at which time the *classification* of the School commences.

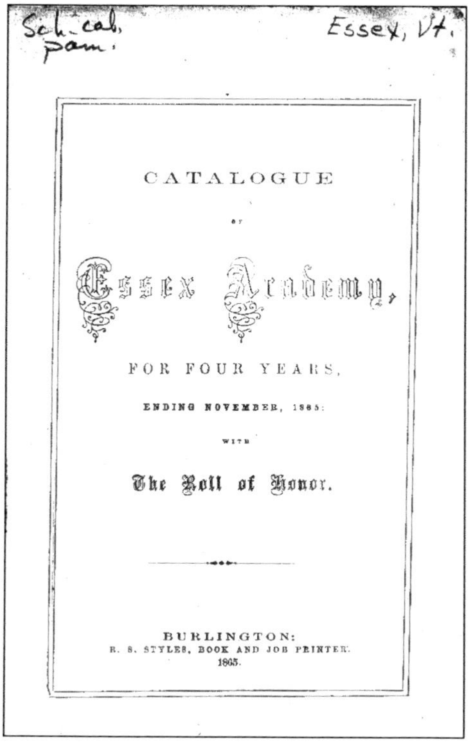

Sch. cat. pam. Essex, Vt.

CATALOGUE

OF

Essex Academy,

FOR FOUR YEARS,

ENDING NOVEMBER, 1865:

WITH

The Roll of Honor.

BURLINGTON:
R. S. STYLES, BOOK AND JOB PRINTER.
1865.

In 1862, the Chittenden County Institute came under the charge of Asa Sanderson and was renamed the Essex Academy. Behavior of the students was governed by the simple rule "do right." Students were "not expected to be absent from their rooms in the evening, or to attend parties or places of amusement, without permission." An 1865 catalog contains an honor roll of 21 former students who fought in the Civil War.

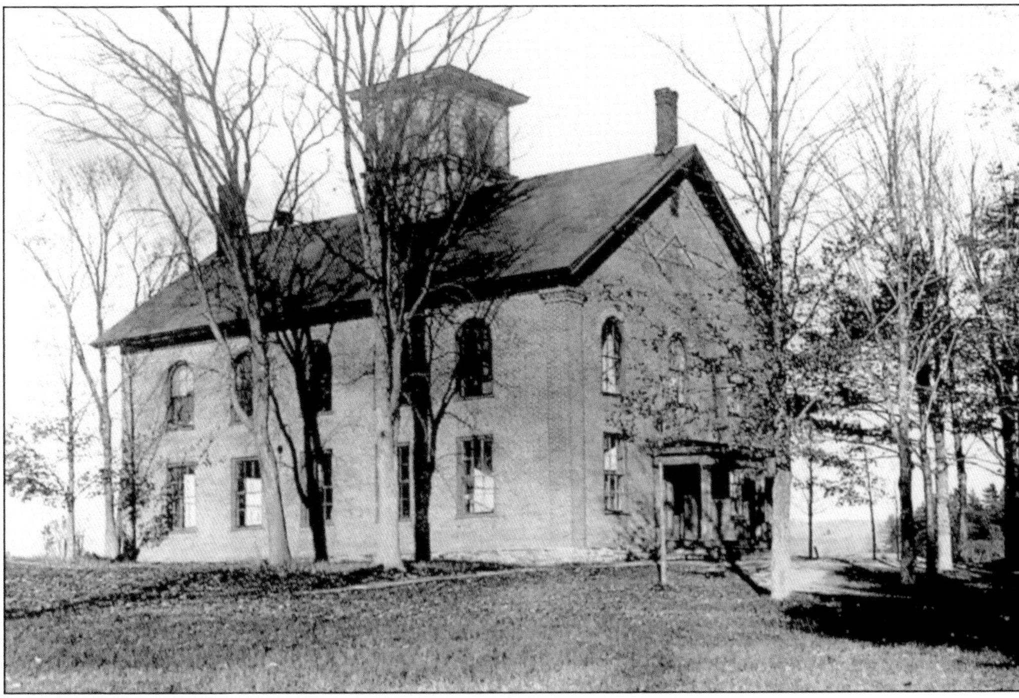

The Essex Classical Institute was located on the corner of Browns River and Bixby Hill Roads. The original school building was destroyed by fire in 1868. A community effort led to the rebuilding and to a name change to the Essex Classical Institute in 1874. Later, the building was incorporated into the town school system. It was torn down in 1972; however, the board of trustees still functions today as a scholarship committee.

—AT THE—

Essex Classical Institute,

CLASS DAY EXERCISES OF '96.

AT INSTITUTE HALL,

Thursday Evening, June 4th, 1896.

The 12 members of the Essex Classical Institute class of 1896 invited the public to a series of events to mark their commencement: baccalaureate, in the Congregational church; class exercises (music, class history, recitation, and class prophecy); graduation exercises; and a concert. Every member of the class read an essay or performed an oration at the graduation. The class motto was "Here we Launch, Where shall we Anchor?"

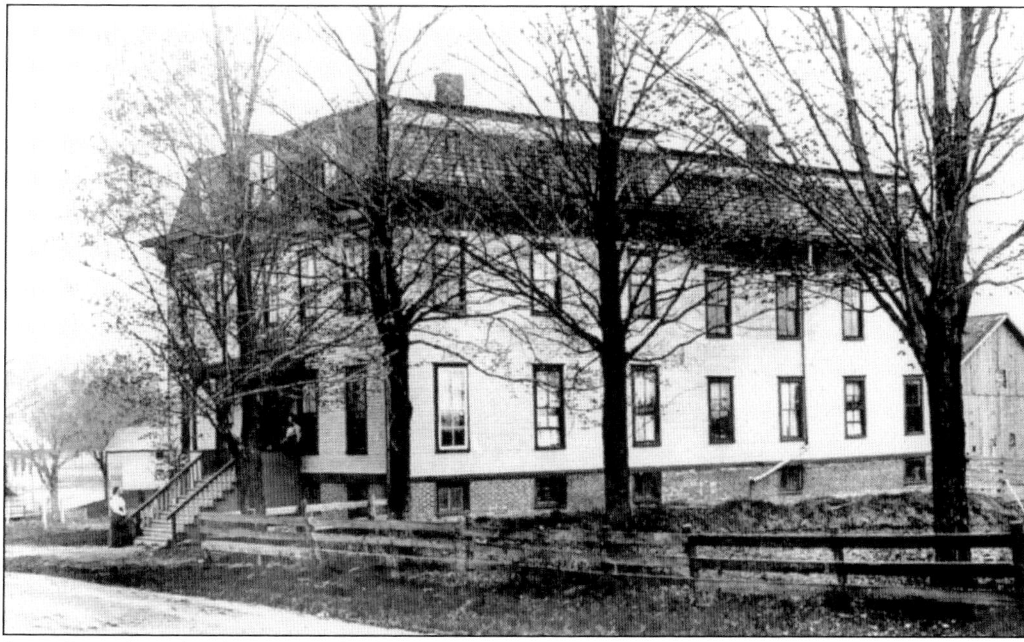

In 1874, a boardinghouse was built for teachers and students of the Essex Classical Institute. Early financial difficulties meant it was not fully utilized by the school. After 1884, Mary Fletcher donated $2,000 to help the trustees buy the house. The building still stands on Bixby Hill Road.

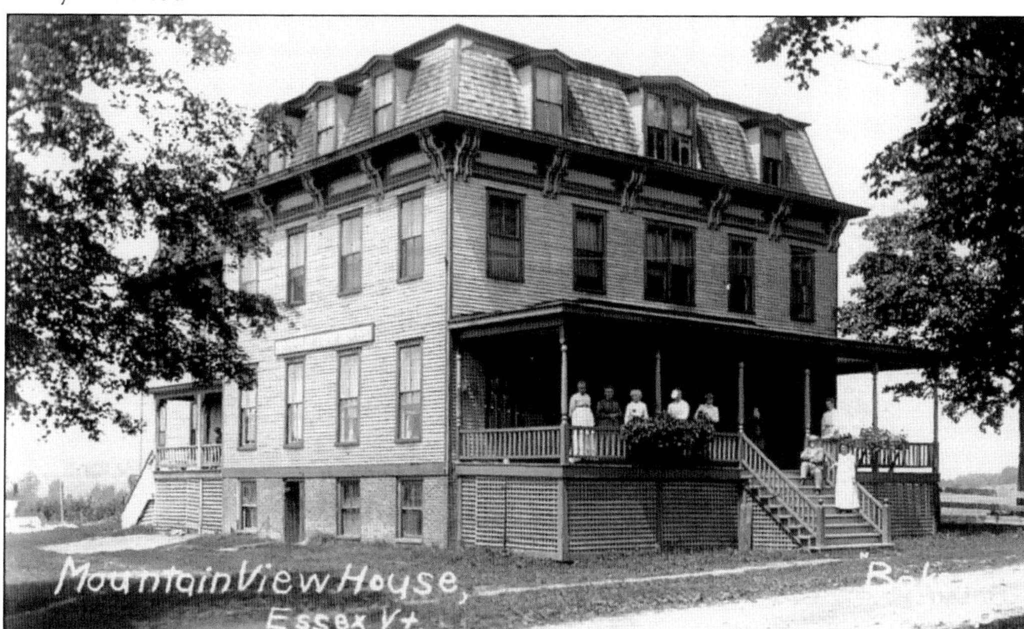

The Essex Classical Institute boardinghouse was later operated as the Mountain View House, "600 feet above sea level." Its location close to Fort Ethan Allen and Burlington, with bus service several times daily, and high, cool, airy rooms with electric lights, telephone, and radio and spacious verandas "make this an idea [*sic*] place to spend the summer months." In the 1950s, it became the Maple Leaf Nursing Home and was converted into apartments in 1966.

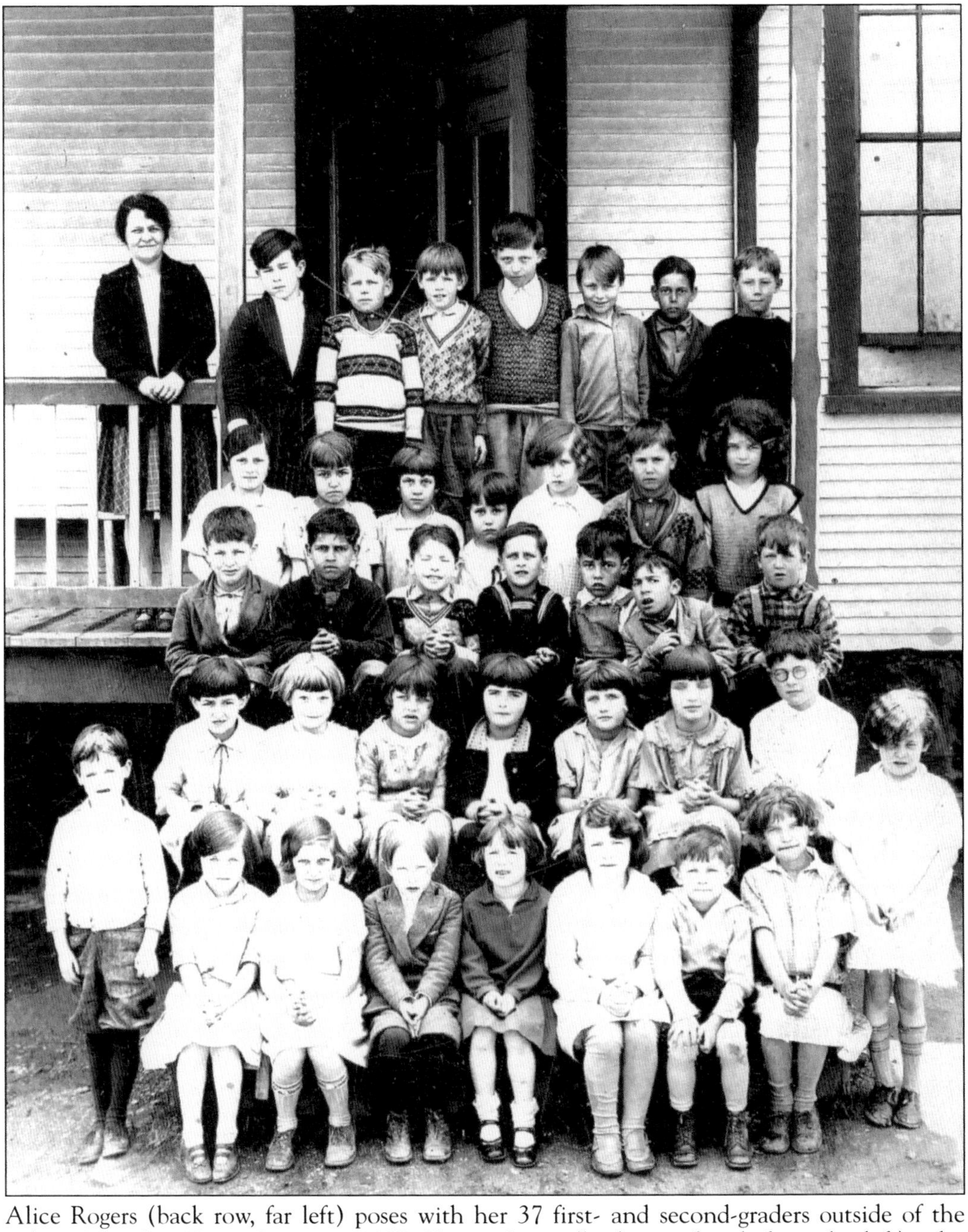

Alice Rogers (back row, far left) poses with her 37 first- and second-graders outside of the White School in Essex Center c. 1927. Horace Jones (back row, fourth from the left), who lived on Brigham Hill, remembers traveling to school by a horse-drawn barge. He likened it to a stagecoach. In the spring, a fence might have to be cut so the barge could go out into a meadow to avoid the mudholes. Mr. Flynn would also take students in an old touring car. When he let loose with a mouthful of tobacco juice, it would sometimes land on the students in the back seat. In the winter, travel was by a horse-drawn double sled with straw on the rack. Horace brought his meal in a metal lunchbox, usually a peanut butter sandwich, because his father bought it in large buckets. Other, less fortunate students had lard sandwiches.

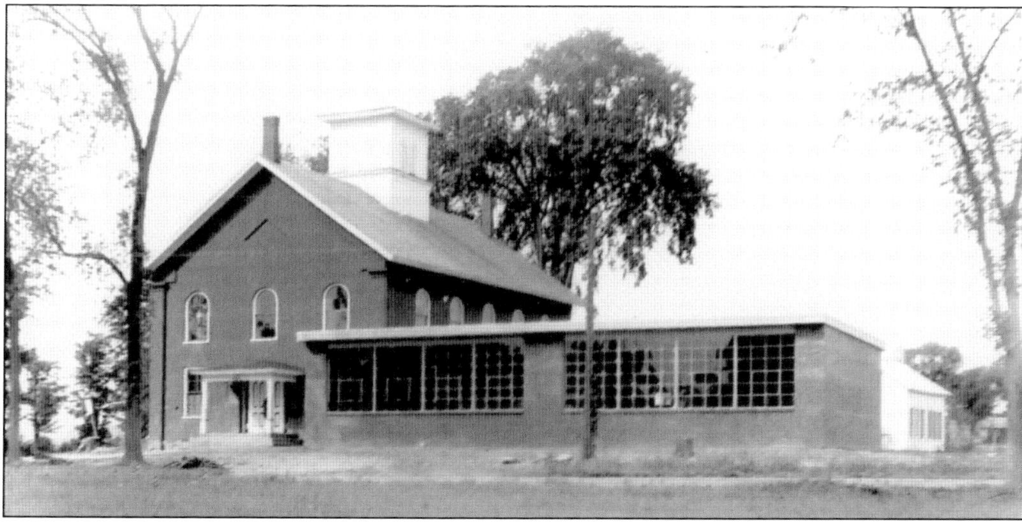

The Essex Classical Institute building required several additions to keep up with the increase in population in the 1950s and 1960s. This addition was approved on June 29, 1951. A 1957 addition created six more classrooms. Before the 1965–1966 addition of 11 classrooms and a library, classes were held in the basement of St. Pius X Church, the White School, and the overcrowded institute building. (Photograph by Evans Knapp.)

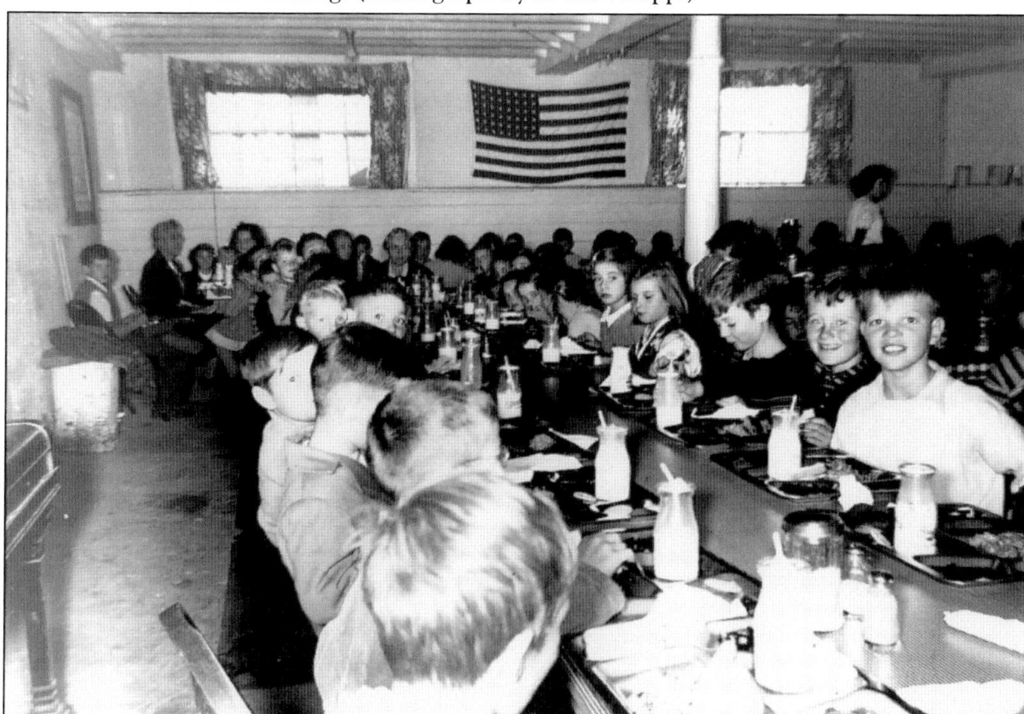

The Essex Center PTA started the hot lunch program for schoolchildren in 1949 in the basement of the Congregational church. About 180 students were served a hot meal for 15¢. At that time, the building housed a community center. It was used during World War II for Red Cross activities and as an air-raid shelter. It was also a meeting place for other community groups. (Photograph by Evans Knapp.)

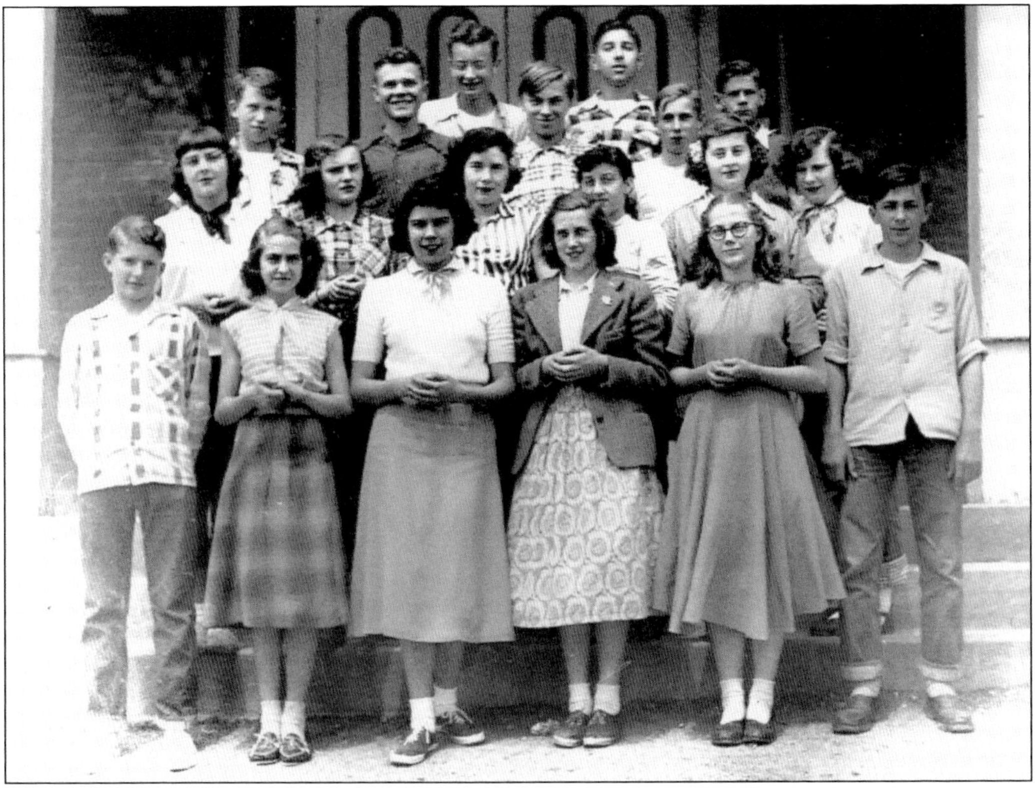

The 1953 Essex Center School eighth-grade graduating class includes, from left to right, the following: (first row) Richard Kenney, Pauline Sole, Pearl Naylor, Katrina McLaughlin, Barbara Bowman, and Laurence Miller; (second row) Evelyn Jerome, Georgia Buzzell, Marjorie Desso, Martha Provost, Rocklyn LaVigne, and Nancy Pariseau; (third row) Stanley Mayo, Philip Bixby, Ray Bowman, and Leon Lestage; (fourth row) William Desjardins, Raymond Charbonneau, and Walter Kellogg. (Photograph by Evans Knapp.)

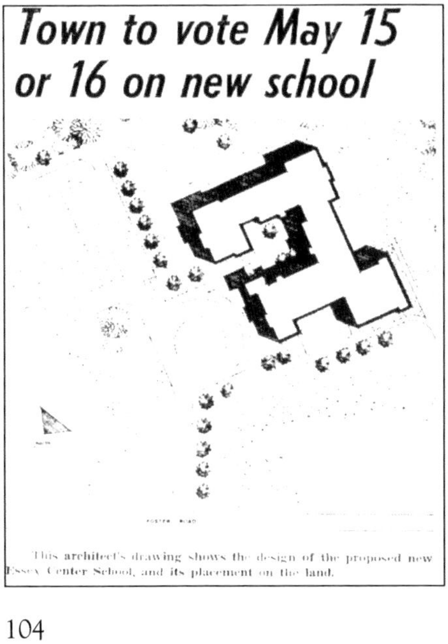

Town to vote May 15 or 16 on new school

This architect's drawing shows the design of the proposed new Essex Center School, and its placement on the land.

The town purchased property on Foster Road from Place's Livestock Exchange for a new middle school. The exchange used 575 hogs to dispose of garbage from Burlington. After cholera struck and the hogs had to be destroyed, the garbage piled up. The ensuing legal tangle threatened the construction of the school. The town and the exchange soon settled their differences in court, and voters approved the bond issue in May 1968.

Maple Lawn Academy operated for only a short time—*c.* 1897 to 1900. Under the same name, Fannie A. Stevens moved her school to South Hero in 1900 and ran it successfully until 1911. As to the naming of the school, Stevens replied, "Because there are a lot of maples in Essex Center." The building is now a residence on Sand Hill Road.

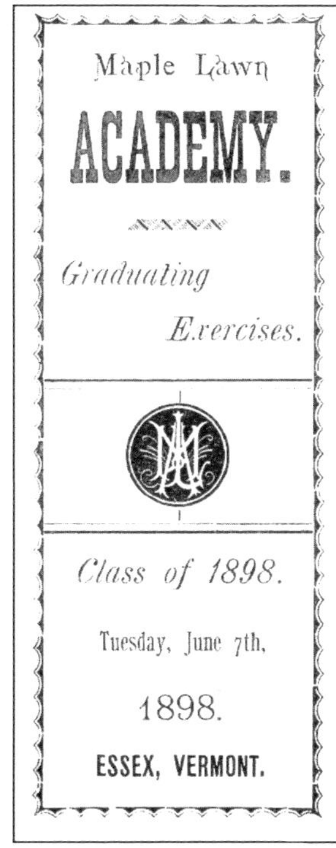

Maple Lawn

ACADEMY.

Graduating

Exercises.

Class of 1898.

Tuesday, June 7th,

1898.

ESSEX, VERMONT.

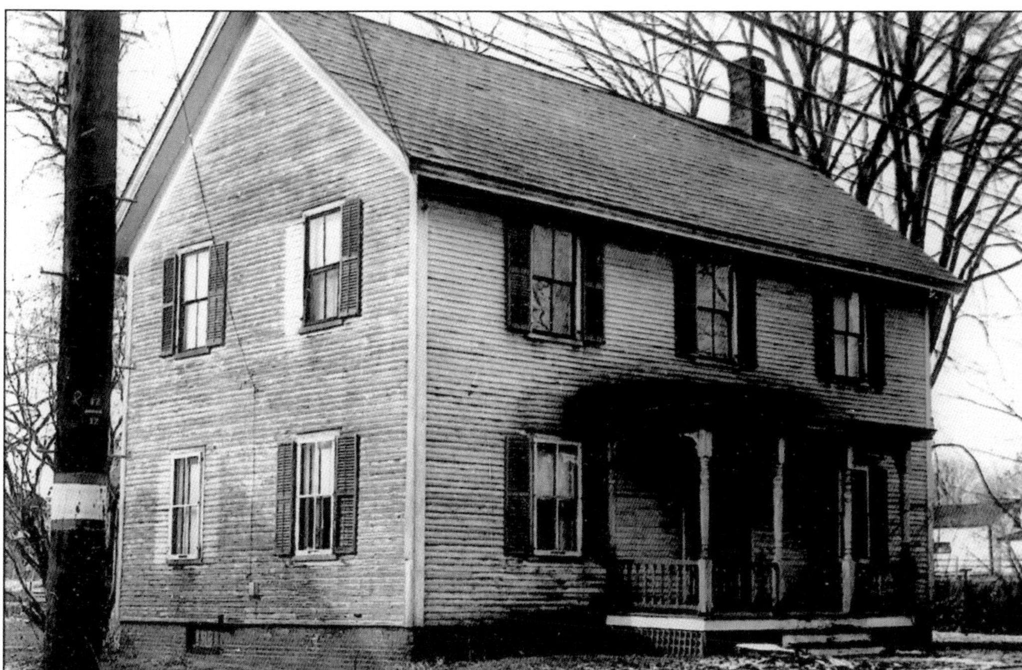

The Anna Early house, on Park Street, was built *c.* 1840 and served as a school from *c.* 1860 to 1873. At this time, its enrollment far outreached its capacity, and the Park Street School was built to handle the needs of all the schoolchildren in Essex Junction. Most recently, this building has served as the home of the Discovery Museum and now as the Northern Vermont Tradeswomen.

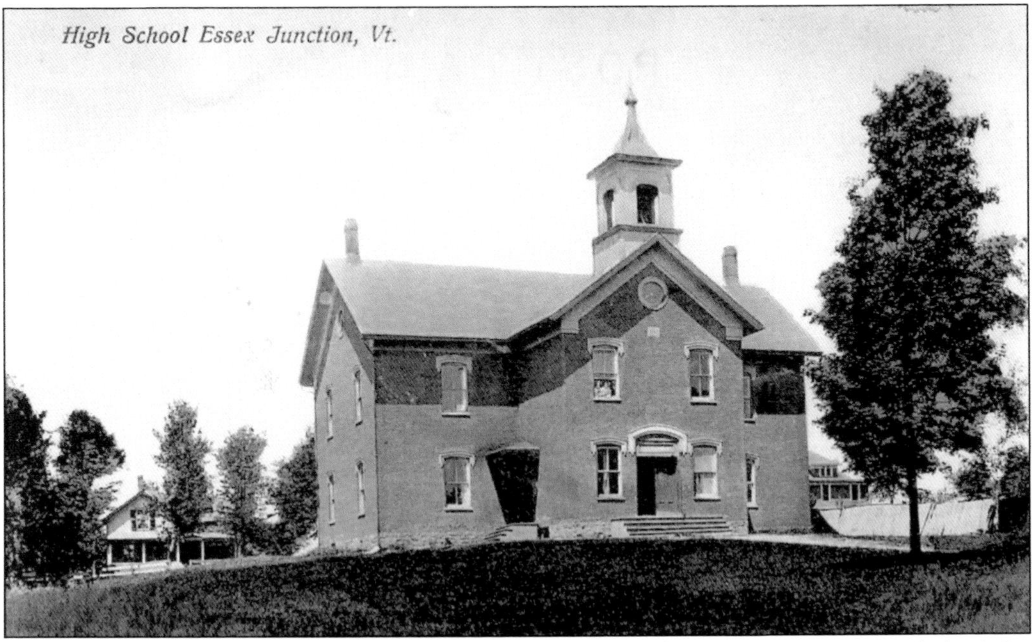

The Park Street School, in Essex Junction, was built for $8,000 in 1873, a symbol of the prosperity the railroads brought in the last half of the 19th century. Remaining with the school district, it continues to serve educational purposes with an alternative high school program and a preschool. There has been much debate recently about the fate of the building, which needs major renovations.

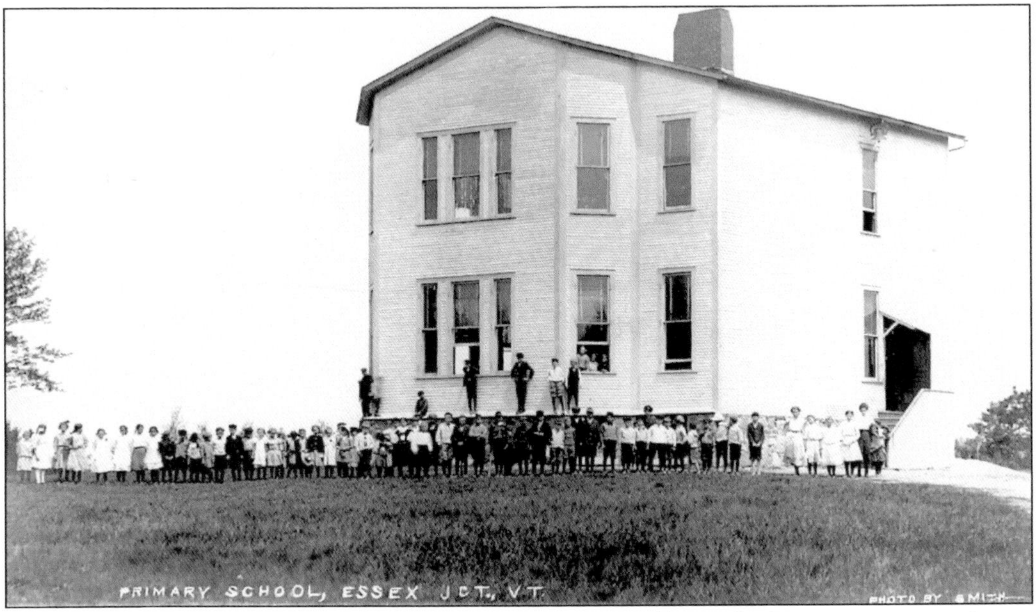

This school's façade has disappeared, but the structure still stands. It was constructed as a one-story building on land deeded by Daniel Macomber on a hill above the village. The Park Street School was overcrowded; this primary school was the answer. A second story was added c. 1903. In 1912, it was doubled in size and was bricked over to become the Prospect Street School, later named the Fleming School.

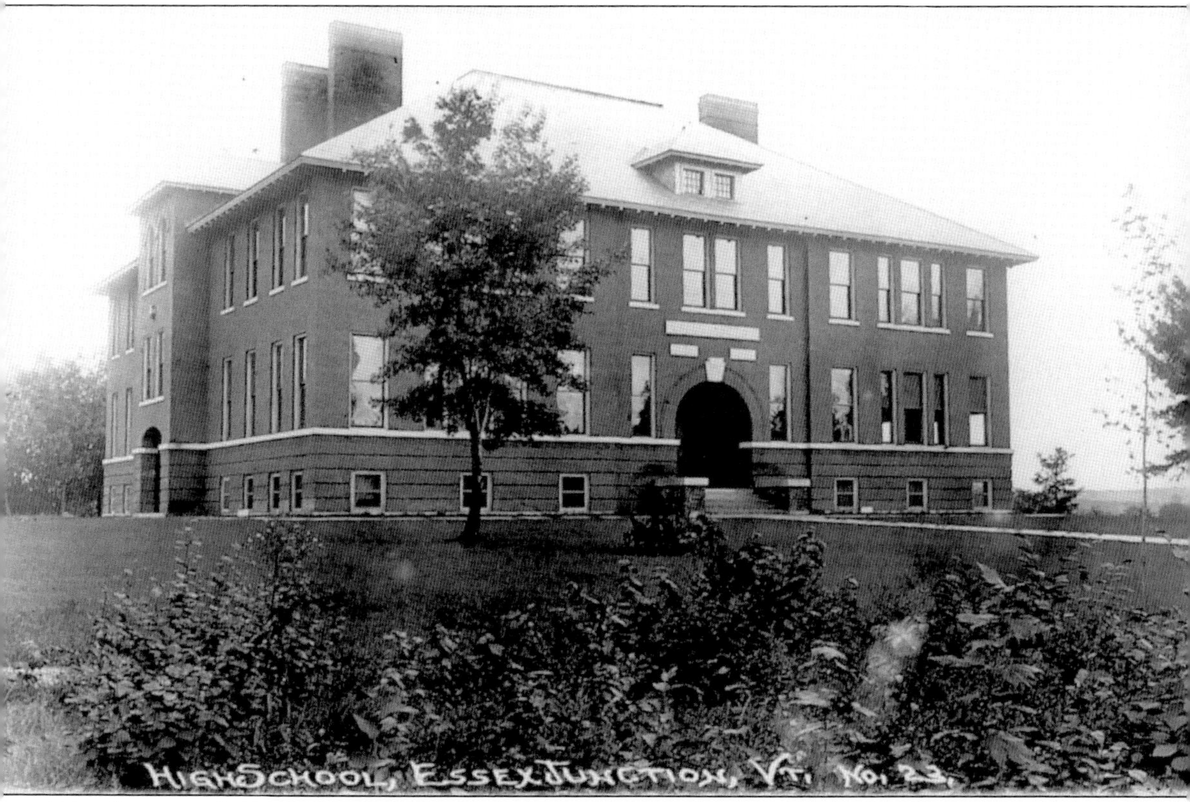

The Prospect Street School, built for $40,000 in 1912, served high school students until 1957. Commencement exercises from June 7 to 12, 1931, included a baccalaureate sermon by Rev. R. H. Mercer in the assembly hall, the commencement ball in the Colonial Theatre, Class Day at High School Park, the alumni banquet at the Lincoln Inn, graduation exercises in the assembly hall, and a class trip to Camp Sunrise in Benson. Noah Thompson recalls, "In 1932 the high school students occupied the top floor and grades three through eight had the lower floor. . . . There was no gym. . . . Music, art and special activities were at a minimum. Boys and girls basketball and boys baseball were the only organized sports." An auditorium-gymnasium was dedicated on April 15, 1951. The school was named the Fleming School in 1973 after Thomas Fleming, custodian there from 1944 to 1967. Today, it serves fourth- and fifth-graders.

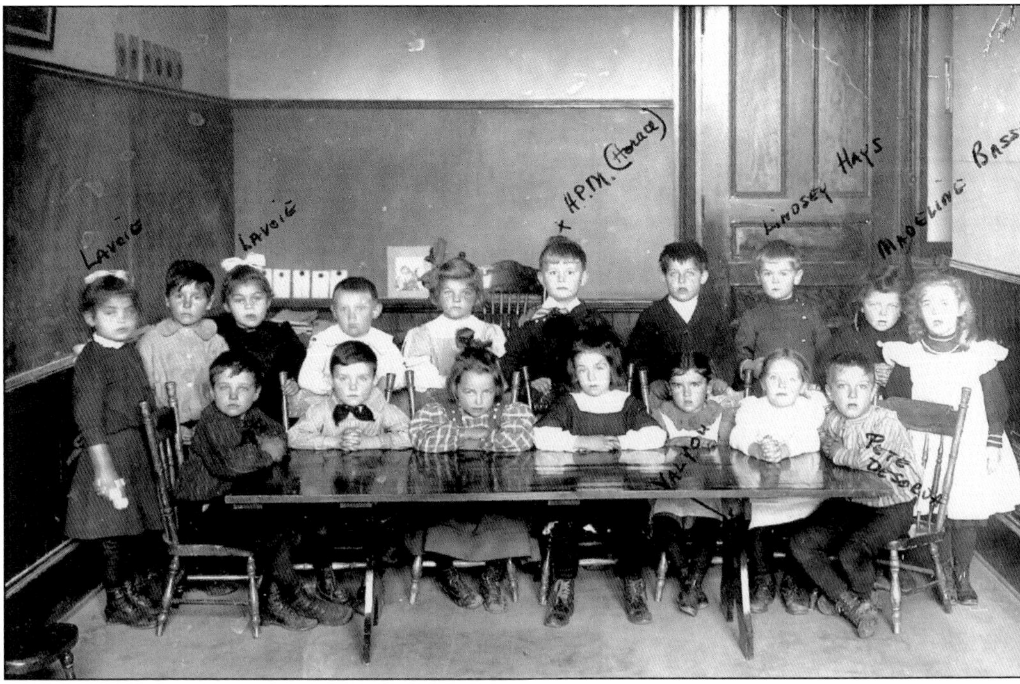

This class photograph was taken *c.* 1907. Horace P. Marvin appears in the back row, sixth from the left. Horace was the oldest of three sons of Dr. David and Marion Marvin. Dr. David Marvin, a prominent Essex Junction civic leader, was head of the Department of Pharmacology and Therapeutics at the University of Vermont. Horace received a medical degree from that university, served in the military, and later became CEO of a Denver hospital.

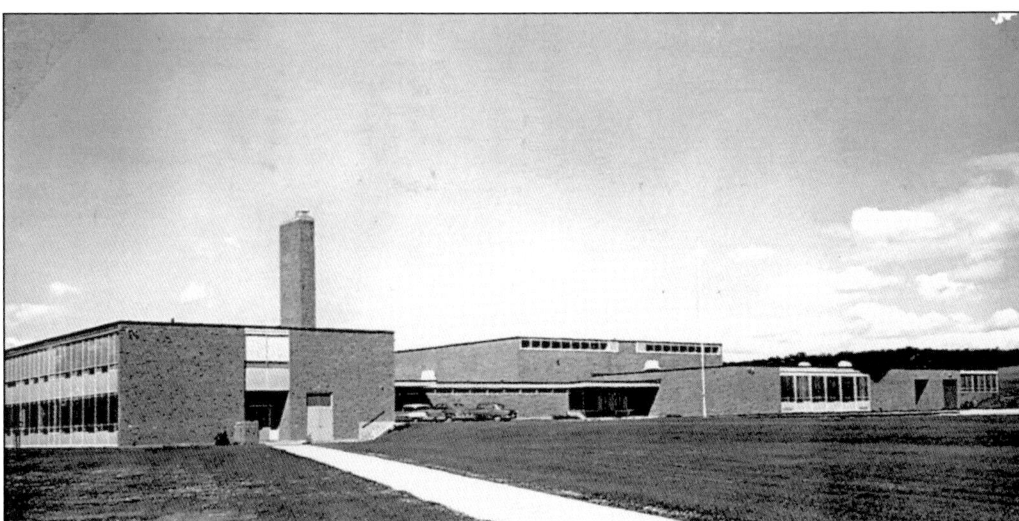

The new $700,000 1957 high school in Essex Junction had 17 classrooms. The layout of the building "separates classroom activities from those activities which are noisy and disconcerting to classroom study." In the activities wing were the gymnasium, cafeteria, kitchen, shop, and music room. This building served as the high school in Essex Junction until the Community Educational Center opened in 1970. It is now the Albert D. Lawton Intermediate School.

The First Congregational Church of Essex Junction was formed out of the Union Church Association between the Methodists and Congregationalists. This building was completed in 1869 as a wood-framed structure at a cost of $7,826.06 on two lots deeded by Byron Stevens and Enoch Howe.

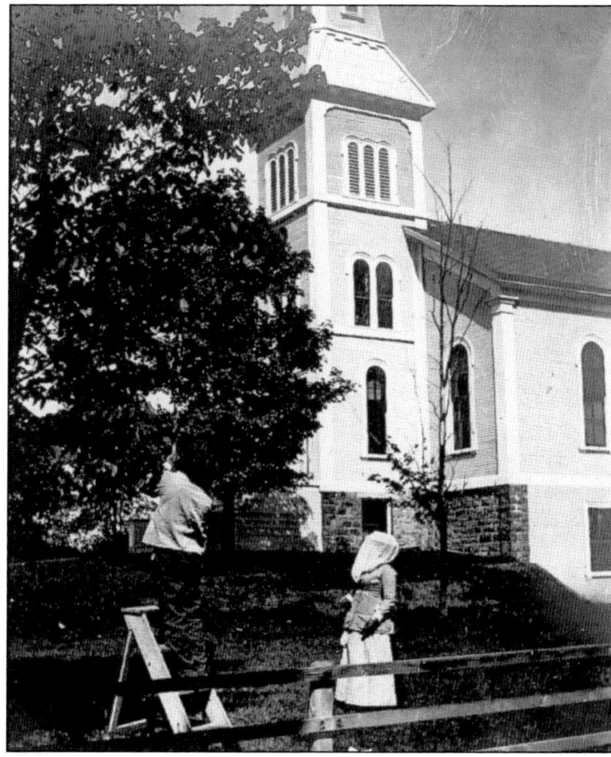

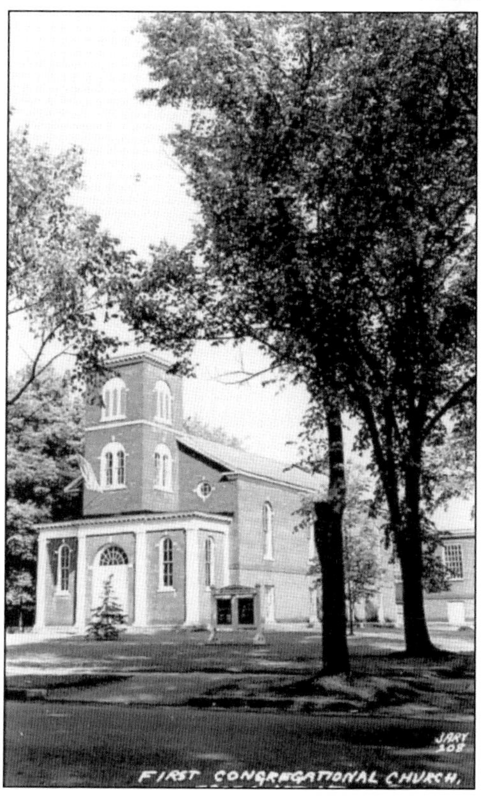

In 1879, the Baptists completed their own church and withdrew from the Union Church Association; the Methodists followed in 1898. In 1913, this church was incorporated as the First Congregational Church of Essex Junction to clear up any remaining confusion from the original denominations. In 1914, brick was built over the clapboard exterior, and a parish house was added. Further renovation to the parish house was done in 1961.

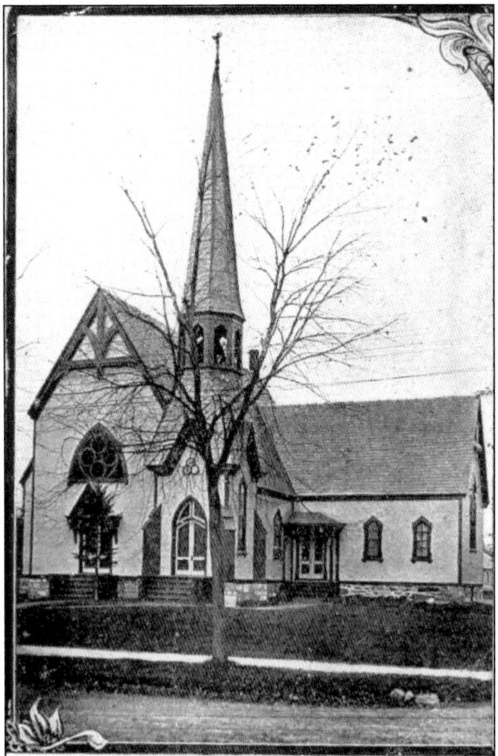

BAPTIST CHURCH, ESSEX JUNCTION, VT.

The Baptist group in Essex Junction was formally organized as a mission of the church in Essex Center in 1873. This building was constructed on Main Street, and the group was recognized as the Second Baptist Church of Essex in 1874. The congregation disbanded after selling the building to the Masons in 1927. In 1959, the Calvary Baptist Church of Essex Junction was formed.

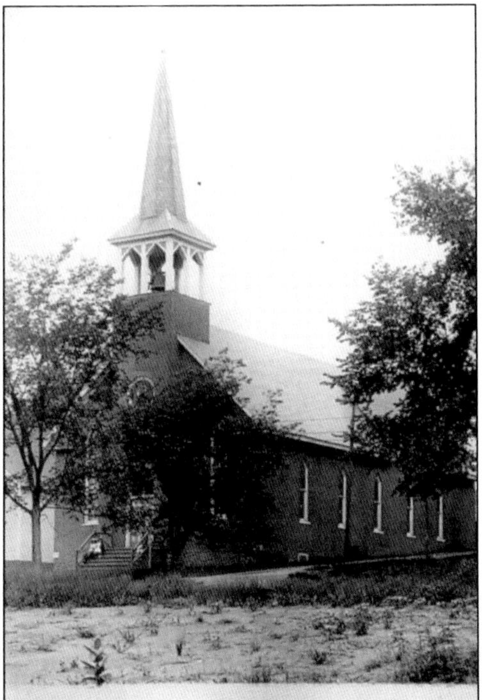

P8472 Catholic Church, Essex Junction, Vt.

Mass was first celebrated in the newly constructed Holy Family Church on Christmas Day 1893. The church is located on Lincoln Street. Up until the mid-1950s, members of the parish were mainly French Canadian immigrants. With the rapid growth of the Essex area since then, several parishes have been established from this one, including St. Lawrence Parish (also in Essex Junction), started in March 1966.

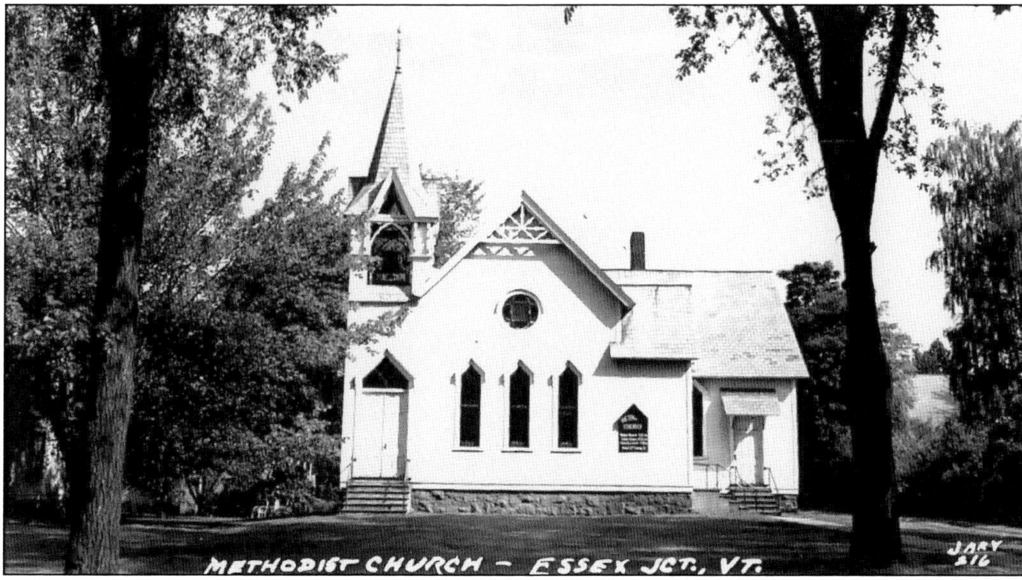

This building was built on Main Street for the Essex Junction Methodist congregation in 1897. An Estey organ was purchased in 1904, and a bell was obtained in 1924 from a former church in Weston. In 1958, the church became independent of its Williston affiliation and had its own full-time pastor. Since the church moved to its new building on Maple Street in 1966–1967, the Calvary Baptist congregation has been located here.

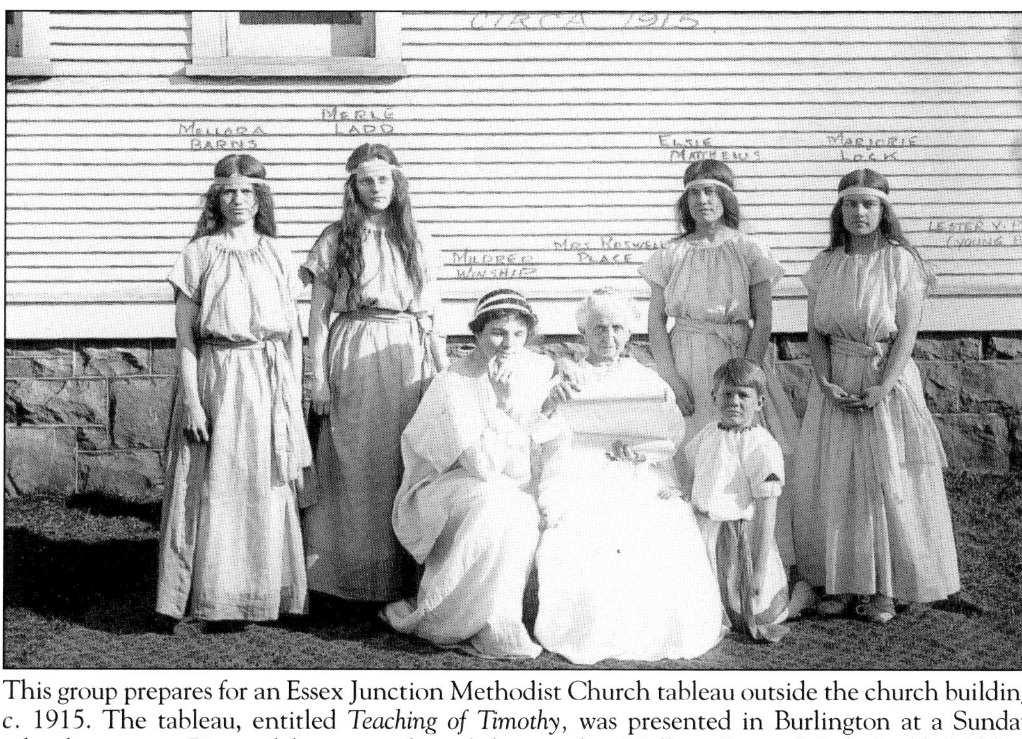

This group prepares for an Essex Junction Methodist Church tableau outside the church building c. 1915. The tableau, entitled *Teaching of Timothy*, was presented in Burlington at a Sunday school pageant. Pictured here are, from left to right, Mellora Barns, Merle Ladd, Mildred Winship, Roswell Place, Elsie Matthews, Marjorie Lock, and Lester V. Peck (kneeling).

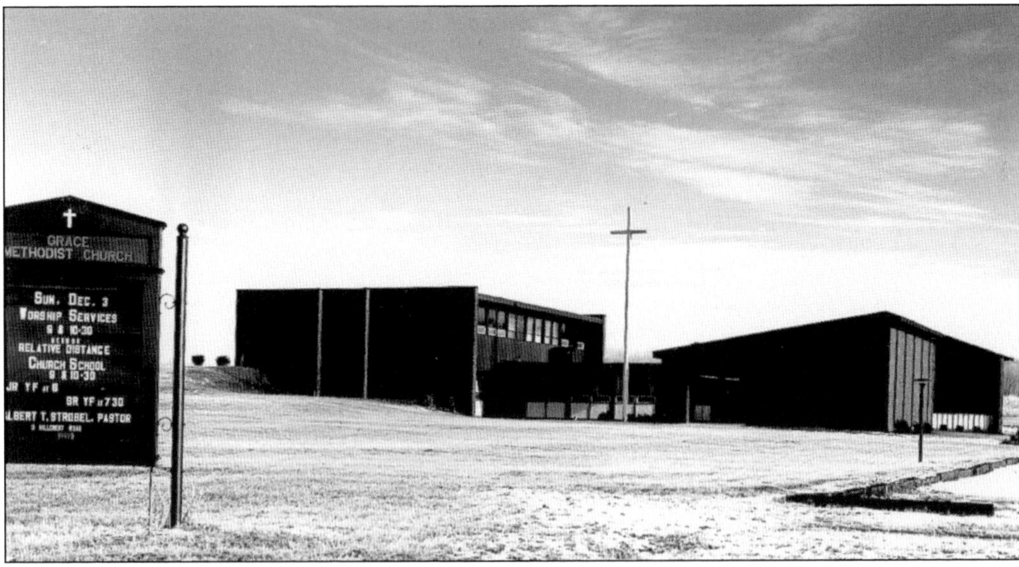

The lack of room at the first Methodist church building on Main Street led to the 1966–1967 construction of the Grace United Methodist Church on Maple Street on an almost four-acre lot. The new church was consecrated on March 3, 1968, by Bishop Lloyd Wicke. An educational wing with additional classrooms, offices, and storage was completed in 1994. (Courtesy William P. Hall.)

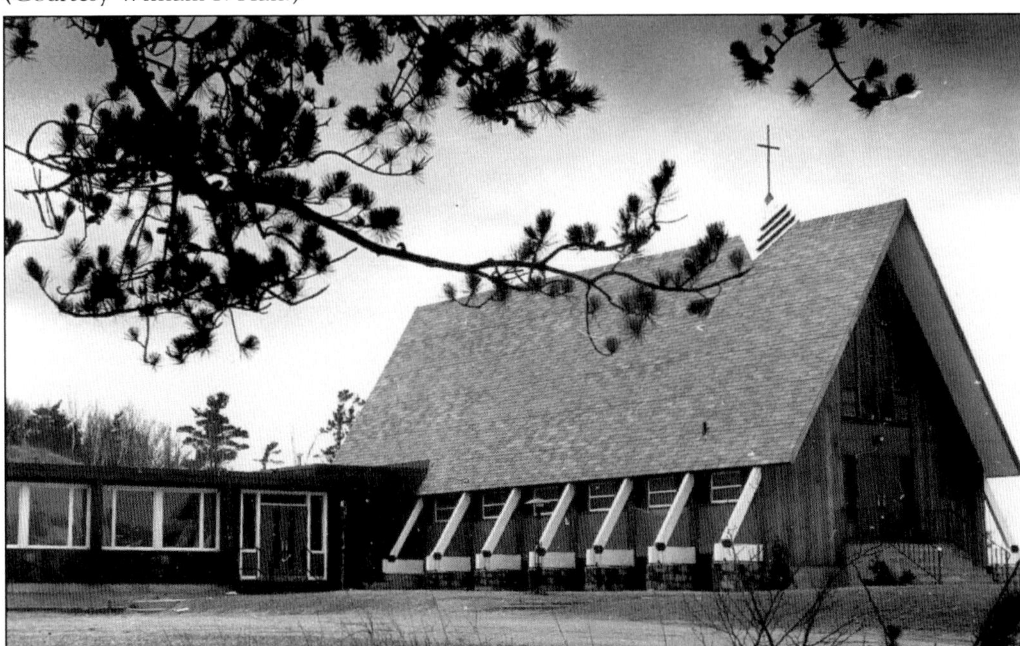

The first services for St. James Episcopal Church were held in 1951 in the Masonic temple and later in Lincoln Hall. Giles Willey gave the church the land adjacent to the fairgrounds in 1958. The new church building, shown here, was dedicated in September 1959. The church school wing was built, and St. James was formally accepted as a parish in 1964. The new rectory was built on church land in 1966.

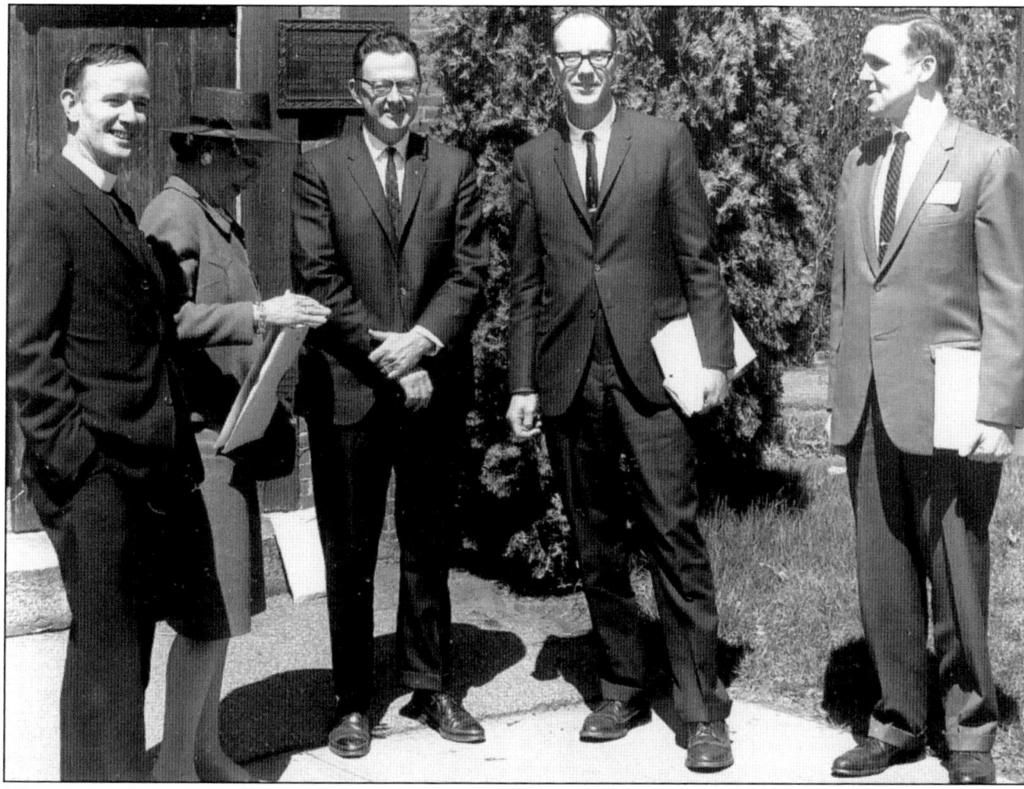

These people were influential in getting St. James Episcopal Church established and thriving. Pictured c. 1965 are, from left to right, Rev. Alexander Smith, Carlotta Raine, Newell Briggs, Kyle Scott, and Warren Bundy. Reverend Smith, the second full-time priest, ministered the congregation for more than 25 years.

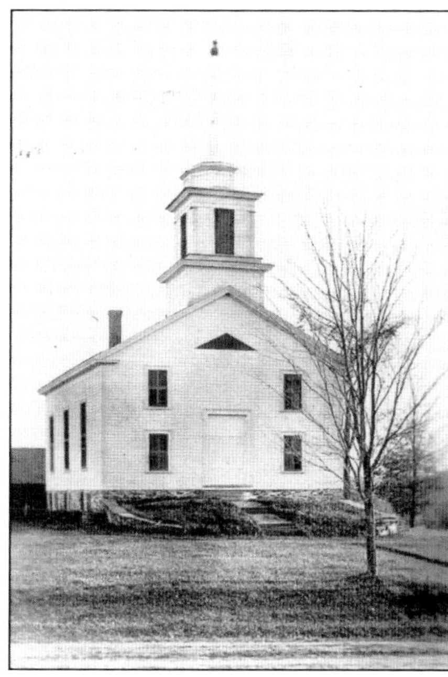

The First Baptist Church of Essex appears here c. 1910 across Browns River Road from the Essex Classical Institute. The Baptists organized on November 5, 1801, and erected their first building on this site in 1827. That structure was destroyed by fire in 1839. The building shown here lasted from c. 1840 to 1928, when it was torn down.

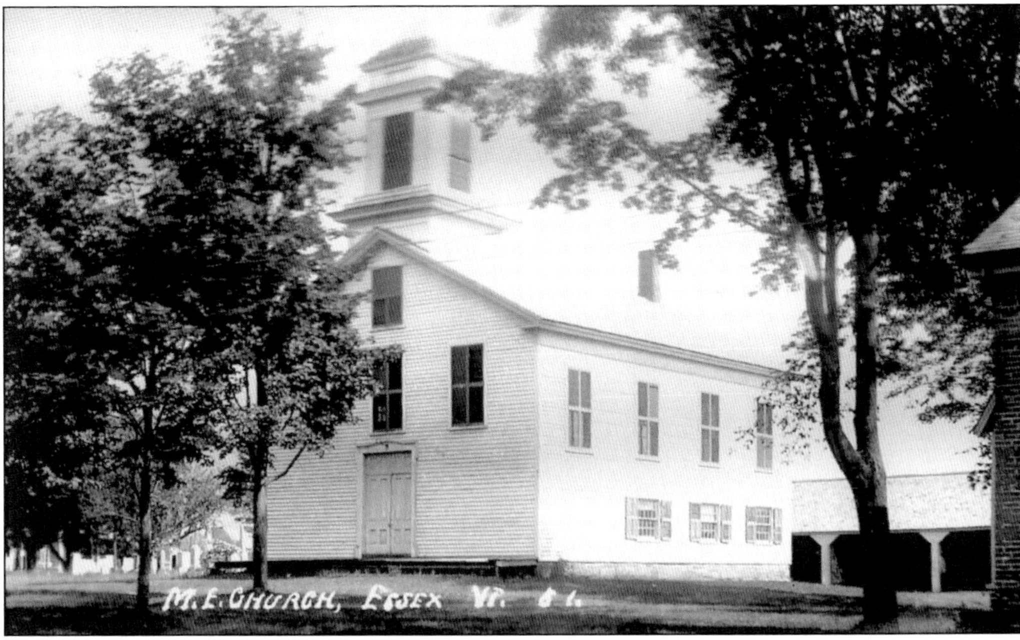

This is the United Methodist Church in Essex Center *c.* 1908. Methodists officially organized in December 1829. This church was constructed in 1839 on property given to the church by neighbor Joseph Fairfield. The property was deeded over to the church when the building was completed by benefactors Joseph Fairfield, Loren Tyler, George Whitney, and Benjamin Joslin.

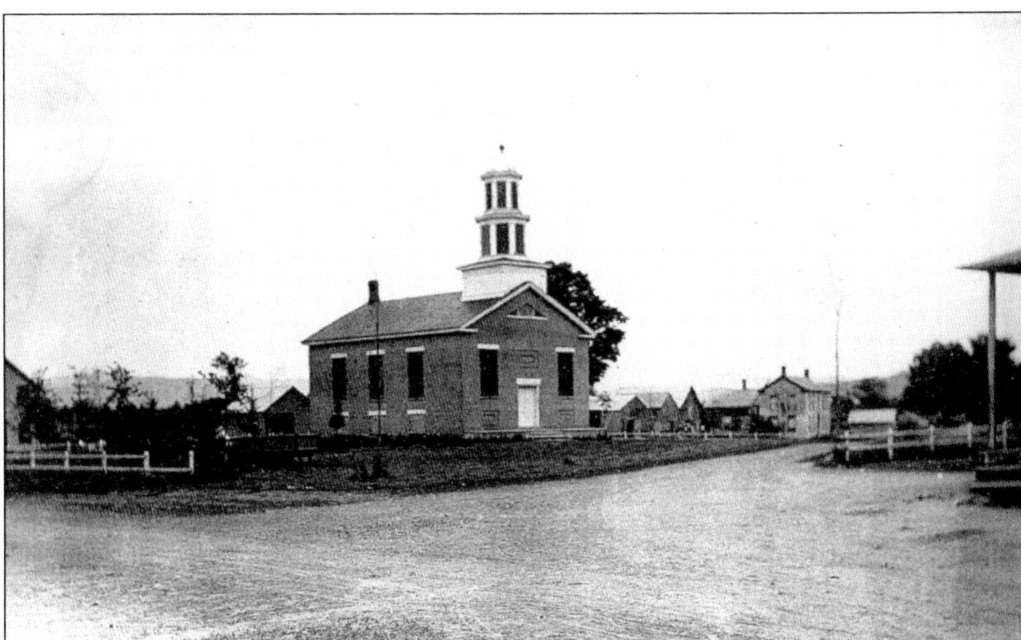

The Congregational church in Essex Center was built in 1839 to replace a white-framed 1803 building that had burned down. Congregationalists worshiped here up to 1941. Town meetings were also held here until 1873.

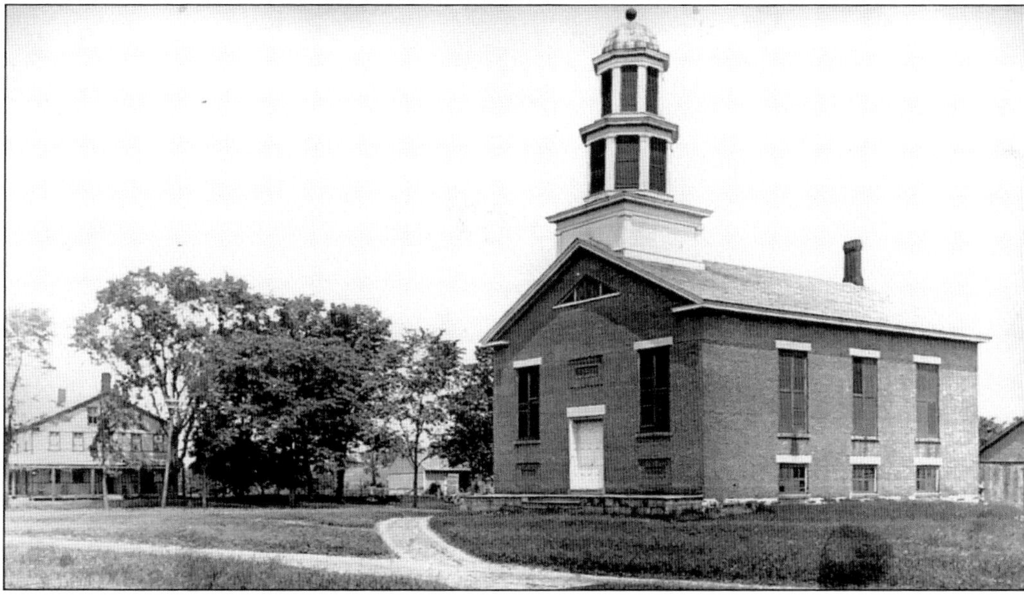

The Roman Catholic Diocese subleased the Congregational church until St. Pius X was opened. The Calvary Baptist used it from 1964 to 1969, then Essex Alliance, and lastly the United Pentecostal Church. In 1986, a new copper roof was added, and in July 1987, a bond was approved for converting the building into the Essex Free Library. It has remained the dominant building on the Essex Common.

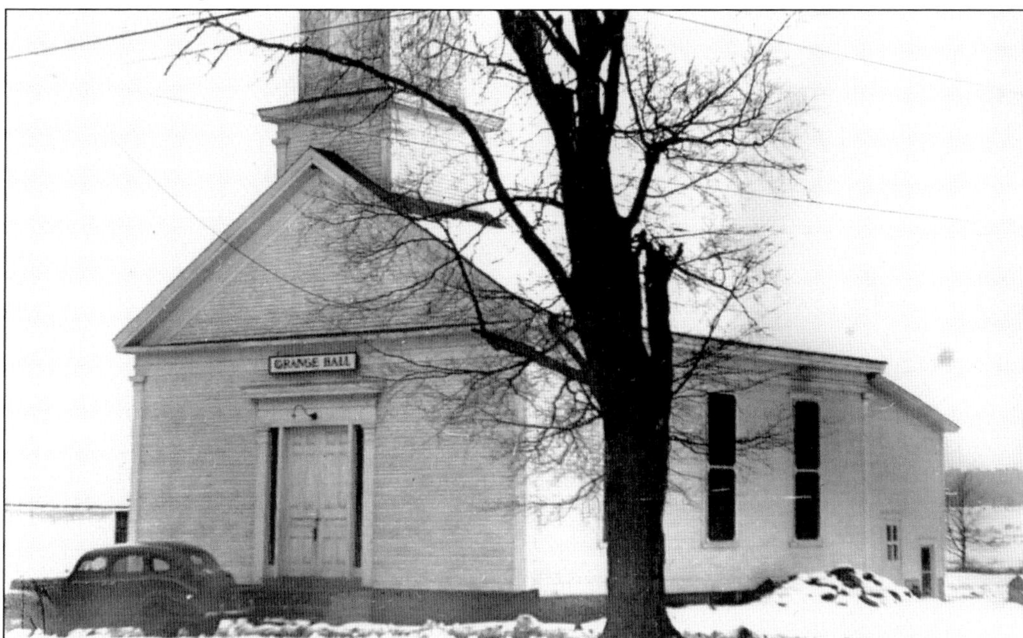

The Universalists built this structure in Essex Center in 1859. The congregation was very active during the early years of Essex; however, the group did not grow, as the members lived in all corners of the town, making regular attendance at church sometimes difficult. Membership reached a high of 52 in 1875. After 1895, services ceased. The Essex Center Grange bought the building in 1901 for $400. (Photograph by Evans Knapp.)

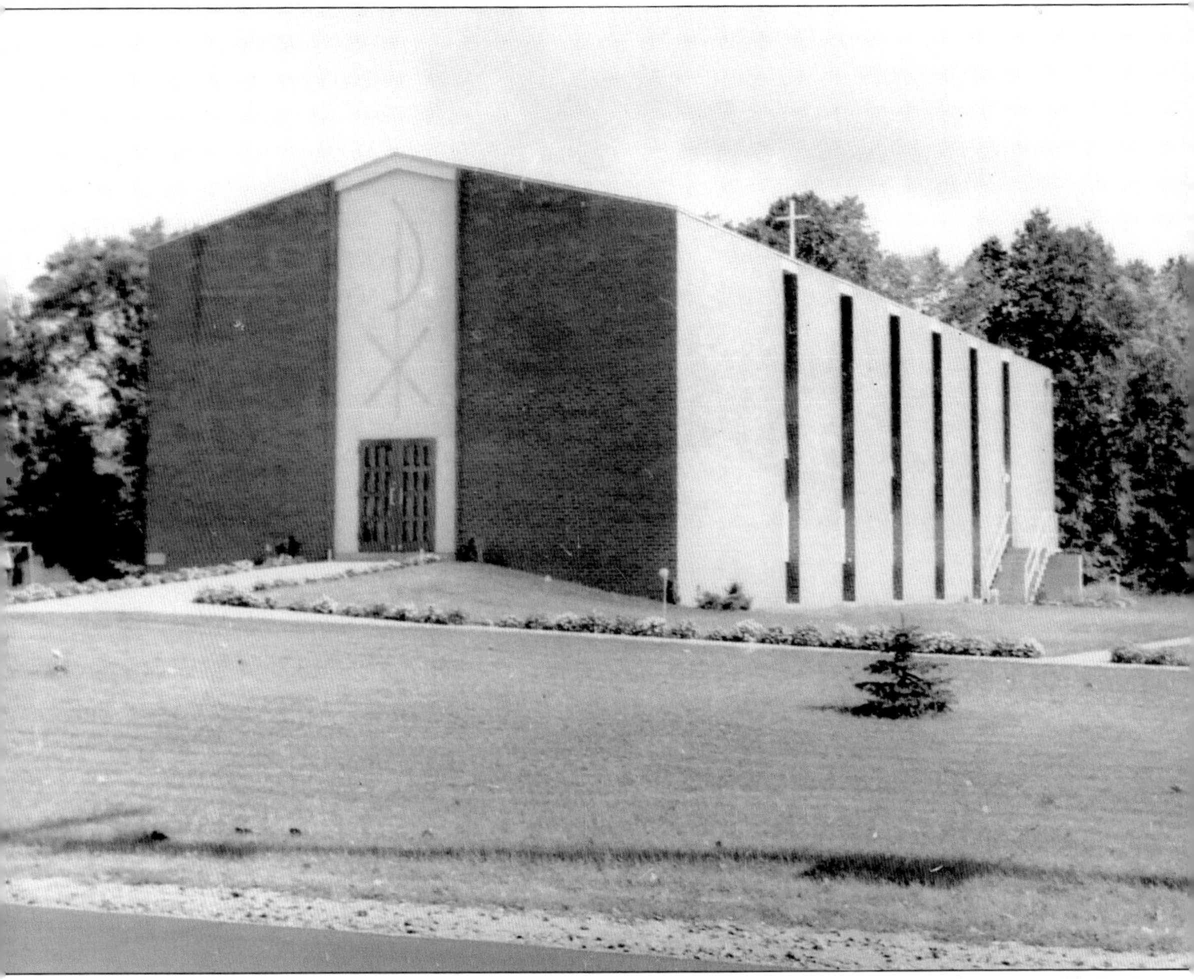

With crowding at the Holy Family Church in Essex Junction, the St. Pius X parish was established in Essex Center. The first mass was held in the Grange Hall in 1957. The initial mass in this new building was celebrated by Fr. James B. Murray on May 11, 1961. Two wings were added in 1991–1992. Currently, there are 2,836 parishioners. (Courtesy Betsy [Thrasher] Melvin.)

Six

Fun and Celebration

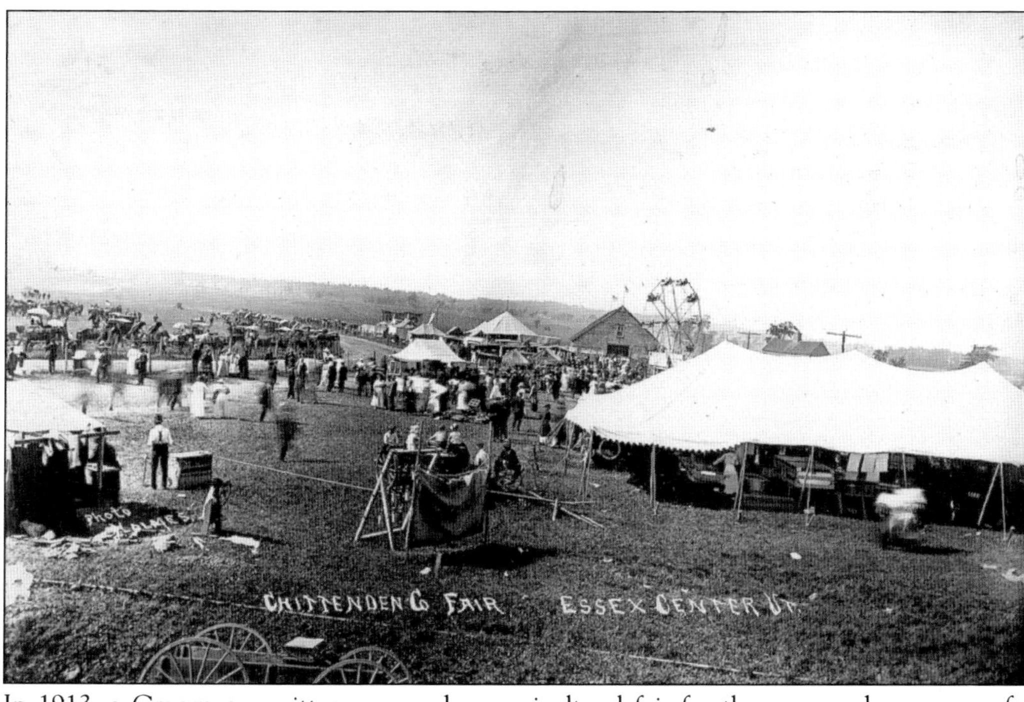

In 1913, a Grange committee proposed an agricultural fair for the area, and every year for the next eight years, a three-day fair was held. The first agricultural fair, later known as the Chittenden County Fair, was held in 1914 and made a profit of $286.58. In 1915, with land rented from C. F. Chapin for $100, permanent buildings were erected off Towers Road.

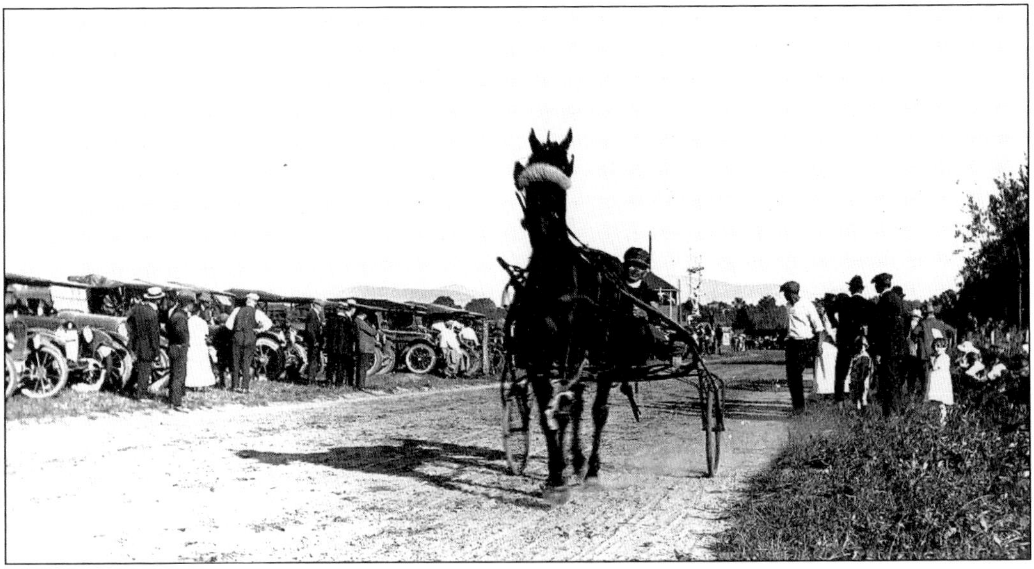

Essex Center Grange No. 155 was started in Essex Center in 1893. It was an early center of social activities in the community, with dances, picnics, and dinners held there. Sponsoring a fair was a major undertaking for the group. Horse racing occurred on a half-mile track laid out on a large field along Towers Road. Julia Fifield, who attended the fair, recalls this was the prime attraction for the men.

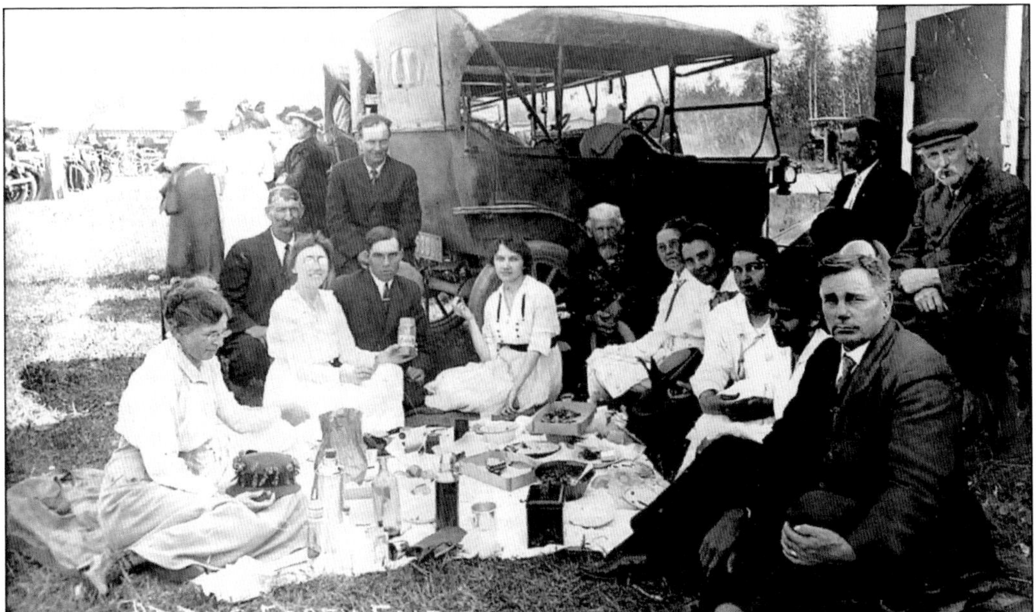

The Grange hosted the fair until 1921, when it sold out to the Champlain Valley Fair, because the soil at the fairgrounds was poor, the fair was increasing in size, and the site was not centrally located. The Grange used the money to fix up its hall. Here, people picnic "at the Essex Fair, Essex Center, VT, 1916."

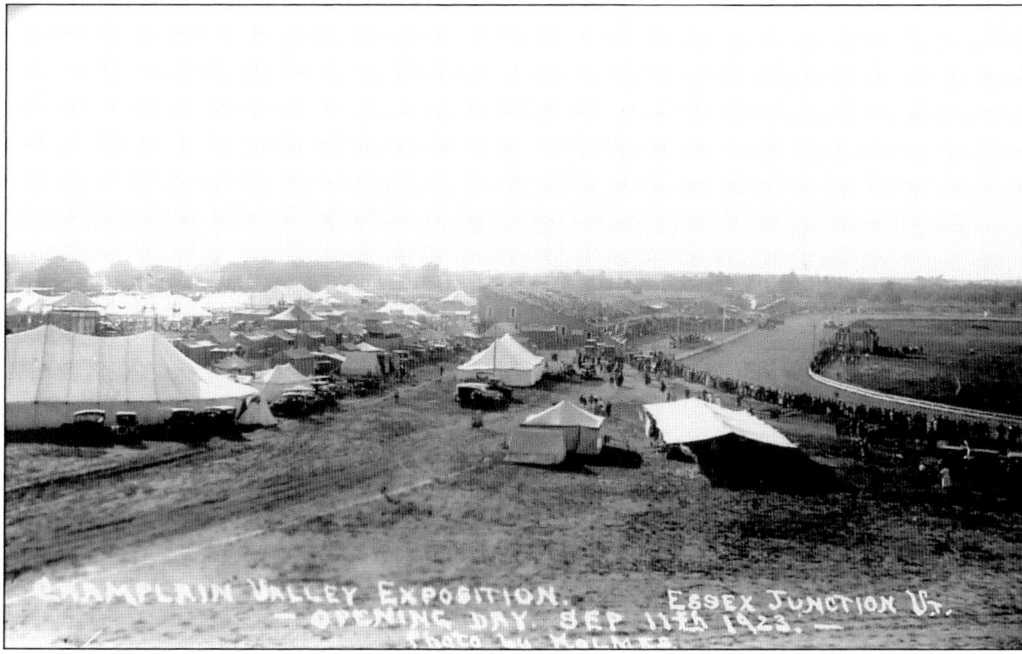

This view looks west on opening day of the Champlain Valley Exposition, September 11, 1923, in Essex Junction. The Essex Center fairgrounds had hosted the 1922 fair, as the horse track at the new site in Essex Junction was still being completed. The first year's attendance was 56,997, and the fair made a profit of $7,357.

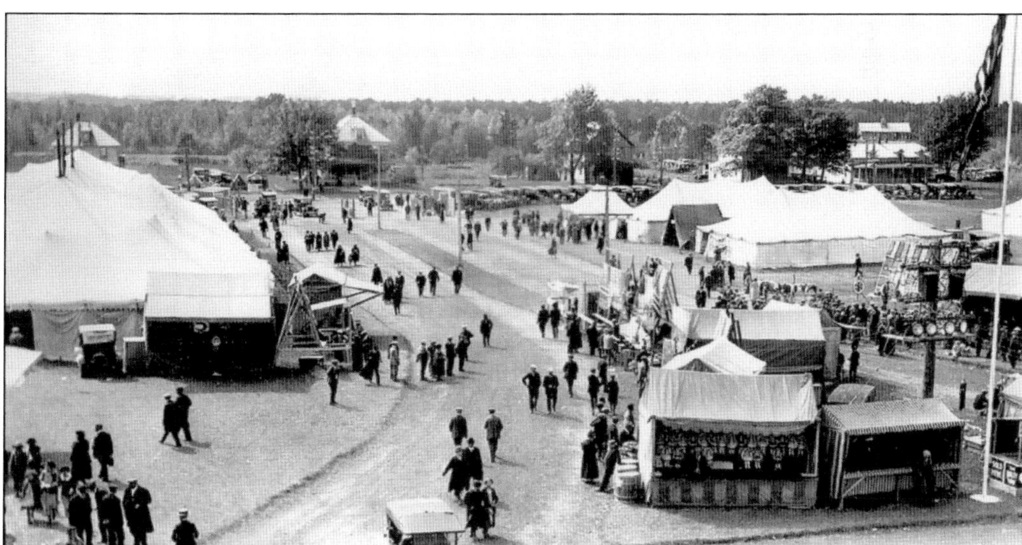

Shown here is a view of the fair in its early years. Pearl Street and the main entrance are in the distance.

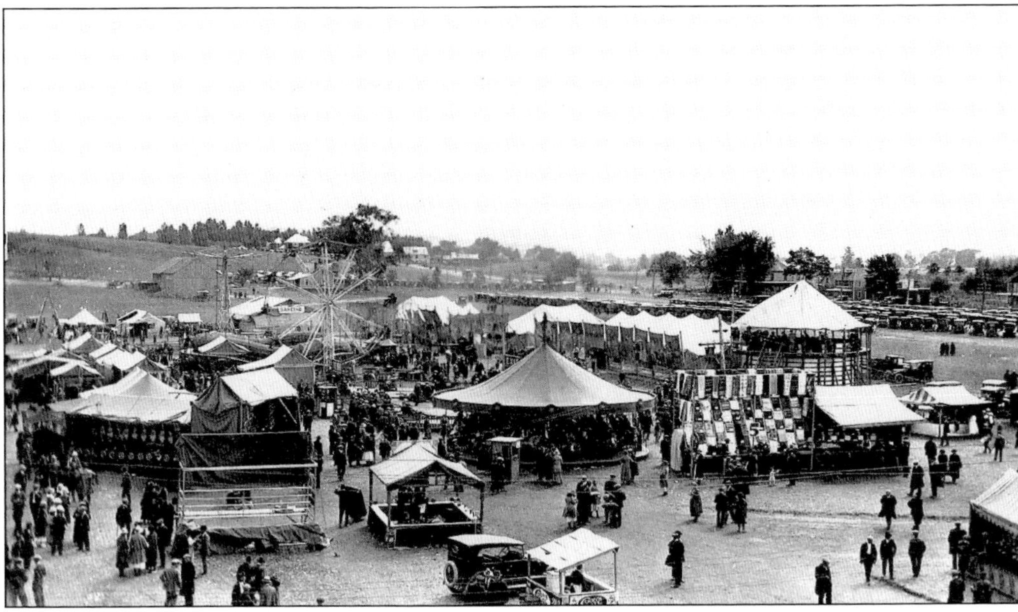

Since 1923, the Champlain Valley Exposition has been held every year, offering something for everyone: exhibits of crafts, paintings, culinary skills, horticulture, and livestock. Also to keep one occupied are the midway, free entertainment, grandstand shows, motor sports on the track, and fair food. Harness racing's heyday spanned the 1920s to the 1950s.

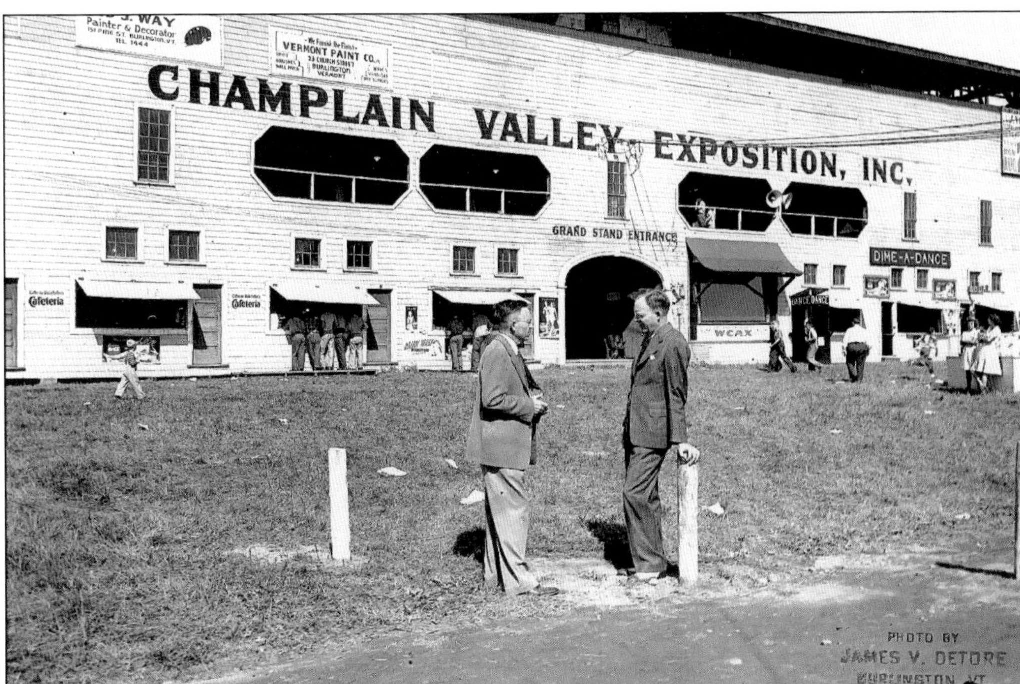

Harris K. "Had" Drury (left), fair manager from 1937 to 1973, and James S. Grow, treasurer from 1934 to 1940 and from 1956 to 1966, have a quiet moment at the 1939 fair. On July 11, 1965, the grandstand in the background burned. A new grandstand, holding 3,000, was built in 1966.

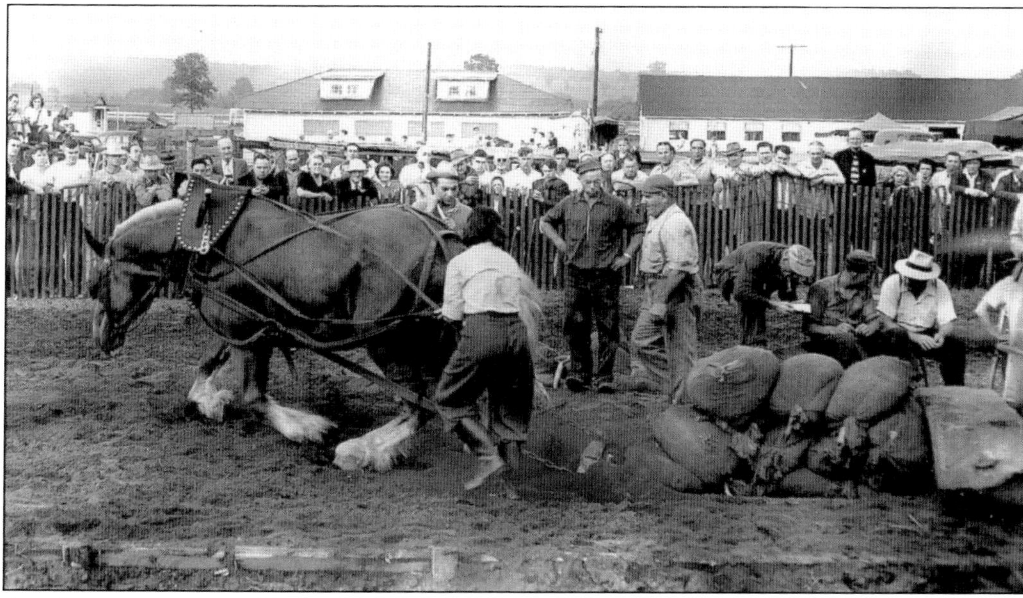

Another attraction at the fair is the test of strength for horses and oxen. Here, Jeanette Pyle and horse Mike compete in a special "lady drivers of single horses" class. The photograph was taken in the late 1940s or early 1950s. Mike was half of a free-for-all class blue-ribbon team and won the single class with ease.

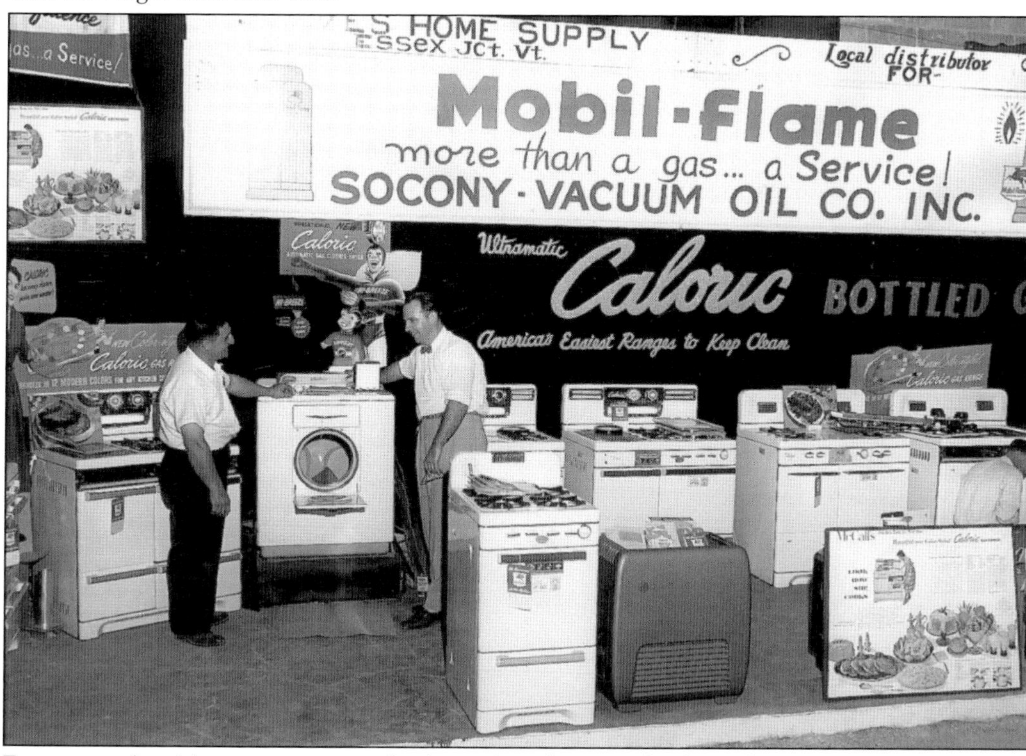

Every year, local businesses set up displays of products at the fair. The owner of Steve's Home Supply, Anthony "Steve" Stevens, stands to the left of a washing machine, with a representative from the Caloric Company on the right, in the 1950s.

1773. 1883.

THE ONE HUNDREDTH ANNIVERSARY

OF THE

Settlement of the Town of Essex

Will be celebrated at

ESSEX CENTER, Sep. 2, 3, and 4, 1883.

The Exercises will commence Sunday Evening, September 2, with a UNION RELIGIOUS SERVICE at the CONGREGATIONAL CHURCH, in which the Pastors of the several churches will participate. A Discourse appropriate to the occasion will be delivered by REV. JOHN COWAN. The music will be under the direction of E. F. Garvin.

Monday Evening there will be a

GRAND CONCERT AT THE TOWN HALL,

Commencing at 7 o'clock sharp, by the HOWARD OPERA HOUSE ORCHESTRA, of Burlington, and a CHOIR OF SINGERS improvised for the occasion, who will "tune the music of ye olden tyme," and intersperse their music with Recitations and Readings.

Admission FREE to all who hold CENTENNIAL Tickets. All others 25cts. each.

The dawn of TUESDAY, the "election day" of the Fathers, will be ushered in with a

Salute of Fifty Guns,

and a like salute also at evening, under the direction of JOHN McGREGOR, ESQ.

The Public exercises of the day will be held at the CONGREGATIONAL CHURCH, commencing at Half-past Ten A.M., when a Historical Address will be delivered by

—{ L. C. BUTLER, M.D. }—

Other appropriate exercises will also take place.

At the close of services at the Church, DINNER will be served at the TOWN HALL, FREE to all who are provided with CENTENNIAL Tickets.

Former citizens of the town and strangers, who may be present, are requested to report their names to the Secretary of the committe, A. B. HALBERT, Esq., at the earliest moment possible, and will be provided for to the extent of the seating capacity of the Hall.

The dinner will be followed by the presentation of sentiments, and by speeches, under the direction of the PRESIDENT OF THE DAY and M. A. BINGHAM, Esq.

By the courtesy of the Central Vermont and Burlington and Lamoille railroads, free return checks will be furnished to all who pay full fare from any point on those roads, coming to this Centennial.

The arrangement of the trains is such that people can reach here in season for the exercises of TUESDAY and return after they are completed.

L. C. BUTLER, Chairman,
A. B. HALBERT, Secretary,
C. H. NICHOLS,
D. H. MACOMBER,
S. G. BUTLER,
W. J. BEACH.
} Committee of Arrangements.

Essex, Vt., August, 1883.

Essex was chartered in 1763. Some temporary settlements existed in 1773, but it was not until 1783, after the Revolutionary War, that permanent settlement took place. So why, as shown here, was there a celebration of "the one hundredth anniversary of the settlement, 1773–1783"? It is interesting to note all the festivities taking place in Essex Center rather than Essex Junction, and the prominent role played by Dr. Lucius C. Butler.

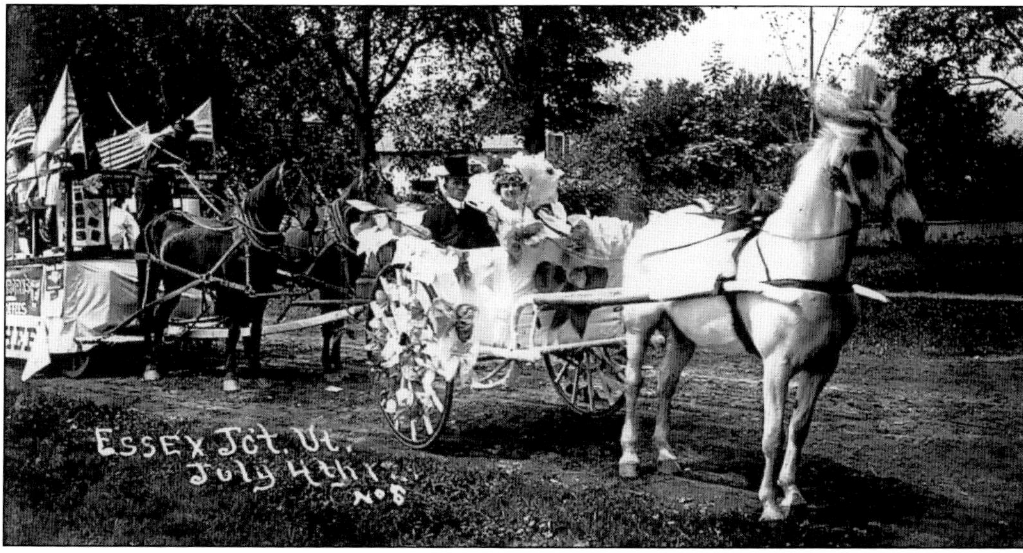

As well as horse-drawn carts, the July 4, 1912, parade had 20 decorated automobiles carrying dignitaries, the 10th Cavalry Band, floats advertising stores and products, "a daisy chain of young ladies, an ivy wreath of boys; a float by the Knights of King Arthur; boys on bicycles; real clowns; [and] suffragettes, few but enthusiastic." The festivities were topped off with a "scientific" baseball game between the Fats and the Leans.

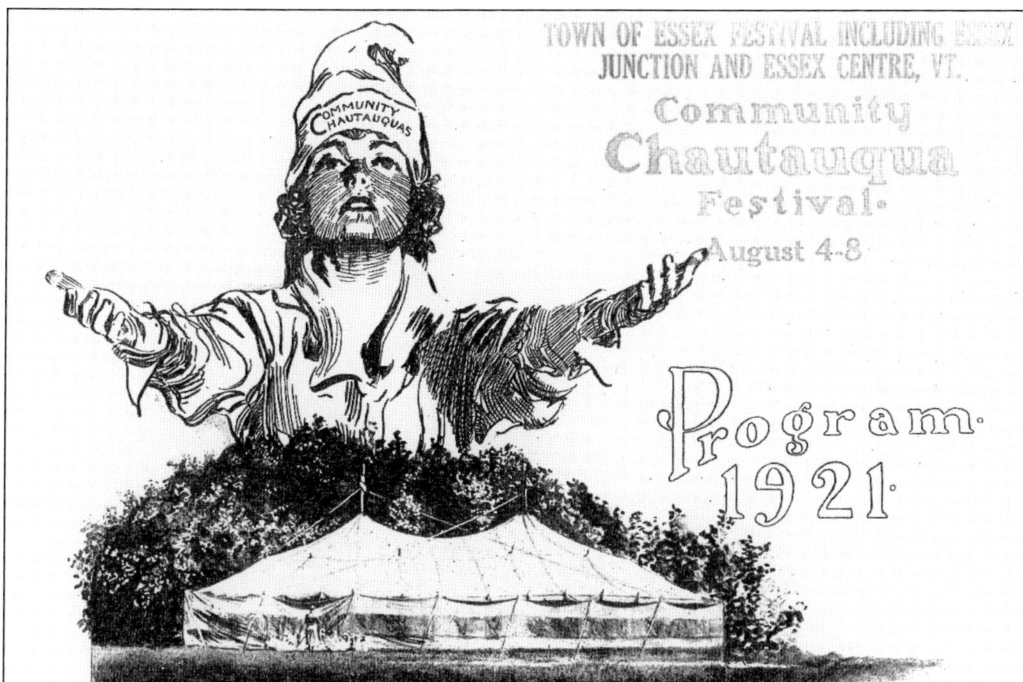

Over four days in 1921, this Chautauqua Festival featured a recitation by Bill Bone, music by the Filippino Quartet, and a comedy called *Her Husband's Wife*, among other acts. Chautauquas were traveling groups that operated from 1903 to 1930. Particularly active in rural areas, they moved from town to town, giving lectures, concerts, and recitals in a tent. The increased popularity of radio was one factor in their demise.

HILLIKER'S GARAGE

MOVING AND LONG DISTANCE HAULING A SPECIALTY.
WE BUY, SELL AND EXCHANGE AUTOMOBILES

PEARL STREET — — — — ESSEX JUNCTION

THE MEN'S CLUB MINSTRELS

1924 EDITION

Benefit of State Children's Aid and Men's Club
DIRECTION O. GREENE BURNELL

Thursday and Friday Nights
NOV. 20 and 21, 1924

PARISH HOUSE, ESSEX JUNCTION

Rugg's ECONOMY STORES

Minstrel shows were put on by a variety of community groups in Essex and Essex Junction. The show included the typical format of white performers in blackface mimicking African Americans in stories, song, and dance. They persisted in the community well into the 1950s. This one by the Men's Club charged a 50¢ admission for adults and 25¢ for children. O. Greene Burnell was the director.

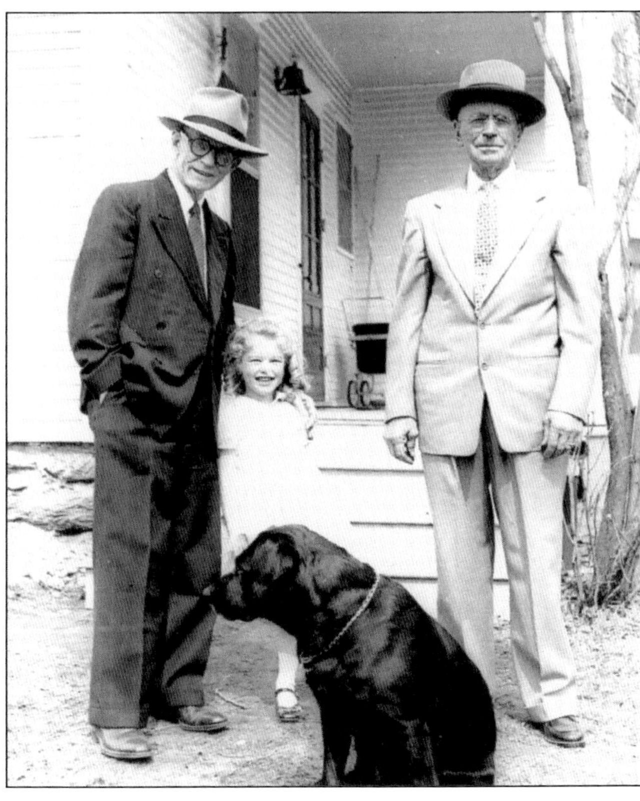

From left to right, O. Greene Burnell, Martha McLure, "Captain," and Judson Hilliker appear at 32 Pearl Street c. 1956. Burnell was an experienced vaudeville actor who directed minstrel and other community shows. His early roles, starting c. 1900, included assisting in a magic show with then famous magician F. Richard Davis and singing illustrated songs. For years, he was the telegraph operator at the railroad station.

In 1959 and 1960, the Essex Center Community Council sponsored a festival. This one was held on Saturday July 30, 1960, in Essex Center, starting with a parade and ending with a street dance. Betsy (Thrasher) Melvin was the chair of the festival for the council. There were also booths, an open house at the library, pony rides, exhibits, and sales of art, crafts, and antiques at the town hall. (Courtesy Betsy [Thrasher] Melvin.)

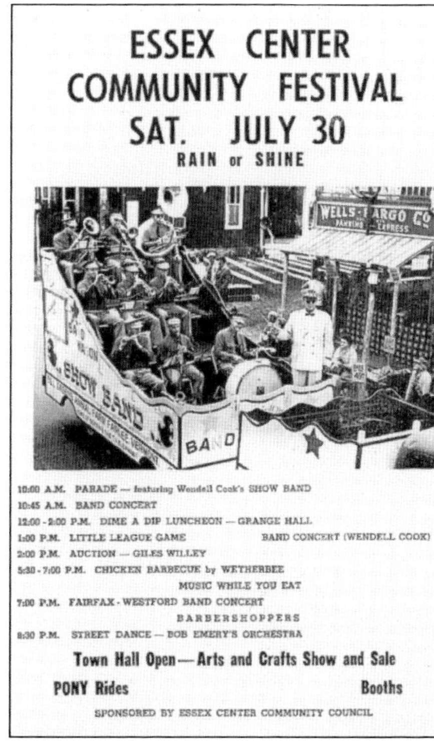

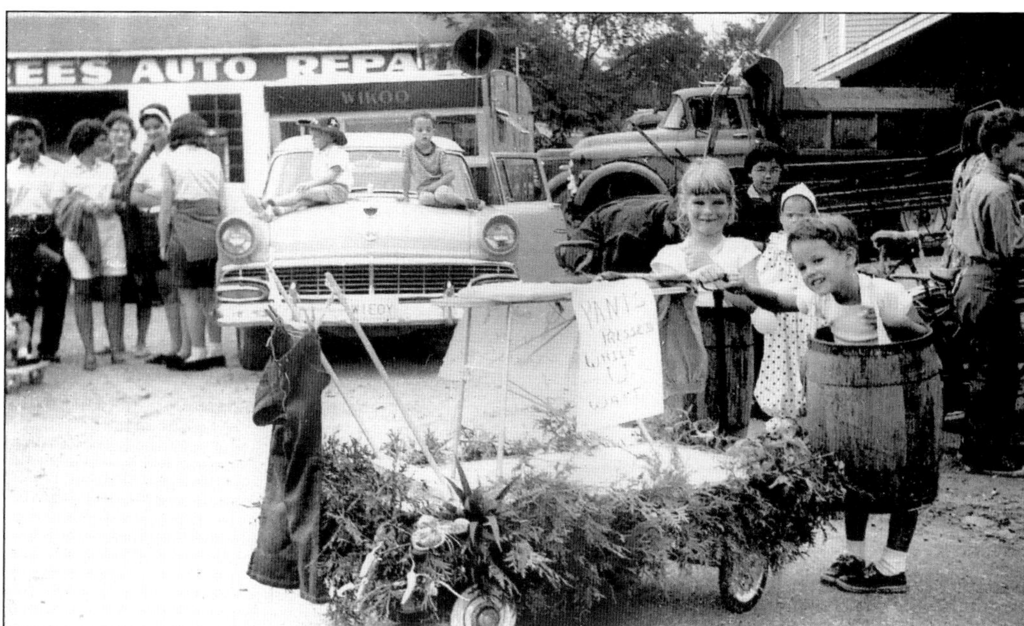

"Pants Pressed While U Wait" was the winning children's float at the 1960 Community Festival. Julie Page (right) waits for her pressed pants from Jennifer Whitcomb. Because it was a rainy day, the booths had to move into the school. There was a wishing well by the PTA, souvenirs by the community council, chess by Phil Kolvoord, an auction with auctioneer Giles Willey, and a concert by the Fairfax-Westford Band. (Courtesy Betsy [Thrasher] Melvin.)

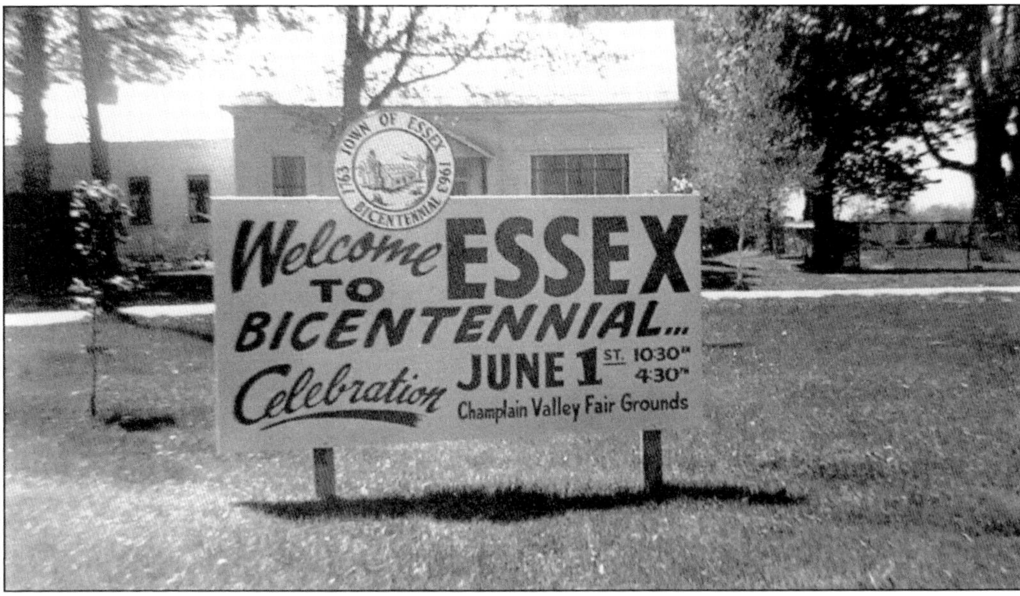

On Saturday, June 1, 1963, Essex Town celebrated its bicentennial. The junior chamber of commerce planned the parade, and the Lions Club organized the afternoon program at the fairgrounds. "Bands played, young gymnasts tumbled, boys climbed a greased pole, and for the icing on the cake, the ladies of the Women's Club put on a fashion show featuring old time clothes," reported the *Suburban List*. This sign was on the Essex Center Common.

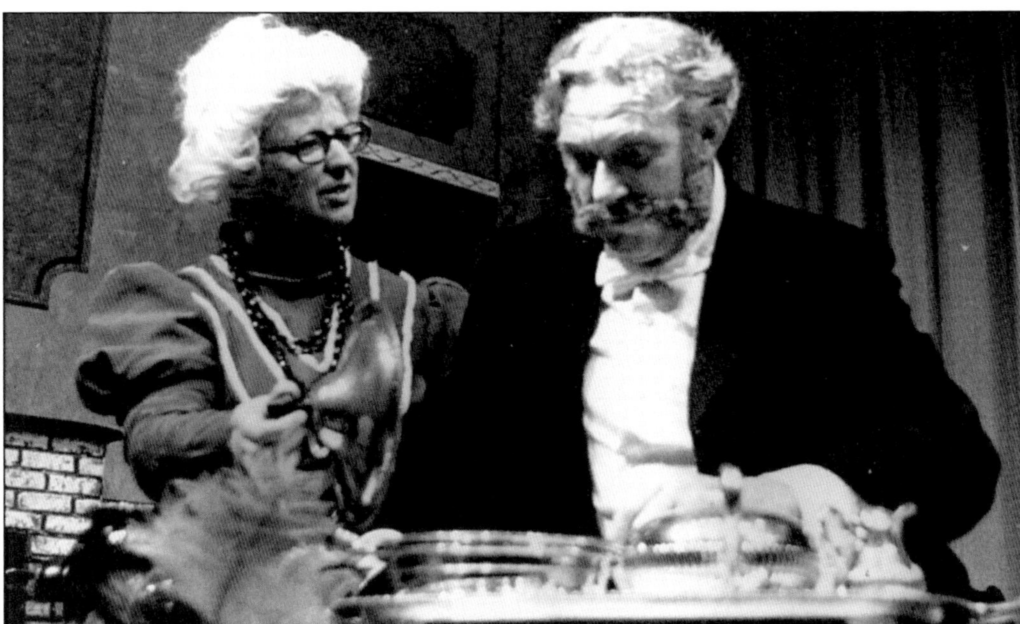

The Essex Community Players was started in 1958 by Phil and Bess Cohen and about 15 of their friends and neighbors, under the name Essex Players. Memorial Hall in Essex Center became home c. 1966, and the group's name was changed to the Essex Community Players. This April 1971 production of *Strange Bedfellows* shows Marjorie Sylvester (left) and Charles Ketchum in costume. The group continues today with several productions each year.

Sixteen-year-old Ann Bergeron was selected the first National Grange Princess on November 17, 1961, representing the Essex Center Grange. She won the title for her performance in the key youth achievement project, which required exemplifying the seven basic keys of fellowship, activities, fun, recognition, leadership, service, and membership in her Grange, community, church, and home.

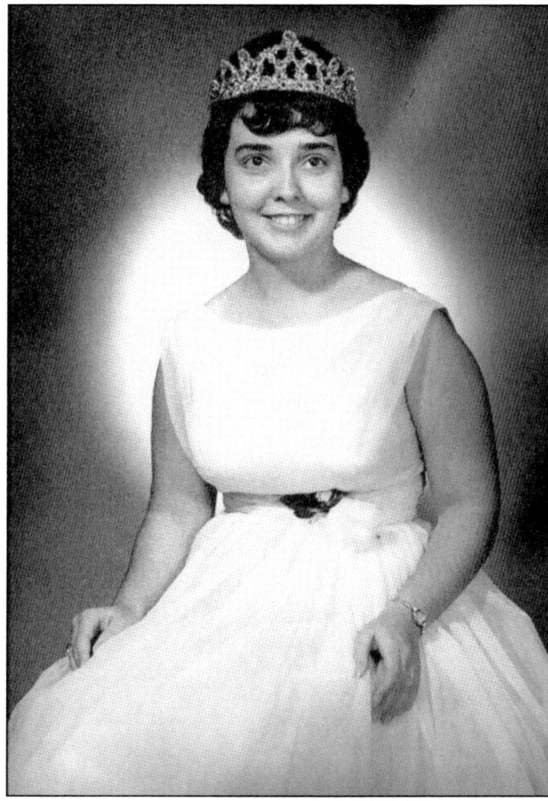

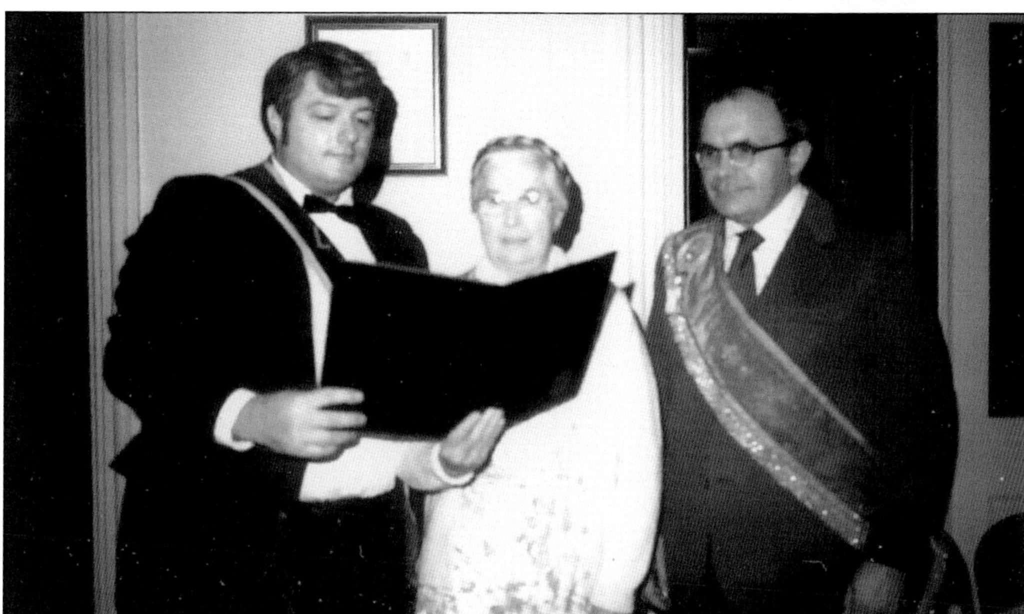

Blue Spruce Grange No. 547, started in Essex Junction in 1976, presents Mildred Barnes with its Community Citizen's Award in 1977. Shown, from left to right, are Lawrence Yandow Jr., Blue Spruce Grange lecturer; Barnes; and Kermit Richardson, National Grange lecturer. Barnes held a wide variety of offices in the village and town from 1921 to 1966.

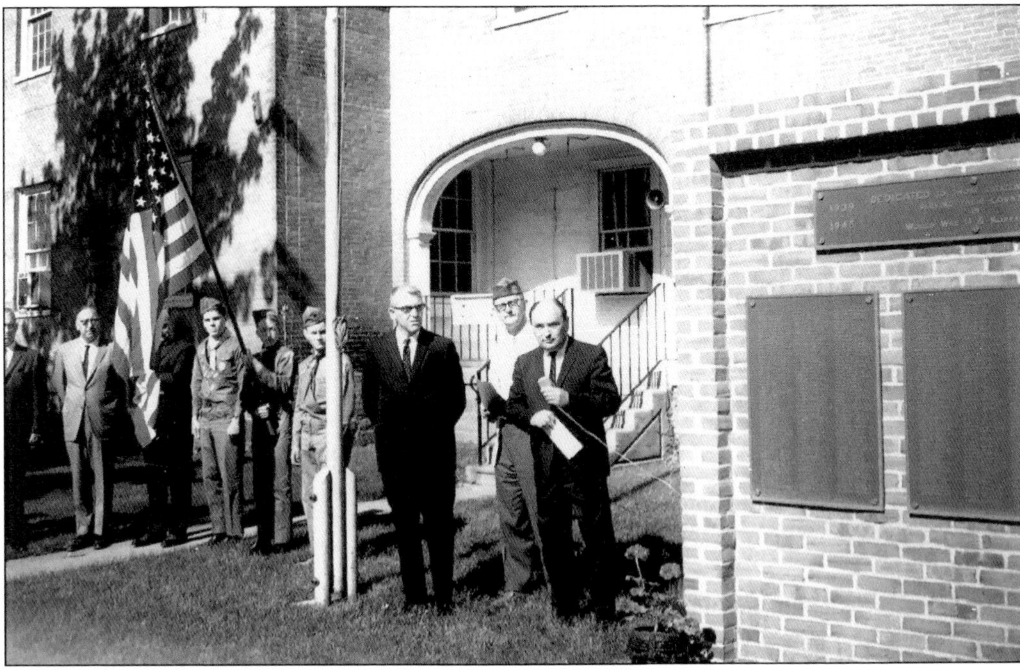

The Essex Junction Lions Club participated in the Memorial Day 1966 services honoring veterans. Standing in front of Lincoln Hall are, from left to right, unidentified, Gene Adorisio, unidentified, three unidentified boy scouts, Max Reader, Pete Blanchette, and Ed Freidman (king lion). The Essex Junction Lions Club was chartered in February 1948 with 58 members.

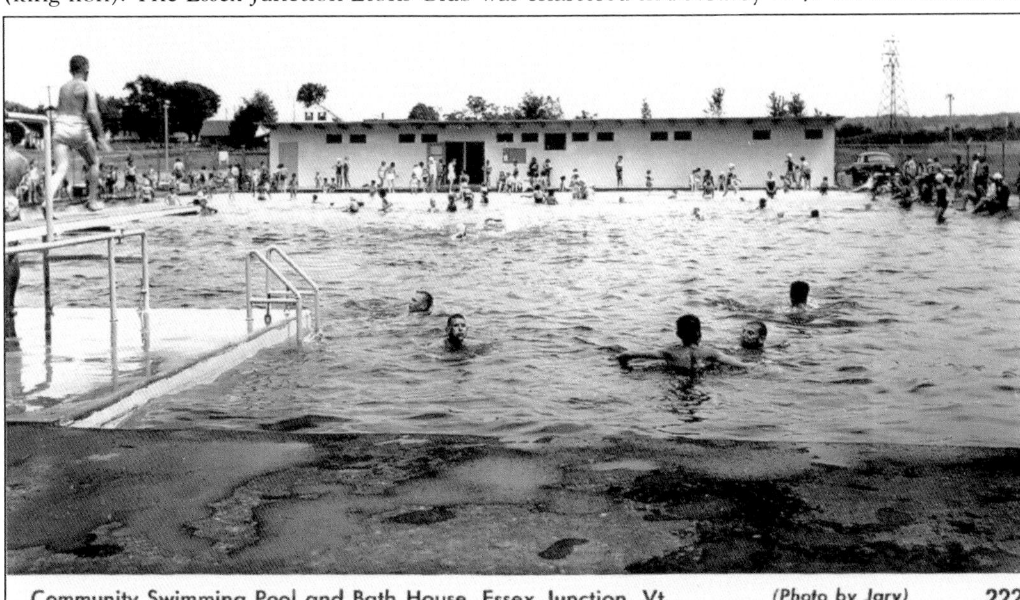

The Essex Junction Lions Club sponsored and built the community swimming pool on Maple Street in 1952. Over the years, the club has provided support for many community projects, including holding glaucoma clinics, upgrading recreation facilities, renovating the basement of the Brownell Library, and erecting monuments to honor war veterans. The group's latest project is the Veterans Memorial Park at the Five Corners.